Peter Lorange

University of Pennsylvania

CORPORATE PLANNING

An Executive Viewpoint

PRENTICE-HALL, INC., Englewood Cliffs, New Jersey 07632

Library of Congress Cataloging in Publication Data

LORANGE, PETER.
   Corporate planning.

   Includes bibliographical references and index.
   1. Corporate planning. I. Title.
HD30.28.L67   658.4′01   79–22348
ISBN 0–13–174755–X

Editorial production supervision and interior design by Pamela Wilder
Cover design by Lana Giganti
Manufacturing buyer: Harry P. Baisley

Printed in the United States of America

10 9 8 7 6 5 4 3 2

Prentice-Hall International, Inc., *London*
Prentice-Hall of Australia Pty. Limited, *Sydney*
Prentice-Hall of Canada, Ltd., *Toronto*
Prentice-Hall of India Private Limited, *New Delhi*
Prentice-Hall of Japan, Inc., *Tokyo*
Prentice-Hall of Southeast Asia Pte. Ltd., *Singapore*
Whitehall Books Limited, Wellington, *New Zealand*

Contents

6 Managing the Evolution of the Corporate Planning System   209

7 Executives' Roles in Planning   253

8 Corporate Planning—A Synthesis   279

To Richard F. Vancil

Preface

This book presents advanced concepts for the design, implementation, and use of corporate or strategic planning systems. It attempts to present a unified concept of corporate planning based on a comprehensive conceptual scheme. Also, however, the book draws on advanced corporate practices so as to reflect the best of practitioners' viewpoints. There has been a strong surge of interest in corporate planning during recent years in the corporate world as well as within academic circles. New or modified approaches to planning issues emerge at a frequent rate, manifested by an abundance of books, articles, consultants' pamphlets, speeches, seminars, etc. Not unexpectedly, there is a sense of fragmentation in the corporate planning field, resulting from the many disjointed inputs that are emerging. This book attempts to offer a unified approach to corporate planning, partly by synthesis of pertinent aspects of the present body of knowledge but partly too by offering conceptual developments.

The book has three main uses: a textbook for graduate and advanced undergraduate students in a course on corporate or strategic planning or business policy; a practitioner's handbook for line managers who are in positions where they are "users" of planning systems, particularly senior executives at the general management levels; and, finally, a guideline for staff planning executives who will be in need of prescriptive advice on specific systems design issues.

As a text, the book is aimed primarily at a graduate or advanced undergraduate course in strategic planning (corporate planning, long-range planning). I have used the text extensively for a second-year Master's program course at the Sloan School, M.I.T. With the growing recognition of planning systems' roles in corporations' strategy formulation and implementation, the text is also well suited for use in a course on business policy (corporate strategy), either as the primary text for such a course or as a supplemental text to more traditional policy texts. Finally, I have used the text extensively in executive programs, in the United States as well as in Europe and South America.

For senior line executives, the book provides a useful exposition of how corporate planning can be made to work as a management tool, with its potentials as well as limitations. We see planning becoming a key part of the management "culture" of many corporations. The book is a primer for the managers who aspire to perform effectively within such an emerging culture.

Corporate planners have an increasingly important and challenging role to play. Not only will they be expected to better tailor-make the design of planning systems to the particular corporate setting they are in; even more important is their role in managing the evolution of a planning system so that it will stay effective and reflect changing environmental challenges. The book provides operational guidelines for situational design of planning systems and for evolving the systems design over time.

Without the help and support of a number of persons, this book would not have been written. I am deeply indebted to Richard F. Vancil, not only for his detailed comments on an earlier draft of this manuscript but also for the strong positive influence he has had on my thinking in general. Martin Dalgleish and Allan T. Malm also provided detailed comments on the manuscript. Others who have provided valuable inputs include Ben C. Ball, Edward Bowman, Herbert Harris, Arnoldo C. Hax, Harold E. Klein, William F. Pounds, George Steiner, Michael Treacy, and John T. Wheeler. All these persons deserve my warmest thanks. Although I benefited greatly from all this help, the caveat must be added, of course, that shortcomings and errors in this work are mine alone.

Judith Weitzman skillfully edited the manuscript, and Christine Hardiman and Joseph O'Sullivan superbly typed numerous drafts. I am thankful to them for providing such skillful help.

My thanks also go to those who reviewed the manuscript. They are Professors S. Alexander Billon, University of Delaware; Charles W. Hofer, New York University; Jules J. Schwartz, Boston University; and Melvin J. Stanford, Brigham Young University.

Peter Lorange

Purpose of Corporate Planning: Strategic Decision Making

Introduction

Corporate planning, also called strategic planning, is a tool to aid management in strategic decision making. The purpose of strategic planning is thus to accomplish a sufficient process of innovation and change in the firm. This book deals with concepts and methodology for formal planning systems. The purpose of these are to support and enhance the total planning process. Consequently, if a formal system for strategic planning does not support innovation and change, it is a failure. An activity that does *not* aid in the strategic decision making of the firm is not corporate planning, even though it may seem to involve many of the "right" elements of planning, such as elaborate five-year-plan documents. The five-year plan often does not influence strategic decisions; key executives rely on other decision-making aids. Effective corporate planning does not have to be elaborate or complicated, but it must be logical and focused on the strategic decisions that will have to be taken.

The thrust of this book will be to operationalize the concept of corporate planning as a strategic decision-making tool, i.e., on how a formal planning system can be designed to motivate and support this process of strategic change. We think that there are at least four aspects of corporate planning's role that need clarification:

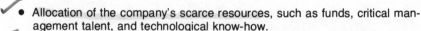

- Allocation of the company's scarce resources, such as funds, critical management talent, and technological know-how.
- Assisting the firm to *adapt* to environmental opportunities and threats, identify relevant options, and provide for an effective strategic fit with the environment. This should be interpreted in a broad sense. The strategic behavior of successful companies deals with the creation of new opportunities through development of superior product systems, through interaction with government and society at large, and so on. Adaptation covers all strategic action that improves the company's relations to its environment.
- Coordinating strategic activities so as to reflect the firm's own internal strengths and weaknesses in order to achieve efficient internal operations—integration.
- Instilling an approach of systematic management development by building an organization that is learning from the outcomes of its past strategic decisions so that it can improve on its strategic direction—a strengthened sense of professionalism with respect to strategic management.

One might presume that from a chief executive officer's (CEO's) point of view resource allocation is the only purpose of planning. For him adaptation, integration, and management development are vehicles for changing his organization in an intended direction. The planning system's role is to operationalize this.

Let us discuss each of these aspects of corporate planning as a strategic decision-making process.

Allocation of Strategic Resources

Resources—most obviously funds but also critical management talent, technological know-how, and, potentially, other resources—will have to be allocated in order to carry out a strategic decision. Let us discuss briefly a few examples of such allocations.[1] For instance, the CEO and senior management of a divisionalized company may be deciding whether to make a major commitment to expansion within one or another existing division or a somewhat more evenly split resource commitment to both divisions. Another alternative might be to invest in an acquisition. Decisions of this type will represent an option of senior management to redistribute the emphasis on the firm's different businesses; thus the discretionary resource allocation tool might have a profound impact on a company's strategic direction. Another instance of strategic resource allocation might be when a division manager decides how much of the discretionary funds generated from his leading product line should be returned to the same product line in order to protect its future position versus how much he wants to divert into the development of new product lines. Again, the resource allocation choice, this time with regard to the allocation of scarce resources among product/market alternatives within a division, might have a profound impact on the strategic direction of the division. Even when it comes to a particular product line there might be radically different alternatives for allocating resources to build up competitive strength, ranging from a heavy investment in R & D (research and development) to taking over a competitor who already possesses a valuable skill, from establishing a strong competitive position in one selected market to investing in a more diversified distribution system, and so on. The allocation of strategic funds will again shape the strategy, this time for a particular product line.

As alluded to, a strategic resource need not be funds only but any resource that can be disposed of in a discretionary manner by the firm's management to create value to the firm. A list of such strategic resources might look as follows:

1. *Funds*. These will have to be available for discretionary use. Thus, funds that are accumulated in a country from which they cannot be transferred but that will have to be reinvested internally are not a strategic resource. Similarly, although a joint venture might be highly successful, the funds flows generated might typically not be disposed of at any of the owners' free discretion. Instead the more modest dividend payments become a strategic resource to the parent companies.
2. *Management skills*. Managers are also scarce resources to the extent that they can be transferred from one area to another and that they frequently represent a scarce input factor for a particular company. For a company which has an ample number of qualified managers to pursue its present strategic direction management skill is not a strategic resource. To underscore this, excess management cannot be sold to other corporations, only transferred from one usage pattern to another within the same organization. It is in the latter form that it becomes a strategic resource. Typically, in past planning practices, corporate plans have been focused around funds almost exclusively. Critical management talent, however, might be an even more central strategic resource in many companies, and this should be reflected in realistic strategic plans.
3. *Technological know-how*. This is also a potentially important strategic resource. A company may possess a particular technological skill, say within a particular product area or in terms of a specific process technology. This skill should be made use of by choosing a strategic direction in such a way that it can benefit the organization. It is important to see technological know-how as a resource which must be maintained; if not, it might easily become depleted.

In particular instances there might be other strategic resources in addition to the ones mentioned under resources (1) to (3). For instance, such a supporting element as superior location may be a strategic resource in some instances. Business contacts may also frequently be an important strategic resource. Connections with the right persons in government positions can also be of significant strategic value. Excess production capacity and manpower can in themselves under certain circumstances be strategic resources. Even tax shelters can sometimes be

To be a STRATEGIC Resource, a resource must be available for discretionary transfer w/i or w/o a company.

transferred and used elsewhere and as such may be seen as a strategic resource. Energy is also now and then potentially a strategic resource, provided that freed-up energy can be transferred from one part of a firm's operation to another or sold to outside users. These and other examples do not, however, represent strategic resources in the more typical settings, since they can not then be transferred in a discretionary sense. It should be stressed that one should critically examine what constitutes the relevant set of strategic resources in each corporation's specific setting.

We should, however, normally focus on discretionary funds, critical management talent, and technological know-how as the primary resources that we have to allocate strategically. The allocation of resources, either through investments or discretionary expenditures, is the demonstration of strategic direction—intended or not intended, explicit or implicit. Thus, the corporate planning process must be focused on the allocation of strategic resources; the resource allocation pattern is the key output of strategic planning.

Adaptation; Identification of Strategic Options

Strategic success in most instances will require that the firm systematically look for opportunities and/or threats in its environment to come up with the best alternatives for the firm to pursue. This outward-looking search is crucial to improve the firm's chances to take more advantageous directions and to employ its resources in such a way that they yield the best return.[2]

Adaptation may be seen as the antithesis of extrapolation. Too often plans are developed based on extrapolating from the past to determine the activity levels of the future. The epitome of this can be found when activity-level forecasts in the plan increase in a harmonious manner, say linearly or with a steady, fixed percentage every year. Even in cases where the plan is not built up around such visible extrapolations, there might be a strong element of mental extrapolation behind the development of the plan. For instance, we may have become familiar with how a business has been developing in the past. Consequently, we wish that such a pattern will continue; we are comfortable with a scenario that we feel we can understand and relate to. Such extrapolation-based planning was probably not all that worthless during the relatively stable decades of the 1950s and 1960s. However, in a post-OPEC, post-recession environment belief in undisturbed growth seems far less relevant. Thus, a focus on adaptation to emerging environmental opportunities and/or threats has become more and more a critical element of planning.

Planning should facilitate an assessment of one's strategic exposure to opportunities and threats in the future and unlatch a creative process to take advantage of this. Planning should never become an extrapolative, creativity-dampening process. Needless to say, those companies that do relatively better than their competitors in instilling an adaptive planning mode are more likely to excel in an unstable environment. Paradoxically, for the sophisticated, well-managed company environmental turbulence represents a welcome opportunity to move ahead.

Adaptation might take place in several ways. It might be an assessment of opportunities to move into a new business, including acquiring another company; or it might be an opportunity to improve one's position within one of one's present businesses, say by bringing out a new or modified product line or by breaking into a new market; or, it might be an adaptive assessment that is bound primarily to a particular function, such as a new technology opportunity that seems to be emerging for R & D. Adaptation might also take the form of a defensive move, such as the divesting of a business.

Adaptation might not be equally important for all companies. Some companies may enjoy more than ample opportunities without carrying out an elaborate formal adaptation process. One example of this might be a company within a highly specialized segment of the electronics business, where demand is developing so rapidly that all the company's attention and resources are channeled into following up on the present business opportunity. Another example of relatively low adaptation pressure might be for a company within the oil-based energy field. At least until recently the selling of the finished oil products was less of a problem; the company's efforts would concentrate on how to increase oil output by getting more oil out of the ground and/or by streamlining production. Still other companies may have done such a successful identification of opportunities in the past that they have a backlog of opportunities and can de-emphasize further adaptation efforts somewhat. An example might be an R&D-intensive company which has had a number of new product successes and does not have the capabilities to follow all of them through. A final situation might be a company which does not have discretionary resources of any significance to commit during the foreseeable years, either because of a weak economic position which will call for consolidation rather than expanding or because of a recent major commitment which will consume all of the firm's discretionary resources.

It also follows that the need to adapt might change over time. For instance, the continued potential for growth and expansion within a business which has been highly successful up to the present might slacken off, or technological innovations and/or entry of new companies might weaken the firm's position. Thus, while the company's mode of succeeding in its business previously was relatively straightforward, an increased need for adaptation is now created in order to maintain an updated competitive strategic approach. Another example, which is very common, is a firm whose product lines may be shifting somewhat from a rapid growth mode toward becoming more mature as times goes by. This requires relatively fewer investments to be "plowed back" into the business for the maintenance or increase of its market share as well as the establishing of a production and/or R&D position in order to continue in the business. The firm's cash-flow position will change in terms of increased flexibility to allocate discretionary funds. However, an increased adaptation need has thereby been created for identifying viable options for allocating resources to achieve the best possible continued growth.

Integration; Narrow Down Options

A third important purpose of planning is to provide for an orderly evaluation and choice of alternatives to establish a direction which reflects the firm's own internal strengths and weaknesses. Thus, the *integration* purpose of corporate planning is to facilitate the narrowing down of the options in such a way that a basis can be provided for achieving an efficient course of operation.[3] Integration, then, is concerned with developing ways of achieving a strategic direction, always attempting to build on the firm's strengths and avoid its weaknesses. As such we might say that there *is* an extrapolative element in integration, namely, how to achieve one's strategic goals in the most economical way by building on one's present thrust and avoiding unnecessary changes in one's mode of operation.

Integration can take several forms: a dominating aspect of the integration planning process in the *strategic programming process,* which emphasizes the development of strategic programs to achieve particular objectives. Typically there are many ways to achieve a particular objective, but identifying and choosing among these alternatives often comprise a time-consuming and difficult process. The preparation of an operating budget or action program in itself represents the culmination of the integration planning process in that the budget represents the iceberg of which the agreed-upon strategies for the firm are the tip.

There are important relationships between the adaptation and integration purposes of the corporate planning activities. While adaptation implies a focus on where the firm is to go, integration focuses on how to get there in the most efficient manner. Thus, above all, the two purposes complement each other. A corporate planning activity that addresses the adaptation issues of identifying the key options but fails to narrow down these options through an efficient integration procedure does not provide a useful strategic decision-making support; issues are left hanging in the air. Similarly, a good integration approach which is not complemented by effective adaptation is equally unsatisfactory; by not systematically assessing the opportunities of the business environment one will easily end up with a "garbage in–garbage out" performance of one's firm. Although both adaptation and integration thus are critical aspects of planning, there are three aspects of the relationship between adaptation and integration which might call for differing degrees of emphasis between the two modes.

First, when the *absolute* emphasis is high on adaptation aspects of planning, then the absolute level of integration emphasis will have to be high too; this is merely an issue of capacity balancing. For instance, a large, diversified corporation which is operating multinationally within several highly volatile businesses will have a higher absolute need for paying attention to adaptation than a company operating within a set of businesses that are relatively mature and, say, within the domestic market only. Further, when it comes to the integrative aspects of planning, too, namely narrowing down the strategic choices in such a way that the firm's own strengths and/or weaknesses can be brought to bear, the first company will have to put more emphasis than the second company on this too, with a considerably more multifaceted set of strength/weakness considerations to take into account.

However, we still have to address the issue of the *relative* emphasis between the adaptation and integration dimensions. A company may be in a situation in which it needs to emphasize adaptation more vigorously, say because it is accumulating resources at a faster rate than it can utilize them. Adaptation planning should be emphasized relatively more than integration planning in such a case. Another company, however, may be in a tight financial situation due to a series of competitive setbacks. Relatively more emphasis on integration would be appropriate in such a case.

Finally, although a company may be in a position calling for both a particular absolute level of adaptation and integration emphasis as well as for a particular relative adaptation/integration planning balance, this will probably change over time, given that the needs of the firm will probably change, reflected in improved or worsened economic conditions, due to shifting environmental opportunities and/or threats and/or changes in the firm's internal strengths and/or weaknesses. For instance, a European-based corporation in the automotive business had relatively less need for both adaptation and integration planning a few years ago than it probably does today, then enjoying a relatively stable home market and high growth in its major export markets. With the emergence of fiercer competition both abroad and at home, with fundamental changes in the climate for doing business, and above all with the uncertainties resulting from an unclear energy policy, the absolute level of planning needs will probably have increased. At the same time there has probably also been a relative shift in emphasis from vigorously going after new *adaptive* opportunities, in terms of markets and model changes, to paying very close attention to internal *integrative* planning issues—above all in order to keep one's break-even point under control in response to slackening demand, rising labor costs, and increasing government intervention, which causes less flexibility in trimming the size of work-force and/or plant shutdowns. Thus, the absolute emphasis on planning as well as the relative balance between the two planning purposes should probably change over time. In fact, this calls for an approach for managing the evolution of the planning system so that an appropriate absolute emphasis as well as a relative balance can be maintained.

Management Development

A fourth purpose of corporate planning focuses on top management's need to develop the capabilities of its subordinates. Planning is a vehicle for providing more effective managerial learning, so that the executive team of a company can systematically increase its strategic decision-making capabilities over time. A properly designed and executed strategic planning approach might do this in two ways.

First, the process of developing a plan and discussing it will provide an executive with the opportunity to think through his strategic setting in a relatively systematic and complete manner. Stating his strategy and plans in an explicit way and communicating these to others might provide a valuable learning experience, particularly during the first planning tries.

Potentially an even more important aspect of learning is planning's role as a self-improving system. By stating a strategy and a set of strategic programs for achieving it, a basis has been provided for monitoring subsequent progress toward these goals. Subsequent analysis can be made of why a particular strategic program did not fulfill expectations. Experiences can thus be accumulated in a systematic manner so that past errors can be avoided in the future. Further, experience can be gained about how to react to adverse development and important steps taken toward making the corporate planning system a self-correcting system.

The learning and self-improvement aspect of planning underscores the important roles of performance monitoring and management motivation within the context of planning. We are dealing with an integrated, closed-loop process; strategic direction is initially set out through the plans and is being updated and improved through subsequent monitoring and control. The managers involved must of course feel that they have sufficient personal incentives to act in a way which actually facilitates the carrying out of corrective actions and learning.

Above all, then, the planning system should instill a management style that fosters professionalism within the corporation. This takes the form of an accumulation of strategic understanding and strengthened aptitude toward managing strategically among a relatively large management group. Also, it facilitates the transferability of strategic skills from one manager to another. Thus, planning may be seen as a vehicle for facilitating normalization of strategic management tasks within a firm. This might become an increasingly important factor for several reasons. First, given the dying out of the "old, entrepreneurial salts" who managed the business on their own, senior management transition from founder-entrepreneur to professional manager might be eased. Further, given the need to "bring up to speed" managerial talent that has been brought in from outside the company, a relatively rational and explicit management style might be highly beneficial. Also, given the need to avoid disruption when transferring managers internally, a common frame of reference to shared understanding of the firm's strategic directions might be essential.

Outline of Book

All four specific purposes for corporate planning that we have discussed are merely aspects of the overall purpose of the corporate planning activity, namely, to improve strategic decision making within the company. The purpose of this book is to operationalize the design and implementation of corporate planning systems that can provide effective support in this goal. Our focus will thus be on the planning system. Focusing on systems design is appropriate, of course. It needs to be quite explicit that the designer of the system should work in close connection with the line management. We shall make frequent reference to this designer throughout the book in order to clarify the design choices he must make.

The book addresses the issue of how to complement good substantive strategic decision moves. A corporate planning system alone cannot provide for corporate success; the quality of the strategic decisions is what matters. Many a company has prospered without a formal corporate planning system, because of intuitively sound strategic decision making by the "old salt" senior management of the company. Similarly, a good planning system cannot substitute for the lack of strategic savvy on the part of management. It seems reasonable, however, to see a planning system as a useful complement which might improve the batting average of the management. Also, the planning system might be an important factor in making the strategic management of a company less dependent on the highly individual personal leadership style of a particular chief executive, thus improving the firm's ability to cope with management transitions. As discussed, new management talent will function more effectively within a corporate managerial setting that is somewhat structured in terms of its planning system's guidelines for strategic decision-making than in a highly individualistic, even at times eccentric corporate setting. This, however, must be seen in a realistic context: Live managers do differ in their leadership styles, and this factor must be ground into the design of any planning system that they will use. Given the present state of the art, it seems as if corporate planning is a tool which is likely to give management a competitive advantage; since corporate planning is no longer in its infancy, it seems unlikely that senior management can afford to dismiss it. There is just too much evidence of its usefulness to permit this.[4]

The approach to be taken in this book is based on the belief that the needs for planning will differ from company to company as a consequence of differences in strategic situational settings. Thus, a planning system should be tailor-made to possess the unique set of capabilities needed by a given company. Hence, it is highly unlikely that there might exist a universally acceptable, standardized approach to planning. Despite this, we shall attempt to develop a generally applicable unified set of concepts for a contingency-based approach to the design and implementation of corporate planning systems. This approach is based on an initial conceptual framework for planning which sets out a few general propositions about designing a planning system. From this initial base of general components for planning, a series of steps will be suggested for tailoring the planning system to the strategic needs at hand.[5]

The outline of this book, then, is as follows: We shall start out in Chapter Two by introducing a conceptual scheme for corporate planning. We have been involved in the development of this scheme over a number of years and have implemented it in large, complex corporations several times. Our experience is that it is particularly useful to have an overall conceptual framework explicitly established when attempting to develop a corporate planning effort, given the complexity of such a system; the many elements of the system which will have to be fitted together in a consistent manner; the many executives who will have to be exposed to parts of the system and therefore must understand its rationale; as well as the political implications of strategic decisions calling for a need to develop and communicate an overall set of rules for executives' behavior in the planning process.

Having established our conceptual approach, we shall argue that a logical and often necessary step will be to carry out a strategic position audit of the firm's strategic planning needs, the topic to be discussed in Chapter Three. This is important for three reasons. First, a clear and explicit perception of the opportunities and threats in one's environment as well as one's own strengths and weaknesses, i.e., one's strategic position, might be one of the most essential prerequisites for making good strategic decisions. Second, the strategic audit might point out inconsistencies between one's strategies and illogical aspects of one's organizational structure. Third, the strategic position will provide one of the most important determinants for tailor-making the corporate planning system to the given situational setting; i.e., it will establish a focused set of needs for planning.

Our first step in modifying our general conceptual planning scheme to the particular situation will be to discuss a series of pitfalls that we have experienced when designing corporate planning systems—the topic of Chapter Four. Each of these problems relates specifically to a particular aspect of the planning process, and we shall point out what seem to be reasonable guidelines for handling each of them. Thus, we shall develop what amounts to a first checklist to determine the usefulness of the design of the corporate planning system.

There is another important aspect of the issue of designing a useful corporate planning system, namely, to tailor-make further the design of the system to the particular situation, i.e., to attempt to build into the planning system specific *capabilities* that reflect the particular needs of a given firm. This relates to the balance between adaptation and integration planning, a consideration that comes up after all the pitfalls have been handled, as an attempt at further sharpening and improving the planning system's design. In Chapter Five we shall discuss this.

Since planning needs will change over time, we shall also discuss the issue of how to manage the process of modification or evolution of the corporate planning process. What might be a useful design approach one time might be less appropriate during a different time period. The issue, thus, is to manage the system so that it maintains its usefulness, which might be seen as a third phase in the successive steps to add company-specific tailor-made focus to the planning approach, a topic to be discussed in Chapter Six.

Given that a strategic planning process, like any decision-making process, is behavioral in nature, we shall continue with a discussion of what might be appropriate *roles* for various executive groups within the firm: line vs. staff, senior management vs. division management, general business divisional management vs. functional specialists, planning staff vs. other staff, and so on. These role examples will stress the crucial need of seeing planning within an organization as a mainstream decision-making process and not as an ivory tower exercise detached from the line. Also, we shall stress the necessity of a clear division of labor among managers when it comes to being responsible for various aspects of planning. This will be the topic of Chapter Seven. Finally, in Chapter Eight we shall undertake a brief summarizing of the planning approach proposed in the book.

Summary

In this opening chapter we have stated the overriding purpose of corporate planning as we see it and as we shall advocate it in this book, namely, to assist a company's line management to carry out its strategic decision-making task. It might be argued that this task has taken on added dimensions of importance as a result of an increasingly violent and unstable environmental setting. We shall take an operational approach to strategic planning which centers on the firm's allocation of resources and which attempts to facilitate a modification of the firm's strategic direction so as to adapt to emerging opportunities and/or threats in the environment. Also, however, we shall emphasize the need to take into realistic account the firm's internal strengths and/or weaknesses when choosing among strategic options; thus, we shall advocate an approach which stresses this relationship between the adaptation and integration aspects of the firm's planning.

The focus of the book will be to bring up issues for discussion that might be useful from several types of executives' points of view, of relevance either in terms of their desire to make more effective use of planning as a strategic decision-making tool or to improve the planning process itself. Corporate planning systems can be designed only on the basis of heavy involvement from line managers themselves. Their leadership style and outlook will have to be reflected in any system they will use. CEOs and general managers thus need the kind of information found in this book. Corporate planning managers and their staff members will also find the diccussion in this book relevant in a functional sense.

There will of course not be a set of definite do's and don't's in the field of corporate planning, partly because the area is so new that more definite and universal approaches have not yet emerged but above all because of the need to tailor-make the planning approach to the particular corporate setting at hand. Thus, although we shall see examples of emerging, relatively general planning principles in this book, we shall never expect planning to lose its high degree of contingency-based tailor-making character, with few stable and lasting solutions. Despite the embryonic state of the art of corporate planning we shall, however, attempt to discuss approaches that are founded in actual corporate practices, not in abstract theorizing.

NOTES

1. The resource allocation purpose of strategic planning has been stressed by several authors; see, in particular, Norman A. Berg, "The Allocation of Strategic Funds in a Large Diversified Company" (unpublished Doctoral dissertation, Harvard Business School, 1963); Joseph L. Bower, "Planning Within the Firm," *American Economic Review*, LX (May 1970), 186-194; Joseph L. Bower, *Managing the Resource Allocation Process: A Study of Corporate Planning and Investment* (Boston: Division of Research, Harvard Business School, 1970); and E. E. Carter, "The Behavioral Theory of the Firm and Top-Level Corporate Decisions," *Administrative Science Quarterly*, 16 (1971), 413-428. A relatively more heavy emphasis on process-related aspects of planning has been made by Allan T. Malm, *Strategic Planning Systems* (Lund, Sweden: Student Litteratur, 1975, see Chapter Eight in particular) and E. Skinco, "Intuitive-Anticipatory Versus Formal Strategic Planning," *Strategic Managerial Planning* (Oxford, Ohio: Planning Executives Institute, 1977), pp. 26-34.

2. The dual concepts of adaptation and integration have been discussed by several authors, although frequently with the use of different wordings. See Ralph J. Cordiner, *New Frontiers for Professional Managers* (New York: McGraw-Hill, 1956); Alfred P. Sloan, Jr., *My Years with General Motors* (New York: Doubleday, 1964); P. R. Lawrence and J. W. Lorsch, *Organization and Environment: Managing Differentiation and Integration* (Boston: Division of Research, Harvard Business School, 1967); P. R. Lawrence and J. W. Lorsch, "Differentiation and Integration in Complex Organizations," *Administrative Science Quarterly* 12 (June 1967) 1-47; James D. Thompson, *Organizations in Action* (New York: McGraw-Hill, 1967); Eric Rhenman, *Organization Theory for Long-Range Planning* (New York: Wiley-Interscience, 1973); Clay D. Whybark, "Comparing an Adaptive Decision Model and Human Decisions," *Academy of Management Journal*, 16 (Dec. 1973), 700-703; Jay W. Lorsch and Stephen A. Allen, III, *Managing Diversity and Interdependence: An Organizational Study of Multidivisional Firms* (Boston: Division of Research, Harvard Business School, 1973); Allan T. Malm, *Strategic Planning Systems: A Framework for Analysis and Design* (Lund, Sweden: Student Litteratur, 1975); and Richard Normann, *Management for Growth* (New York: Wiley-Interscience, 1977).

3. See Note 2 for discussions of integrative aspects of the planning tasks. Also see S. R. Wilson and John O. Tomb, *Improving Profits Through Integrated Planning and Control* (Englewood Cliffs, N.J.: Prentice-Hall, 1968), and A. H. Van der Ven, A. I. Delbecq, and R. Koenig, "Determinants of Coordination Models Within Organizations," *American Sociological Review*, 41 (April 1976), 322-338.

4. For a review of studies of planning systems' usefulness, see Peter Lorange, "Formal Planning Systems: Their Role in Strategy Formulation and Implementation," in *Strategic Management: A New View on Business Policy and Planning*, Dan Schendel and Charles Hofer, eds. (Boston: Little, Brown, 1979), 226-241.

5. The approach to be taken to strategic planning in this book is an extension of a conceptual scheme developed by R. F. Vancil and P. Lorange; see Richard F. Vancil and Peter Lorange, "Strategic Planning in Diversified Companies," *Harvard Business Review*, 53 (Jan.–Feb. 1975), 81-93. The notion of interrelationship between a firm's capabilities and strategic setting has been discussed in H. Igor Ansoff, R. P. Declerck, and R. L. Hayes, eds., *From Strategic Planning to Strategic Management* (New York: Wiley-Interscience, 1976); Peter Lorange,

"Diagnosis and Design of Strategic Planning Systems in Diversified Corporations," *Sloan School Working Paper* (Cambridge, Mass.: Sloan School of Management, M.I.T., 1977); and Peter Lorange, "An Analytical Scheme for the Assessment of a Diversified Company's Corporate Planning System: Needs, Capabilities, Effectiveness," *Sloan School Working Paper* (Cambridge, Mass.: Sloan School of Management, M.I.T., 1977).

A Conceptual Approach to Corporate Planning

Introduction

As discussed in Chapter One, the purpose of the present chapter is to present a conceptual model for corporate planning as our first step toward an operationalized planning approach.[1] This model, then, will serve as a starting point or skeleton for the planning system in that it will define certain dimensions of a planning system and identify certain characteristics that seem to be more or less universally applicable. In subsequent chapters we shall discuss how to build on the framework developed here in order to achieve a more focused or tailor-made planning system with capabilities that match the specific needs of a given company.

The conceptual scheme for planning to be advanced in this chapter is based on the premise that a planning process should have an explicit focus, indicating which executives should be involved in the various aspects of the planning tasks as well as when these tasks should be dealt with. Thus, we shall propose a conceptual model for corporate planning which provides for communication, information handling, interaction, iteration, and decision consensus among the various managers of a corporation. This is done by employing a division of labor among managers at several organizational levels for different aspects of strategic responsi-

THE THREE (3) BACKBONE ELEMENTS OF CORPORATE PLANNING

bility. Also, we shall introduce several stages of focus so that the planning system will have the desired adaptation, integration, and learning capabilities. In this chapter let us first discuss the concept of levels of strategy, then the concept of stages in the planning process, and finally the information-handling characteristics of the planning process. These represent the three basic dimensions in the scheme, the three backbone elements of corporate planning. When discussing each of these three elements, however, we shall find it useful first to introduce the particular concept as such and then to discuss how it can be applied or interpreted in real corporate settings.[2]

Three Levels of Strategic Planning: The Concepts

Let us at the outset consider a typical divisionalized corporation. We shall find that such a firm provides an excellent vehicle for introducing various types of planning. The book, however, is not restricted to deal with divisional firms only; we focus our initial discussion around such firms only for reasons of expository convenience. We find that divisionalized firms will be engaged in several different businesses, each carried out by a general management unit called the division management. The corporate headquarters will attempt to provide a useful overall corporate setting by creating a meaningful balance among the divisions. Within each division there will be specialized departments that perform the various functional tasks, such as marketing, manufacturing, and R&D. The strategic tasks of each of these three major management groups will be different; each group will be faced with key strategic decisions that in their own way will be critical for the success of the company; however, the strategic variables in focus will not be the same.

corporate level: portfolio strategy

At the corporate level the primary strategic task will be to develop a favorable portfolio strategy for the diverse business activities by providing a balanced set of "legs" for the company to stand on—balance between growth and profits opportunities, degree of economic and political risk, and so on.[3] The corporate level will be concerned primarily with strategic resource flows to and from the various businesses and providing a strategy for improving the quality of the portfolio. A central issue to be dealt with here is to determine from which business sources excess strategic resources should be taken and to which businesses they should go, or, in other words, which of the company's businesses seem to provide the best basis for growth and which businesses might be required to curtail growth. The former would typically receive a net influx of strategic resources, while the latter would be giving up some resources. The strategic resource that typically would be the focus of a portfolio strategy analysis is of course the pattern fo funds flow.

A key issue is to determine the riskiness of the portfolio. How much do the various businesses interrelate? Are they subjected to largely the same or different business cycle patterns? To what extent are they relying on the same type of competition? These and other questions can be raised and analyzed at the corporate level in order to come up with a portfolio strategy and plan. In Chapter Three we shall examine approaches for analyzing the corporate portfolio strategy planning need. At this stage it will suffice to acknowledge the nature of the strategic planning task at the corporate level: What should be the balance between one's businesses? Where should one expand, and where should one contract? Where should excess funds go, and where should these funds come from?

division level: business strategy

The next level of strategy will be at the division level. Here the strategic task is to determine how the particular business can succeed. The variables here are how to improve the competitive position of one's own business, how to concentrate on future developments of the business within segments that seem more attractive, and how to develop business activities that are complementary to other activities already pursued, such as utilization of plant, equipment, or sales organization. We shall denote the strategic planning task at the division level as the business strategy development task.

It is important to stress the difference between the strategizing tasks of the corporate portfolio and the division's business. The former, having delegated the operating business responsibility to the various divisions, deals with how to contribute to the success of the company by putting emphasis on a reasonable pattern of business. The latter deals with how to succeed against one's competition within a given business.

Most businesses will have more than one product or one market, and so we may want to consider the division's business strategy as a portfolio of products and/or markets, i.e., another portfolio strategy analogous to the corporation portfolio strategy. We shall call the planning of the product/market elements within a division *business element plans*, as distinguished from the overall *business family plan* of the entire division. To consider a division's business strategizing as another portfolio planning situation is not, however, a realistic analogy for the following two reasons.

In the corporate portfolio the elements will be business families that are more or less self-contained and independent of other business families. Thus, a particular division can perceivably be sold without much effect on the other businesses' operations. Within a division, though, various products and/or markets will typically be more interdependent, since they will be largely supported by the same functional organization. If one product and/or market is sold or closed down, the functions will feel the effect immediately in terms of utilization impacts on their functional capacities. Also, a line of products may typically be marketed vis-à-vis the customer as a family, and it will be important to be able to offer a reasonably comprehensive line.

Second, just as corporate management interacts downward in the organization pyramid with a series of general or division managers (excluding for now the Group Vice Presidents, whose roles we shall return to later), each representing a business strategy, so each division manager interacts downward in the organization with a series of functional managers as well as product/market element managers none of whom, however, is a full-blown strategic manager. Thus, the division manager is the lowest general manager in the organization; his portfolio of products and/or markets represents trade-offs within his business, a strategic task distinctly different from the corporate level's task of developing a sound portfolio of autonomous businesses. As we shall see in Chapter Three, entirely different analytical techniques will be employed in assessing the corporate strategic portfolio position than with each division's product/market strategic business portfolio position.

functional level: strategic programs

We have already alluded to the third level of strategic tasks, namely, those faced by the various functional managers (such as marketing, manufacturing, or R&D) within a business. Here the task is to contribute to the strategic success of the business by focusing on the particular strategic variables in the domain of a particular functional manager. However, the key to strategic success is widespread cooperation and coordination; functional strategic plans generally do not contribute to business success in isolation but only as part of interfunctional strategic programs. For instance, a typical way to strengthen the position of a business might be to develop a new product. This will require close cooperation among the various functional departments; the strategic task is to plan the cross-functional program. To start out with strong functional plans, on the other hand, would probably inhibit the implementation of strategic programs. There are many examples of strategic programs failing because they cannot be reconciled with each of the functional plans and the strong vested interests of the functional departments. It is thus critical to recognize that the functions' strategic roles are *derived* from the business strategies they are to support. The functions represent resources which should be put to use in such ways that strategic programs are launched which contribute toward the implementations of the particular business strategies.

We have now identified three levels of strategies and strategic planning in the firm. It should thus be a requirement that a corporate planning system be hierarchical in that it reflects a division of labor in strategy formulation, implementation, and planning. At the corporate level the focus should be to develop an overall portfolio strategy which should reflect a desired risk/return balance among the firm's various businesses. This is the strategic management task of the CEO *par excellence*. At the division level, in contrast, the task will be how to succeed relative to one's competition within a particular business. Since the division manager should be the one who understands the intricacies of this business, the division of labor within the firm calls for each division manager to be responsible for the strategic success of his own business, within the context of the corporate portfolio strategy. In developing a business strategy the division manager will of course collaborate closely with his product/market managers (if such positions exist), so that his business family plan becomes a reconciliation of several business element plans. At the functional level within a division the various managers will bring their specialized skills to bear on aspects of the planning of strategic programs, complementing the division manager's general management role.

We shall claim that this three-level hierarchy of strategies is relevant in most corporate settings. In some corporate settings where there is one business only, typically smaller companies, there will only be two levels of strategy in that the portfolio level is informal. Such situations are more or less analogous to a division's business planning and should not require further discussion. In large, complex organizational settings, we might be led to believe that there should be more than three levels of strategy. In the next section we shall discuss several examples to illustrate whether a recognition of more than three strategic levels might be appropriate. As we shall see, this will rarely be the case.

Three Levels of Strategic Planning: Implementational Considerations

In this section we shall discuss whether there are instances when it would be appropriate to have more than three levels of strategy in the corporate planning system. Toward the end of this section we shall also briefly touch upon the instances where the strategic levels get truncated to two. We shall discuss three types of settings when one might assume that there should be more than three levels of strategy. One is the so-called group structure, typically within very large and/or highly diversified companies. Does this call for a group plan and a group strategy, i.e., a separate strategic level between the corporate portfolio and the divisions' business strategic levels? A second type of setting refers to the role of the so-called product/market elements within a division, as already touched upon. Does this call for a business element strategic planning task below the divisional business family planning and distinct from the (cross-) functional programming? A third setting occurs when we have a so-called matrix structure, such as can commonly be found in multinational corporations. Does the adding of, say, a geographical area dimension imply an additional strategic level?

group level:
part of portfolio strategy sphere

Starting with the so-called group phenomenon, we shall claim that the group rarely or never represents a fourth strategic level generically different from corporate portfolio strategizing or divisional business strategizing but that the group's planning efforts invariably can be seen as part of one of the other two. In instances in which group planning can be seen as an extension of corporate portfolio planning we typically have a highly diversified company where it would be difficult for the CEO to interact directly with each operating division, largely due to sheer lack of time. So instead the CEO creates groups in which a group vice president interacts with a smaller and manageable set of divisions on behalf of the CEO and the corporate level. It is important to recognize that the group thereby handles a part of the corporate portfolio and not a group portfolio of its own; the strategic problem is not to develop a series of partial group strategic plans reflecting a balanced trade-off between the expansion patterns for the groups' businesses. This would imply that each group would have to define its own businesses for expansion as well as for funds generation independently of the other groups, without being familiar with the growth and funds generation opportunities elsewhere in the company. As a consequence there would be a danger that some groups would be expanding businesses that might be less favorable to the company as a whole than other growth opportunities in other groups. Similarly, some businesses that might have been designated to provide funds within a group might not be the most advantageous sources of funds when seen in an overall corporate context. Also, a group portfolio strategy might be less amenable to encompassing selected risky investments, given that such a risk would have to be absorbed by a smaller number of businesses than if seen as part of the entire corporate portfolio. Thus, group strategies are likely to result in suboptimal resource allocation decisions, which might also result in too conservative a corporate portfolio strategy. So it is not an answer to propose that the corporate strategic portfolio can be developed as a portfolio of groups; these are already too aggregated. Strategic portfolio trade-offs must be made from a corporate viewpoint and must be based on the complete set of businesses as building blocks, not partial subsets.

By means of the following example we shall explore some potential problems of a perceived fourth level of planning in connection with a group structure. A company with 2.0 billion dollars in annual sales had been reorganized into three groups some years ago. Two of these groups were considerably larger than the third, one being involved in pulp and paper manufacturing activities, including heavy emphasis on end-use conversion through eight different divisions, and the other being involved in various metals-processing manufacturing activities, again spanning a fairly wide spectrum of activities through nine divisions. The third group was within a diverse area of emerging growth opportunities, primarily based on plastics, many of the businesses of its four divisions having developed as offshoots of the activity bases of the old businesses. Senior management was motivated to ease operations-related time loads by instituting the three groups. A number of unforeseen issues did, however, surface when the corporate planning system was modified to reflect the new organizational structure. First, the group managers were asked to take over large parts of the roles previously held by corporate management in the planning process. To free corporate management's time was one of the main reasons for delegating portions of the planning responsibility. The group managements responded to this task by instituting group staffs of their own to facilitate the execution of their "semicorporate" planning tasks. The issue that soon arose was what should be the role of each group management in strategic resource allocation; should this be addressed by each group as the new group structure setup implied, or should at least the major resource allocation trade-offs be referred to corporate management? The company experimented with both approaches, but neither yielded satisfactory results. In the former case three group portfolios were emerging, as a result of considerable efforts by the group managements to develop portfolios that were reasonably balanced in risk/return as well as in funds accumulation/funds utilization. Thus, the senior management at the corporate level was no longer able to see the overall pattern of business strategy trade-offs; instead they were faced with deciding on resource allocation trade-offs among three groups. Given that each group aimed at presenting a relatively balanced portfolio, there was not much of a substantive role left to corporate management in the resource allocation process, potentially its most effective tool for strategic change. As mentioned, the alternative approach tried was to have corporate management jointly involved with group management in the major resource allocation decisions. Here, too, however, corporate management was suffering from not having the entire business portfolio pattern clearly at hand; ad hoc and sporadic corporate involvement could not be a substitute for systematically viewing each resource allocation within the context of the overall strategic portfolio pattern. In Chapter Six we shall consider further the subject of operational solutions to prevent the groups from becoming what might be seen as strategic filters.

group level:
part of business strategy sphere

In other instances a group may contain a set of *divisions* in a highly related set of businesses. This may, for instance, have come about by a series of acquisitions of a number of smaller firms within more or less the same business, as proliferations into related business lines, and/or as geographical extensions. What often becomes apparent here is that each division cannot develop a business strategy independent of the other divisions. On the contrary, by not coordinating the strategies of the divisions a major competitive advantage might be wasted—typically the very rationale for carrying out the acquisitions in the first place. The result is a lot of overlap, competition with oneself, and so on. In instances like this the group itself is indeed one business. As such it should carry out the business strategizing and planning; whether or not the divisions should be kept depends on what would be a rational way of organizing the functional, product, and market activities within the business. To allow each of the divisions to develop its own strategic business plans and have the group create a higher-level strategic business plan would make little sense; again we have only three strategic levels of planning.

An example of this problem could be found in a European-based company which was in the cement business as well as in several segments of the building materials business. The company had been formed through the merger of two previously independent companies, each with its major business emphasis on cement. However, each company also brought into the merger several building materials businesses. Both firms were making sheets for roofing but utilizing competing production technologies. They had also been competing within the market for pre-fabricated concrete elements and blocks; however, the production technologies were even more different, and each had well-established brand names in the marketplace. Finally, each company had several ready-mix concrete plants, some of which relied heavily on delivery to some of the element manufacturers that depended on a process where concrete was a major ingredient. These companies were all maintained as independent divisions after the merger, except for the ready-mix concrete plants, which formed a new division. Coordination between the companies was to be achieved by having all building materials divisions reporting to a building materials group. What happened when the plans from the divisions emerged was that they revealed competitive strategizing patterns which would have a potentially strong negative impact on other divisions within the group. The most extreme examples of this were when (1) the ready-mix concrete division proposed to launch its own element and block production based on an excessively concrete-intensive production process and (2) at the same time the element division, which based its production on a small fraction of concrete raw material, proposed a new plant which due to economies-of-scales production efficiencies combined with an intensified retailer rebate marketing program would enable the division to capture a significant market share increase (but, alas, mostly at the expense of other divisions within "the group"). What was needed in this instance was to consider the group as the focal point for the development of a building materials business strategy and to treat roofing materials, elements and blocks, and ready-mix concrete as product lines within this business.

business level:
family vs. elements

The latest example leads us to consider a second area where we might question whether we are dealing with a fourth level of strategy. As we shall see, however, there are in fact only three distinct strategic levels here too. The problem to be discussed deals with how to consider the strategizing task within a division when the division consists of several product/market elements. We have touched upon this before, but a more extensive discussion is warranted. The product/market elements should be seen as the building blocks of the strategizing task within a division. For each product/market the task should be to develop a pattern for strategic success within this particular business element. An important aspect of this is the establishing of the funds-flow patterns that follow as a consequence of each product/market's business element strategy. For the division, then, a "family" pattern of the funds flows of the product/markets will be developed. However, the task of defining the development of business element strategies should be seen as one part of a division's overall business strategizing task, calling for additional divisional planning steps to modify the "first cut" divisional funds-flow portfolio pattern. The reason for this stems from the typical interdependence among product/markets within a division, as we have already noted. This gives rise to an additional element of divisional strategizing, namely, to develop a consolidation attractiveness dimension which reconciles the strategic roles of the product/markets within the division. Of paramount importance in this respect will be the facilitation of sharing of resources where possible, most notably production but also R&D, distribution and marketing. Also important will be to take advantage of counterseasonal patterns, pursue vertical integration opportunities and to utilize barriers to entry opportunities represented by already established goodwill positions (such as trade names), existing service and distribution channels, and so on. Thus, a consolidated set of the product/markets' business element strategy inputs constitutes a division's business family strategy, and it is not productive to consider individual business elements of such an overall business family strategy as a separate strategic level.

Our previous example from the building materials industry has already illustrated the difficulty that might occur when allowing business element strategizing to fragment a divisional business family strategy. The issue of segmenting a division into a meaningful set of product/market units for the purpose of business element strategizing is a complicated one and central for the development of good strategic planning. We shall discuss approaches for business element definition in Chapter Six. To increase our sensitivity to the complex task of defining product/market building blocks for planning, let us, however, discuss two additional examples. Both illustrate that we are still dealing with the three generic strategic levels despite the appearance of several more levels on the organization charts. The first example relates to a company which is in several areas of the cosmetics and toiletries business, with annual sales of approximately one billion dollars. The company is organized into four *divisions,* one being the dental products division. The dental products division consists of two *groups:* the toothbrush group and the toothpaste group. The two groups have separate product development activities and production facilities. Marketing and distribution are also largely independent for the two groups. Within each group there are three product lines, each headed by a product manager and each aimed at different market segments.

The potential for confusion regarding relevant strategizing elements is amplified in this example by the use of organization unit labels which are not consistent with the ones adopted in this book. According to our terminology, the company would have a corporate portfolio strategy consisting of the corporate level and the four divisions, each of these in fact being a group. The business strategizing task should be carried out by the groups, toothpastes and toothbrushes being the two entirely separate businesses. The three product lines within each of these divisions would be considered product/markets, each warranting the development of its own business element strategy. However, these cannot be dealt with as independent strategic entities; to come up with one integrated, nonfragmented path of direction, these should be seen as planning elements within their respective divisions' business strategizing task. Within each of the toothpaste and toothbrush divisions, functional unit managers should cooperate to develop (predominantly) cross-functional strategic programs to put muscle behind the execution of the divisional strategies.

In this example, we see that what might at first appear as five strategic levels in fact can easily be reconciled into the three hierarchical strategic categories. Needless to say, if we choose not to consider the strategizing hierarchy in such a consolidated form but instead base the planning task on the more extensive five-level structure, there will be serious dangers of a suboptimal portfolio strategy and too fragmented business strategies. We also should be aware of the different usage of organizational labels from company to company, underscoring the need to focus on the generic differences among the components of the organization chart; where in the organization hierarchy is a particular strategic task in fact carried out?

As a second example, consider the formal structure of a high-technology-oriented company with annual sales of around 200 million dollars and a record of rapid growth. The lowest level at which this company requires strategic planning is the *business element*, defined as a business system which involves a single product line or a particular service capability supplied to satisfy the needs of a single market segment. The company has 101 separate business elements. Considerable effort goes into developing an appropriate delineation of what is a useful business element, keeping in mind not only a logical product/market delineation but also attempting to keep the product/market units at reasonable size, not too small to afford a professional management overhead and not too large to be unwieldly to manage. (In this case the average size per product/market unit is about two million dollars.) A separate manager, then, is responsible for each of these business elements. Above the business element level are 27 divisions. Each division, headed by a division vice president, is responsible for a family of business elements. These business elements are related to each other in the sense that they share a large portion of the division's functional capabilities, notably manufacturing and R&D. Often the business elements of a particular division serve related markets, but this is not always the case. Thus, in some instances business elements might draw on a common marketing functional capability and in other instances not. The divisions are parts of seven groups, each headed by a group vice president. However, one of these seven groups is different from the others in that it consists of one division only, this division being considerably larger than the others.

The strategizing task is carried out as follows: The business element managers are charged with developing a business element strategy for their product/markets. Considerable effort goes into this, and a standardized and quite elaborate format is followed. Each division manager develops a strategy for his division by consolidating his business element strategies. The groups then develop their strategies by consolidating their divisions' strategies, and, finally, a corporate strategy is developed as an aggregation of the groups. Two types of problems become apparent. First, splitting the business strategizing task into two by focusing on business element strategies that are "added up" into division strategies results in too much fragmentation in this case. An overly proliferated pattern of disjointed or at best loosely connected business element activities results. There is an unfulfilled need to "pull together" business element strategies into business family strategies at the division level. Second, by splitting the portfolio strategizing task into two by focusing on group strategies and a corporate strategy the portfolio strategy becomes an amalgam of several group miniportfolio strategies, thus preventing senior management from properly considering the entire span of strategic options.

From our discussion of the four examples thus far we see that the creation of additional levels of strategy rarely will be warranted. Neither the corporate portfolio strategy nor the divisional business strategy should as a rule be divided up to create additional strategic levels.

the international dimension

Let us now move to a third, and often more complex, area where one frequently sees a call for additional strategic levels of planning. This relates to the international activities of companies, where unsatisfactory strategic treatment of operations often seems to exist. We shall point out three areas of concern, none of them warranting the creation of an additional level of strategy, as we shall see.

The first issue relates to the question of whether the international activities are part of any of the existing businesses. If so, the international activities should be treated as part of the business plan of the domestic division; unrealistic business plans will emerge if a global business planning point of view is not considered. If, on the other hand, an international activity is not part of any of the businesses but is a business on its own, then it should be treated as a separate division. Typically, a business in a foreign country might be run this way. Particularly for consumer products, even though similar products might be marketed in other parts of the world, strategically there is business independence.

In many situations, however, there might be some degree of interdependence as well as independence, so that it is impossible to judge whether a particular foreign operation should be seen as a separate business division or as part of a worldwide business division that is domestically based. What we might be faced with here is a so-called matrix worldwide business planning setting. Take, for instance, a worldwide product division business which is part of a corporation in which it coexists with several other worldwide product division businesses. It might be useful to explore potentials for coordinating the appearance of each of the worldwide businesses in a given country; however, this will not change the basic worldwide business planning strategic thrust. Take, on the other hand, a company which has several relatively autonomous foreign business divisions. It will of course be important for each of them to be aware of new product developments and even to carry out some worldwide coordination of research, product development, and marketing profile. Again, however, matrix planning does not call for the creation of additional strategic levels; the division's business planning is still the cornerstone of a three-level strategic planning hierarchy. It goes without saying, however, that the execution of a three-level planning approach in such a complex setting indeed will be difficult enough.

Let us as a final point emphasize the relevance of matrix planning to help provide a proper degree of focus at the corporate portfolio level as well as at the divisional business level. In Chapter Six we shall discuss further how to operationalize matrix planning. At the corporate portfolio planning level the various businesses will provide the major inputs. However, we might also want to assess the geographic implications of a particular portfolio, so that political risks and opportunities can be considered on an overall corporate basis. Matrix planning is useful here. At the business planning level of a worldwide business too there might be a need for matrix planning to ensure that the business incorporates functions, products, and countries (markets). While of course the execution of planning will be much more complex in a diverse multinational situational setting, none of these situations will add new strategic levels to the three-level strategic planning approach just developed.

In the appendix to this chapter we have illustrated how to define relevant strategic levels within a multinational corporation by means of an extensive, detailed example. This example is intended to point out some of the complexities of reaching a meaningful strategic division of labor in an actual corporation.

single-business companies

Let us now consider instances when there might be fewer than three strategic levels in the planning process. As should be clear from our previous discussion, when a company consists of only one business there will be no formal strategic portfolio level, as there is no possibility to develop a trade-off strategy with other businesses within the company. Thus, a single-business firm faces a strategic planning task essentially analogous to the business planning task of divisions of a diversified firm. Consequently, there will be only two strategic planning levels in such a single-business company.

Although the size of a company tends to correlate with its degree of diversity, this is not a general rule. There are several large companies that are in one business, or that at least are entirely dominated by one business. Examples can be found within the energy industry, the metals-processing industry, and the transportation industry, among others. Among such large single-business firms there is often a tendency to label a functional department as a "division" and to make the department manager a "division head." For instance, we might have a smelting division, a rolling mill division, and a sales division within an integrated steel company. The use of the word *division* in this context of course does not call for a divisionalized portfolio strategy. We are still faced with a two-level strategic planning task.

We have now completed our discussion of the hierarchical strategy dimension of our conceptual scheme for planning. As we have seen, there are three generic levels of strategy and strategic planning: corporate portfolio planning, divisional business planning, and (inter-) functional programming. We do not find more than these three distinct generic strategic levels even though the actual organization chart might indicate several additional operating levels. In a single-business company only two of the strategic levels will be present. By now, however, it should be clear that a typical evolving organization might provide an extremely complex setting for the development of an overall corporate strategy. The requirement that a planning system be logically clear and specific in terms of the strategic division of labor among organizational subunits within the organizational hierarchy is frequently not met in practice; it is often difficult to get a clear picture of the three levels of strategy and who is responsible for them. We thus have to recognize that while a firm will have a formal organization structure primarily reflecting the operating tasks of the company, there will also be a strategic structure which, as we have seen, does not have to coincide with the formal organization structure. Our conceptual scheme for planning will as one of its major premises be based on utilization of the division of labor that a sharpened strategic focus of a strategic structure provides. Thus, the explicit delineation of the strategic structure with its three strategic levels as distinguished from an often more complex formal organization structure is critical in our planning scheme.

Before turning to a discussion of the second dimension of our conceptual planning scheme (namely, what seems to be a relevant set of stages or steps or planning cycles, for identification of strategic options, for narrowing down these options, and for monitoring progress toward strategy fulfillment), let us briefly restate our definitions of the levels of planning as a way of formally establishing an explicit vocabulary of terms which we shall use throughout the book. These terms have of course been introduced throughout our discussion and examples up to this point. Table 2-1 provides our summary of hierarchical levels planning terms.

TABLE 2-1 Types of Hierarchical Strategic Planning Terms and Their Correspondence with the Operating Organization

Strategic Structure	Operating Structure; Organizational Units
Portfolio strategizing	Corporate Group
Business strategizing: Business family strategy Several business element strategies	 Division Product/market element (also called strategy center*)
Strategic programming	Functions R&D Manufacturing Marketing ⋮

*See Chapter Three for a justification of the strategy center label.

Stages of the Planning Process

We shall propose five stages of planning for identifying environmental opportunities and/or threats, for narrowing down our strategic options to recognize our own strengths and/or weaknesses, for monitoring progress toward the chosen strategic options, and for providing management with incentives for contributing toward the strategic direction, namely, *objectives setting, strategic programming, budgeting, monitoring,* and *linking to managerial incentives.* We shall discuss each of these five stages in turn in terms of their specific individual purposes and their interrelationships.

stage one: objectives setting

The first stage, objectives setting, serves primarily to identify relevant strategic alternatives, where or in what strategic direction the firm as a whole as well as its organizational subunits should go.[4] This is an extremely critical phase of the planning process in that it should set the innovative and creative tone that is a characteristic of good planning. It is at this stage, above all, that the planning process should facilitate a clearer look at environmental opportunities and threats facing the firm. Too often the planning process fails to create this environment-oriented, opportunistic, and creative atmosphere but instead shows a mechanistic, extrapolative dominance. Needless to say, if the planning process should suffer from lack of appropriate openness at this stage, it is likely that the remaining steps of the planning process will turn out to be less useful, too, handicapped by the inappropriate starting position of the planning process.

To facilitate the development of a creative set of objectives it is useful to consider four aspects of the objectives-setting stage. These are an assessment of the opportunities and/or threats facing the corporation as well as its various businesses; comparison of one's own performance criteria with available outside criteria for normal performance to be expected of comparable organizations; delineation of assumptions and constraints for objectives setting, including a consideration of the general economic outlook, the firm's financial position, and social and regulatory factors; and finally, reconciliation with the personal aspiration and style of the CEO and his key management team.

The first aspect of the objectives-setting process, then, is to assess the rationale for the strategic direction of the firm and its businesses by determining how to take advantage of environmental opportunities and threats. This should take place at both the corporate and divisional business levels. The divisional task to search for new opportunities and threats within its business will typically have three aspects. First, a systematic assessment should be made of potential developments with regard to the attractiveness of the business, for instance, which segments of the business seem to have the best growth potential and which segments seem likely to slacken in the future. Second, assessment should be made of the competitive strength of one's own business, for instance, what moves might be likely from present and potential competitors, given their strengths and weaknesses relative to one's own. Third, the opportunities and risks of a fundamental breakthrough of some sort should be considered, such as an entirely new process for making a product, radical shifts in consumer behavior, or sudden raw material shortages. We are of course typically on very soft ground here; scenario building and technological forecasting may be useful tools, but they are typically among the most arty aspects of planning. The strategic position assessment must be precise and specific in terms of the markets and products and must articulate the basic rationales for carrying out business. One should avoid defining business strategy at such a high level of abstraction that it becomes meaningless, an issue to be discussed further in Chapter Three.

One company attempted to have its businesses address the issue of operationalizing their long-term performance aspirations by formulating a picture of where they would be in ten years. The businesses were asked to focus on the opportunities and threats on their business horizon, disregarding their own internal strengths and/or weaknesses for now. It was pointed out to the divisions that the natural tendency might be to do just the opposite, an example of mental extrapolation into the future based on one's present business situation; the danger of this would be to develop a picture of the future of the business based on the wishful assumption that future opportunities and/or threats would be extensions of the present. After taking a context-free look at future opportunities and/or threats, each division was then asked to assess what broad areas of change this might call for to make the necessary reorientation of one's internal strengths and weaknesses.

In this instance, one division, which happened to be in a particular segment of the computer-manufacturing business, identified a need to strengthen its own technological base in the semiconductor area, which was seen as critical for going after opportunities within an emerging segment of the minicomputer business. A rapid move was deemed essential to meet the competition, to "tool up" for a more aggressive performance within the market that the division had identified. The division proposed an acquisition which was subsequently approved and consummated. Needless to say, this type of acquisition was merely a move to develop a better product line position within an existing business faster than through internal development and in response to the more aggressive performance expectations established. Such a business-strategy-related acquisition should not be confused with the role of acquisitions as a way of taking advantage of opportunities and avoiding threats for the corporate-level portfolio, an issue that we shall now discuss.

The corporate-level task of assessing opportunities and threats should include appraisal of the general climate for the availability of new businesses for the company to acquire as well as for new internal business growth opportunities, such as eventually developing a new division. Part of this corporate alternative business opportunity availability assessment procedure also involves assessing the potential for divestiture of a business. It will of course be quite rare that an acquisition or a divestiture actually takes place, but the purpose of this planning activity is to carry out a systematic assessment of opportunities of this kind to determine where the company might go in terms of upgrading the portfolio of businesses. There should be awareness of potential threats to each existing business, too, and awareness that they have to earn their place as part of the corporate portfolio, given the emerging pattern of opportunities facing the company. The notion that some core business should be treated as part of the company forever should be resisted—hence, the ongoing assessment of divestiture potentials. The overall result of this aspect of the objectives-setting process is of course that expectations about what should be realistic opportunities and/or threats at the corporate portfolio level can be appropriately developed.

Many companies fall into the trap of developing their notion of a reasonable set of long-term performance expectations based to a large extent on an *intellectual extrapolation* of the firm's past performance. Instead, a less inhibited assessment of reasonable long-term opportunities and/or threats should lead to the firm's overall performance expectation. Keeping a close eye on performance aspirations of other companies is useful in this respect.

Let us thus turn to a second major aspect of objectives setting, namely, the desirability of comparing a company's own tentative criteria for objectives performance with available performance criteria of corporations and/or businesses comparable in size and types of business involvements. Comparative performance data can be found in such listings as *Fortune's 500, Forbes Annual Report on American Industry*, or stock market reports. This should signal whether the performance of the company as a whole seems up to par, outstanding, or lagging behind. This should give corporate management an indication of the success of the company's adaptive attempts and whether there is an imminent need to strengthen its efforts.

For each of the particular business divisions a similar evaluation of performance can also be made by using the so-called PIMS data bank.[5] Currently over 1200 real-life businesses are contained in the data base, a *business* being defined as an operating unit selling a distinctive set of products to a distinctive market and with a clearly identifiable set of competitors, i.e., what we have denoted a product/market element, chartered with developing a business element strategy. A multiple regression model is used to diagnose strategies at the product/market level, indicating what would be a normal ROI (return on investment) for a product/market element in a particular strategic position (in terms of its market share position, growth, and so on). Thus, for instance, a division manager can compare his own product/market elements' performance records with the norm, again leading to the identification of businesses which might be under pressure to improve their adaptation posture.

The process of making acquisitions and/or divestitures might also shed important and useful light on the company's own performance criteria. To illustrate the positive effects of an ongoing acquisition/divestiture assessment on the establishment of realistic and operationally useful performance expectations as part of the planning process, one highly diversified company with annual sales of approximately two bill-ion dollars might serve as an example. This company receives an average of 12 acquisition leads per week (some relatively preliminary, others considerably more detailed). A separate group within the corporate plan-ning department does the first screening and makes recommendations on each. Relatively few leads will be followed up, but the corporate planning department's acquisition group plays a central role in providing con-tinued analytical support here too. The result of this activity is that a healthy notion of what might be a realistic set of alternatives for modify-ing the present business portfolio with its 3 groups and 52 divisions surfaces. The constant exposure to external business opportunities and reasonable patterns of performance heightens senior management's abil-ity to articulate and express strategic performance standards for its own business divisions. Being able to draw on such external sets of inputs seems to increase corporate management's credibility with its divisions when it comes to communicating and discussing its performance expecta-tions with them. To achieve this useful effect on the corporate planning process, then, a key feature seems to be that the acquisition analysis support function rest entirely with the corporate planning group. The commonly found corporate practice of having a separate corporate ac-quisition group is less likely to provide this positive effect. Such detached groups might also face the problem of not fully comprehending the performance needs of the corporate portfolio pattern and the specific areas in which the portfolio should change. Acquisitions that are strategi-cally detached from the portfolio strategy might result.

A third major aspect of the objectives-setting phase is to make more explicit and to communicate a set of underlying assumptions and con-straints relevant to a feasible corporate strategy. These have at least four aspects. First, the general economic outlook should be considered as a factor that might have a dampening or a stimulating effect on the firm's objectives setting. Expectations about the long-term developments of the general economic climate traditionally play an important role in modify-ing corporations' objectives. Relatively new sources of information for the firm to use in this respect are economic forecasting models such as the DRI (Data Resources Institute) model, the Wharton model, or the Chase Econometrics model.[6] These model services can give forecasts of nar-rower business segments, too, of particular relevance to specific divi-sions.

A second class of constraints would be to state common assump-tions with regard to such items as interest rate, social security expenditure rates, tax rates, currency rates, internal overhead charges, and so on. The purpose here is to see that plans can be developed on the basis of common assumptions, so that they can be compared and discussed on the basis of substantive strategic issues of concern, not bogged down in questions relating to the premises for the plans.

Third, the financial constraints facing the firm—the unused new financing capacity that the company possesses, the cost of raising new capital, and the rate of dividend payouts—should be made more explicit. The firm must decide to what extent to emphasize growth versus ROI, the former typically being a more long-term goal and the latter more short-term. An optimal growth picture can be envisioned based on these factors. It is of course impossible to determine exactly the most advantageous path of expansion based on the amount of funds one should borrow. What is essential, however, is to communicate a realistic view of the financial situation, so that sound strategies can be developed that are consistent with the financial goals and not overly optimistic or pessimistic. In Chapter Three we shall discuss an approach for a strategic audit of a firm's financial position in order to see what particular needs for planning a given financial position might imply.

Finally, there might be a number of nonfinancial constraints that could be important for the development of realistic plans, such as issues relating to social factors, political factors, business ethics, government regulations for setting safety standards, pollution, energy conservation, and so on. These factors will probably become relatively more important in the years to come. Thus far many of these constraints have been seen as negative intrusions by the public sector into the strategic management of corporations. It is probably a competitive advantage for those companies that see these constraints in a positive sense, attempting to build their strategies to neutralize the constraints as much as possible. This is another aspect of the basic challenge of the objectives-setting task, namely, to adapt to environmental opportunities.

A large multinational corporation, headquartered in France, was encountering a lot of problems during the corporate-divisional review of divisional objectives. Many of these problems stemmed from lack of corporate awareness of several types of common assumptions. It took several meetings to clear up the confusion stemming from this lack of compatibility among the various divisions' proposed objectives. After the corporate planning department issued a set of common planning assumptions, much of this confusion disappeared, and there was a better basis for discussion of what might be substantive matters of disagreement. The corporate planning assumptions document contained the following elements:

- A corporate creed, stating in broad terms what type of company it was striving to be. This creed was partly based on the results from a survey about how several levels of management were seeing their company.

- A set of principles with regard to modes of ethically acceptable business conduct and social responsibility.
- A set of definitions of terms. Some of these were verbal, while others indicated uniform ways of measuring quantitative phenomena (such as how to measure relative market share).
- A set of economic assumptions from the corporate economist's office which indicated the discount rates to use in net percent value calculations, the annual percentage increase rate to use for items such as wages and energy, and currency exchange rates to use. The corporate economist's assessments were revised every year and were reviewed and approved by the CEO.

A fourth and final class of issues with respect to the objectives-setting process relates to the role of the CEO and his key line managers. The objectives-setting stage provides a vehicle for the CEO and the division managers to be explicit about their aspirations for the organization: What is the nature of the risk they are willing to take to support a minimally tolerable performance expectation? How can they be more explicit about articulating an acceptable organizational notion of preferred directions?

For instance, when we contrast a well-established firm within a relatively mature business, say, a cement manufacturing company with a relatively new, extremely rapidly growing company within an emerging high-technology business area, we might find significant differences in managements' aspirations: by tradition relatively little willingness to take new risks by diversifying into new business areas in the former case versus much more of a readiness to go after emerging strategic opportunities in the latter; acceptance of relatively comfortable and less challenging performance levels versus striving for even more rapid growth and increase in profits. This aspirations-related aspect of a firm's organizational climate is highly relevant for striking a realistic and useful planning direction. Undoubtedly, we are dealing here with important constraints in terms of setting realistic aspirations for strategic change. Recognizing this explicitly in the planning process of course does not mean that planning should not attempt to improve lackluster aspirations. Rather, it implies that one should attempt to be reasonably explicit about the realistic potential for change in strategic thinking. The pervasive influence of a CEO in particular, who might happen to be an extremely strong-willed individual who sees obstacles as challenges and enjoys pursuing unorthodox opportunities, is probably an extremely influential determinant of the choice of objectives.

Before concluding our discussion of the objectives-setting stage, let us briefly discuss the distinctions between two notions that have become established in the terminology of planning: *goals* versus *objectives*. Objectives, as referred to in this book, are more general statements about a direction in which the firm intends to go, without stating specific targets to be reached at particular points in time. A goal, on the other hand, is much more specific, indicating where one intends to be at a given point in time. A goal thus is an operational *transformation* of an objective; typically a general objective often gets transformed into one or more specific goals.

It is, however, important not to let semantics block one's use of the goals and objections notions. First, it should be noticed that some persons use the words interchangeably and that some label the more general direction-setting expression as a "goal" and the more specific target an "objective," exactly contrary to the use of the words that we have proposed above. Any organization is of course entirely free to use the labels it chooses; however, it should be consistent in its use of the two words. A more important objection about the use of the two words, however, is the fact that they tend to dichotomize when we are dealing with one decision-making process in which the emphasis should be on the transformation from general to specific. Thus, we are dealing with an objectives/goals-setting process in which we emphasize both general and specific elements. The objectives/goals-setting stage is thus one step, not two. The output from this step will be a set of objectives, transformed into more specific goals, specific enough in terms of nonfinancial as well as financial detail to provide an operational basis and focus for developing strategic programs for achieving the objectives and goals. The strategic programming task will be discussed in the next section. Another indication of the degree of specificity needed at the present stage is that subsequently we must be able to measure progress toward the goals, one of the intents of the monitoring stage.

In summary, the objectives-setting stage serves a very important purpose in the planning process in that it facilitates a creative, imaginative, adaptive focus on environmental opportunities and threats. Without this step of identifying and sorting the major relevant strategic options the rest of the planning process is likely to resemble an extrapolative exercise. There will of course be a large element of intuitive managerial talent behind the setting of imaginative objectives. However, we have recommended that it is useful to pay specific attention to the following four classes of issues when developing objectives: a thorough assessment of the opportunities and/or threats facing the company and each of its businesses, the establishment of outside and relatively objective criteria for assessing the company's and its divisions' levels of performance, the delineation of various classes of constraints that need to be observed when developing objectives, and, finally, an explicit recognition of the pervasive influence of the CEO relaying his ambitions and aspirations for his organization, a critical determinant as to whether the objectives will be marked by excellence or mediocrity.

strategic programming

The second stage of the planning process relates to the development of strategic programs for achieving the chosen objectives. We have decided during the previous objectives-setting step where we intended to go; now the issue is how to get there. Execution of the strategic programming process takes place primarily at the functional levels within each of the existing business divisions. The intent and emphasis is on developing long-term programs for achieving internal growth. A separate corporate level set of programs might deal with acquisitions and/or divestitures and/or new business developments that fall outside the charters of the existing businesses; we shall discuss this after having gone through three aspects of ongoing internal growth programming. We shall first discuss some of the basic characteristics of strategic programming, both in general and more specifically for four different types of strategic programs that we have identified. Then we shall discuss the need for evaluating the match between the sense of direction actually provided by a particular strategic program and the strategic goals that the program is intended to help fulfill. The final aspect of our discussion of strategic programming at the functional levels within the businesses will deal with the need to utilize fully one's specialized functional human resources.

A first aspect of strategic programming at the functional levels of a firm's business should be intellectual challenge, calling for imagination, skill, and professionalism. Strategic programs cannot be heavily based on past experience; they are unique, and the challenge is to attack unstructured problems in a novel and imaginative way. Typically, strategic programs are interfunctional in their nature, requiring coordinated inputs from different functions, such as R&D, manufacturing, distribution, and marketing. Programming activities go on all year round; it is a continuous process. Informal elements of communication and interaction are particularly important, above all during the initiating stages. The annual corporate planning process adds to the strategic programming process in such a way that it requires that the status of the programs be written down once a year, thereby providing an inventory of the various strategic programs in process at that time.

Given that there typically will be a large, diverse, and unique set of strategic programs for any company, it is difficult to give useful general examples. However, many program activities seem to fall into the following broad areas[7]:

1. *Existing revenue programs*. One example of this might be the development of a set of marketing programs for the existing product line. This will imply a heavy involvement by the marketing department in working out the basic

concepts of the program, such as advertising theme and selling approach. However, other functional departments, such as production and/or distribution, also will be involved in order to facilitate the availability of the products at the right place and time. Another example might be the development of an improved product, which might be perceived as necessary by the marketing department but which might involve the R&D functions as well as production. In both instances the necessary functional skills must be mobilized to meet the requirements of the particular program. Cooperation among the functional specialists is essential. This type of strategic program tends to focus on how to modify and improve one's product or services in an effort to adapt to emerging environmental pressures, such as pursuing new opportunities or responding to threats. Thus, these programs are primarily aimed at improving the effectiveness of existing business family or business element strategies.

2. *New revenue programs.* One example of this might be the planning and development of new products within the general business area of a division. There will be a need for the involvement of a broader set of functional skills than often might be the case in existing revenue program developments. Also, given that the uncertainty typically will be higher with such a program, making it difficult to specify the exact nature of each function's involvement, it becomes particularly important that such a program be managed on such a basis that a cross-functional and project-focused emphasis can be maintained. Later we shall discuss aspects of how to operationalize these programs, and we shall see the critical importance of a program focus, particularly when it comes to making decisions with regard to major changes in a business's direction, discontinuation, or scaling up. In general we might say that this strategic program type, too, is centered on adapting to environmental opportunities and/or threats by developing new products and/or services, often for new market niches. Thus, the thrust of these strategic programs is to develop new, effective business family or business element strategies.

3. *Efficiency improvement programs.* One example of this might be a program to streamline the production/distribution process, so that the production runs become more economical, and inventories might be trimmed as well. This might involve not only the production and distribution departments but might also require engineering inputs in redesigning the product line, R&D for modifying the product itself so that it can be produced more cheaply, marketing inputs, and so on. The general thrust of this type of program will be on the integrative aspects of planning, on improving processes rather than developing new products, and on providing more efficient strategies not only for each division or product/market element but also for exploting economies resulting from interdependencies among product/market elements.

4. *Support programs.* Some programs might involve the development of better administrative support routines, such as, for instance, an improved management information system. While the data-processing department might take a lead in the system's development, other administrative support functions as well as the business-generating functions will also be involved. In general these strategic programs are intended to improve the organizational climate for developing the adaptive and/or integrative programs that directly affect the organization's competitive position. Most of the support programs tend to be integrative in nature.

A second aspect of the strategic programming process relates to the need to evaluate strategic programs to determine how well a particular program seems to contribute toward a particular goal. This is often a difficult task. There is a natural tendency for each function to develop standards for judging the success and appropriateness of a strategic program which tend to be based largely on criteria associated with each function and not on cross-functional success criteria. Research and development, for instance, might focus on the extent to which the program has been successful in providing answers to some critical but previously unknown technical properties; manufacturing might emphasize the choice of a program alternative that minimizes the constraints of production. None of these concerns, however, emphasizes the overall strategic fit as such. A program might represent truly innovative research breakthroughs without contributing toward the development of a new product for a particular market niche as hoped for. The market potential may in fact be entirely lacking. Similarly, a production expansion program might make sense from a production efficiency point of view, although the market for the expanded production might be lacking. To complement the often partial roles of the functional managers, it is important that the division manager apply his general management viewpoint to the evaluation of strategic program alternatives. It will be one of his key tasks to make a proper selection of program alternatives in such a way that the business proceeds, as intended, toward the stated objectives.

The assurance of focus on strategic programming activities is not easy to achieve. We shall discuss approaches to this later in the book; however, a rather involved example to illustrate the nature of the task might be beneficial to discuss at this stage. We shall, therefore, see how the pharmaceutical division of a highly diversified company, heavily dependent on its R&D function, approaches this. For such a business which will be heavily R&D-intensive relative to businesses in most other industries, it seems paramount that major decisions taken within R&D-dominated strategic programs be resolved in a way that is consistent with the pharmaceuticals business strategy. It is thus particularly necessary to integrate R&D closely with other functions so that the resulting programs fit in the overall business plan. Research and development provides a critical and necessary input for implementing the strategic programs of the business.

As a program of developing a new drug proceeds through the stages of gradual completion—ideas-feasibility check, development, pilot stage, semicommercial stage, commercial stage—two critical issues emerge:

- Should we do this program at all? Does it promise the desired strategic potential in terms of leading to a worthwhile business segment?
- Is the likelihood of commercial success high enough so that we might continue investing in the strategic program?

The decision about whether to continue with a program requires an agonizing judgment: Will the added costs yield enough progress toward reducing the risk of commercial failure? Trade-off considerations of this kind will be central to the strategic program developments and choices.

To assess the strategic impact of a new program, the pharmaceutical company raises two classes of questions as part of its strategic programming process:

1. How is the strategic program expected to lead to modified or new products that fit in present business activities?
2. Does the division have sufficient functional capabilities to solve the strategic programming issues at hand, above all the relevant R&D capabilities?

Before attempting to answer any of these issues the division management makes an assessment of the critical risks expected to be associated with a strategic program. A formal list of factors has been developed for this purpose. This list includes assessment of potential market shares and growth rate, potential unexpected obsolescence possibilities, uniqueness of the technological strengths developed, as well as exposure to environmental regulation. Another checklist attempts to assess the strategic program's potential impact on the present business, i.e., how a business element strategy might fit within the business family strategy. Questions in this respect include assessing the capital needed, constraints problems within the various functions such as marketing or production, new materials availability problems, as well as whether a program seems to have strong organizational support.

We might draw a two-dimensional chart which summarizes the portfolio of strategic programs in terms of the attractiveness of the programs' direction and the strategic fit with existing business family strategy and functional capabilities and skills, as shown in Exhibit 2-1.

We would expect strategic programs that measure high on both dimensions to contribute positively to the implementation of strategies of high-priority business segments, while at the other extreme we would expect a program which measures low on both dimensions to be part of an unattractive strategy that we would not pursue. The difficult strategic choices, then, come for the in-between cases, which need to be managed selectively and which should receive particular attention during the programming process.

It should be stressed that for a strategic programming effort to be successful it will have to utilize strengths of the functional organizational units. Since organizational capabilities, involving "investment" in human resources, can be difficult to build up over a short period of time, it is important not to undertake strategic programs which require functional skills that are weak or nonexistent. Similarly, if a particular organizational

EXHIBIT 2-1 Strategic Programs' Strategic Postures

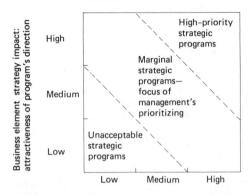

Business family strategy impact:
fit with existing capabilities

skill is seen as a strength, it will be advantageous to pursue strategic programs that utilize this skill. A useful tool for checking whether the strategic programs are consistent with the organization's strengths is a functional strength profile, which consists of assessing one's own strength within each function relative to one's major competitor (or, if one cannot identify one major competitor, relative to the competition in general within the business). Besides providing a better match between the strategic programming activities and the organization's own strengths and weaknesses, such a profile might also provide the basis for a key functional executive development plan for improving one's programming strengths in the long run. It should also be noted that a business now and then might want to acquire another company instead of embarking on the often time-consuming task of developing a set of internal functional skill factors. In such instances, it is particularly important that one's own competence profile and that of the candidate for acquisition complement each other so that one can obtain strengths presently lacking.

Exhibit 2-2 illustrates such a competence curve in the pharmaceutical firm that we discussed earlier. This company had a very strong base in its research capabilities. However, the bottleneck in launching new products successfully was the marketing-related function. This finally led to changes in some of the company's strategic programs, most notably that several new drug programs were pursued through joint ventures with companies with stronger marketing organizations and that licensing was scaled up.

The relative competence strength of each function as plotted on the vertical axis of Exhibit 2-2 cannot of course be measured in precise ordinal

EXHIBIT 2-2 Competence Profile: Illustrating Relative
Strength of Functional Departments'
Capabilities

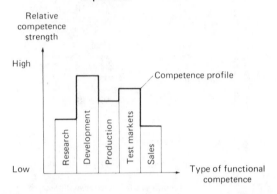

terms. What is useful, however, is even a relatively crude assessment of
how each function's capabilities, strengths, and weaknesses seem to
compare with those of a few of the firm's relevant major competitors. This
will in turn highlight which functions are strong or weak relative to one's
competition.

Having now completed our discussion of strategic programming at
the functional level, emphasizing the cross-functional nature of the process and that it should be carried out with a clear strategic context in mind
and that major differences in functional capabilities should be recognized
in order to utilize strengths and avoid weaknesses, we shall shift emphasis and discuss the strategic programming task at the corporate level.
In this respect, it is important to distinguish between acquisitions which
are alternatives to internal growth strategic programs of a business, as
just discussed, and acquisitions/divestitures of businesses to change the
strategic portfolio balance. While the former is the responsibility of an
existing business division, resulting from an analysis showing that this is
an easier way of attaining the business's objectives than through internal
development, corporate acquisitions/divestitures require a different kind
of strategic programming activity. Typically, this is the major corporate-
level strategic programming activity. (Other activities at the corporate
level might be exploratory R&D to provide "seed" to the divisions for
future products and strategic programs to improve aspects of the firm's
administrative systems.) This programming activity is often somewhat
more standardized than programming within the divisions in the sense
that its focus will be on changing the portfolio balance through acquisitions and/or divestitures as well as new ventures as the dominant
vehicles. For instance, a corporate staff group may be chartered with the
tasks of securing acquisition candidates; analyzing their effects on the

overall business portfolio pattern, particularly the overall financial and risk situation; as well as negotiating. Other corporate groups might decide upon new venture opportunities and nurture those programs from their first stages of development through a corporate internal new ventures division. As soon as the new product has been firmly established the intent is to transform it into an ordinary business division. A third type of corporate strategic programming activity might involve research in a highly exploratory stage so risky that no single division would want to undertake it. This research will have a major effect on the company's business portfolio by providing the basis for new business divisions. It is important that all these programming activities be seen as part of the overall planning process to implement intended portfolio strategy changes.

We have seen several examples of problems being created in the strategic programming phase when the distinction is blurred between the interfunctional programming activities so critical to the implementation of a business strategy and strategic programming activities that are part of corporate portfolio strategy development. In particular there seems to be a danger that corporate programming activities might hamper programming within the businesses. One company, for instance, was very active in its attempts to grow through acquisitions, this activity being spearheaded by the CEO himself. Several of the acquisitions were within business areas that overlapped or were very close to some of its present divisions. When these acquisitions subsequently were handed over to the divisions, the divisions' present programs needed complete overhauls now that previous competitors would have to be integrated into the businesses.

Another company carried out central research which was subsequently handed over to existing divisions. Not only was there strong divisional resentment because it had to pay for an increasing share of the research activity as a project progressed—a more fundamental problem was the poor strategic fit of the centrally developed programs with the business strategies. Central research did not have a close enough understanding of and feeling for the business; the business, on the other hand, put the blame on central research whenever one of its products was in some sort of competitive trouble. In general, extreme care should be taken whenever a significant share of the strategic programming activity is carried out outside the divisions, notably at the corporate level. A clear portfolio focus of intended impact must be demonstrated to be the rationale for the corporate programming activity in each case.

We have now completed our discussion of the second stage of the planning process, namely, the development of strategic programs for operationalizing directions decided upon during the preceding objectives-setting stage. A successful strategic programming effort is of course critical for the development of a useful overall planning approach; even the most brilliant perceptions about strategic direction are useless unless they are followed up by an imaginative implementation effort. The facilitation of strategic progress along an intended path will typically be a long-term effort, perhaps lasting several years. It follows that program specification should not be too overly detailed. However, for the near term a more specific elaboration of the strategic programs is often useful to establish a clear pattern of activities to be carried out, say, over the next year by a wide number of organizational subgroups and in order to specify the nature of various executives' responsibilities. This is the purpose of the third stage in the planning process, the budgeting cycle, to be discussed in the next section.

budgeting

The budgeting stage, also called the operating plan or the action programming stage, is the third step in the corporate planning process. It is closely related to the strategic programming stage: After a set of strategic programs has been decided on, a more detailed set of action programs will have to be established for the next year. As such, the budgeting stage is merely the iceberg reflecting a detailed operations activity pattern for next year which should be consistent with the longer-term strategic programs. The purpose of the budgeting stage then is above all to establish a pattern of activities for the near-term execution of the strategic programs, assigning specific tasks to various organizational units and groups of management, and appropriating necessary financial resources. Above all, it facilitates coordination and integration of the strategy implementation activities.[8]

It is important to see budgeting as the culmination of the strategic planning process. Unless there is a clear and logical relationship between objectives setting, strategic programming, and budgeting, the decision-making purpose which should be the aim of the corporate planning activity will be sacrificed. The three stages of the process discussed so far can be seen as attempting to identify the strategic options and to narrow down these options by gradually eliminating alternatives, thereby adding to the analysis of the remaining options. This can be seen from Exhibit 2-3.[9]

It can also be seen from Exhibit 2-3 that by not allowing for a gradual narrowing down during the objectives-setting and strategic programming stages, virtually the same set of strategic options faced by the firm during the objectives-setting stage will have to be faced by the firm and decided upon during the budgeting stage—strategic options span A versus strategic options span B in the case of prior narrowing down. Thus, an exceptionally high capacity for strategic decision making will be

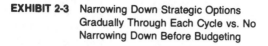

EXHIBIT 2-3   Narrowing Down Strategic Options
Gradually Through Each Cycle vs. No
Narrowing Down Before Budgeting

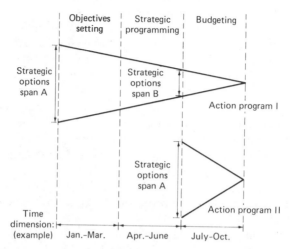

called for during a short period of time. More likely, the quality of strategic decision making will suffer, either because of less in-depth analysis of all relevant alternatives or because several alternatives might not have been identified at all. Thus, action program I of Exhibit 2-3 is likely to be of a better quality than action program II.

It should be noted that while it is essential that some narrowing down is done during the objectives-setting and strategic programming stages so that the budgeting process can be carried out within a relatively well-defined context, it is not possible to provide general guidelines about precisely how much the strategic choices can be narrowed down prior to budgeting. This will vary from company to company depending above all on the degree of complexity and uncertainty associated with the company's businesses. Within relatively stable businesses relatively more rapid narrowing down can take place early in the process, thus providing for a budgeting stage which will be more focused and concerned with fewer alternatives than in the case of more complex and uncertain businesses. We shall return to this issue of systems tailor-making in Chapter Five.

Maybe the most important role of the budget is to provide a blueprint for the actions that each group in the organization will be expected to carry out in the near term. These actions should of course be coordinated so that they add up to an overall integrated action plan for the company. This is probably relatively straightforward when it comes to the corporate and divisional level managers but is likely to be much less clear at the functional level. Given the strategic emphasis on cross-functional program focus, the budgets should, however, complement the strategic programs by restating the short-term program consequences along functional dimensions. Management by objectives (MBO), conceptually linked to the budget, is a good way of doing this. We shall discuss how to do this in more detail in Chapter Four. This gives us a unique and flexible tool for effective determination of each organizational unit's role in developing the near-term actions to be carried out for performance tracking and control. In Exhibit 2-4 we have illustrated this two-dimensional emphasis which is useful in achieving both a cross-functional strategic programming focus and a budgeting focus that unambiguously spells out the action program tasks of each function.

Although the two-dimensional interrelationship that is indicated in Exhibit 2-4 would be the norm in most organizational settings, there are some organizations where the emphasis might be placed almost solely on the program dimension or on the functional dimension. We shall give examples of two extremes when one or the other of the dimensions is virtually absent.

One extreme would be a business that is virtually in an exploratory or embryonic stage of development and which has thus not arrived at a commercialized stage. In such a setting the business activity can appropriately be described as one of pursuing a set of critical developmental programs. Management tasks are based on temporary program organizations, and no permanent functional departments as yet exist. The budget in this case would merely be more detailed specifications of the strategic programs, indicating near-term actions for the temporary organization to follow. Examples of this might be large new business developments, such as an oil company's attempts to develop synthetic fuels from a coal liquefaction process.

At the other end of the spectrum, we might conceive of an extremely stable and well-established business where no new business strategic program is likely to occur. All strategic programs associated with the

EXHIBIT 2-4   Strategic Programming/Budgeting
                  Sequence

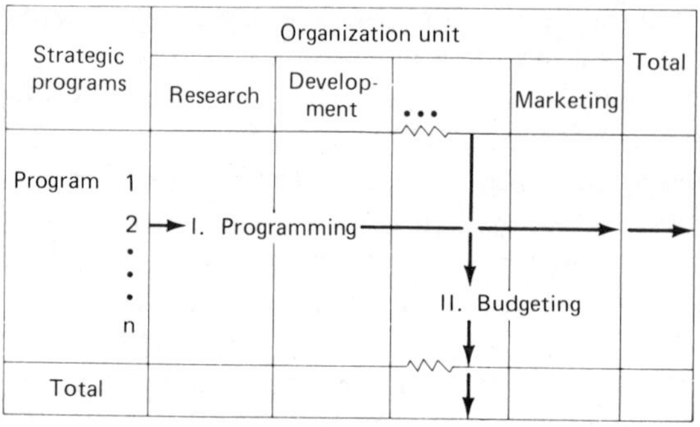

existing business tend to be efficiency developments and are affecting each function in isolation, due to the well-defined way of carrying out business. In this instance both strategic programs and budgets will be developed by the functional departments. Examples of this might be found within the integrated oil industry, the steel industry, or the utilities industry. We might view these industries as extremely stable in their way of carrying out business. In summary, the nature of the strategic program/budget interface will change as we go from a temporary organization (cross-functional dominance of both programming and budgeting) through the normal business cases (cross-functional programming, functional budgeting) to highly stable business settings (functional dominance of both programming and budgeting).

The budgeting process is a critical stage as part of the overall integrated strategic planning systems approach taken in this book in that we shall have to consider the overall completeness and balance of design. However, beyond discussing budgeting to the extent necessary for the overall systems understanding, it is outside the scope of this book to give a detailed discussion of the many aspects of the budgeting process. Let us therefore turn to the remaining two stages of the corporate planning process, which deal with monitoring of actual performance and linking strategic performance to the incentive system. A valid question, maybe, is to ask why these two functions should be seen as parts of the integrated corporate planning system. This will be clear, however, after we have briefly described the two next stages.

monitoring

The monitoring stage is intended for measurement of progress toward fulfillment of the strategies decided on during the three previous stages. Monitoring should play a critical role in facilitating self-corrective improvements of strategies and systematic learning. The measurement of progress should take place for the output of each of the three previous stages, i.e., progress toward objectives fulfillment, toward strategic programs fulfillment, and toward the fulfillment of the operating budget. At the present stage, we shall raise and briefly discuss the types of monitoring tasks we might face, the types of measurements we might employ, and what types of corrective actions might result.[10] In Chapters Four and Five, aspects of this discussion will be followed up more thoroughly.

There are three types of actions that can be taken to measure actual performance relative to a standard (a plan) and observing a particular deviation. One is to take corrective action in time to ameliorate a problem while the implementation of a strategy is still taking place; the strategic goals might still be reached, particularly if necessary corrective modifications are taken in time. We shall call this a *steering control* approach. A

GO-NOGO CONTROL

second result of measuring deviation from a plan is to decide to withdraw from the particular strategy or to continue further. Instead of abandoning a strategy we might also have the opposite situation where we are monitoring a particular economic and/or competitive position before committing significant resources to initiate a particular strategic move. We shall call this an anticipative *go–no go* control approach. Finally, we

LEARNING CONTROL

might be faced with a situation where there is little we can do post facto in terms of modifying or abandoning a strategy as a result of discrepancy between actual and planned. However, a valuable benefit in many such instances is the *learning* that takes place in analyzing what went wrong: What was unreasonable in our assumptions? How did we misinterpret competitive forces in the environment? Which of our own skills did not hold as assumed?

We want to monitor progress toward the fulfillment of the objectives agreed upon during the objectives-setting stage because this gives us the most direct and explicit picture of whether we indeed progress as intended toward our objectives. The task of monitoring the degree of fulfillment of an objective may at first seem operationally impossible, given that an objective typically will specify an intended direction or position to be reached after a considerable time period. It follows that it will be of little practical interest in terms of self-corrective prospects to measure whether we made an objective or not, say, ten years after. However, any objective will be based on certain critical environmental assumptions which must be expected to develop in certain directions in order to render the objective still valid. Thus, changes in one or more of the key underlying factors may call for a consideration of whether and how to modify the objective in question. We thereby have an indirect way of reassessing the relevance of our objectives. A critical part of this monitoring task will therefore be to focus on particular environmental factors. Of the three types of control just discussed—steering control, go–no go control, and learning control—steering control is clearly the most attractive, given that we might have an opportunity to modify our approach before the task has been completed; i.e., we might be able to redeploy resources which otherwise would have been wasted by taking us in an unintended direction. When it comes to objectives monitoring, steering control might be particularly useful. Here we are monitoring progress toward a goal that typically will be several years out in the time horizon before attainment. Thus, we might have time and flexibility to act if we monitor progress toward this phenomenon. Since we are dealing with issues that will be of critical magnitude for the firm, the payoff from this type of performance monitoring might be particularly high.

In attempting to measure progress toward a particular objective, we should take an approach which is tailor-made to the particular critical environmental assumptions at hand. This might imply that we make use of measurements that are not expressed in dollars but in some physical phenomenon or as an index. In performance measures of most kinds there will be a trade-off between the degree of relevance of the measure we choose for reflecting changes in the phenomenon we want to monitor and the degree of objectivity that we can attach to the preciseness of the measure. While more traditional dollar variables are easier to measure objectively, they are not necessarily relevant to measuring progress toward a long-term strategic goal.

Failure to fulfill a particular goal might be due to unreasonable assumptions at the outset which will call for subsequent modification of the goal or it might be due to the organization's lack of ability to implement satisfactory strategic programs. It follows that we have to measure progress of each of the strategic programs to determine whether lack of program fulfillment is a problem and if so, in which strategic program, what particular problem, and what corrective actions need to be contemplated. There is an important and particular consideration to observe when measuring progress toward strategic programs. As already discussed, a strategic program is unique. Thus, it follows that we need temporary performance monitoring systems for each program, in contrast to the monitoring of the major objectives and goals which typically will not change dramatically in general nature over time, although changes in emphasis might occur more frequently. For such temporary phenomena it is particularly important to measure progress toward a completion schedule. A set of milestones will have to be achieved within certain time limits and at specified cost. At particular intervals the strategic program's viability will be reassessed and a decision made whether to proceed, modify, or discontinue. Such progress monitoring is important for a strategic program, given its temporary nature and the interfunctional, project nature of the management groups involved.[11] To monitor critical environmental assumptions behind the mode of carrying out a strategic program will of course be important in this case too.

Monitoring of performance relative to the budget is of course a well-established procedure in many corporations. Performance measurements at this stage offer a unique opportunity to track short-term financial progress, and our measures are relatively more precise than our measurement of objectives and program fulfillment. It is useful to get this information, even though a relatively larger share of it will have to be reacted to as learning control. In fact learning control will be dominant for progress monitoring at this stage, in contrast to the go–no go control dominant in the strategic programming stage and the steering control of the objectives-setting stage.

There is, however, an important modification of the monitoring approach to be made when interpreting short-term performance progress. There might be opportunities to trade off long-term strategic progress against short-term progress, unless the budget-monitoring system specifically also measures changes in the strategic position, so that short-term performance can be interpreted relative to such changes that might have taken place. If not, a business might boost its short-term results by, for instance, trading off against long-term market share through making cuts in its advertising and/or product development expenditures.

Let us now turn to the related issue of motivating management based on how well they perform relative to objectives, strategic programs, and budgets. The feasibility of and basis for performance incentives have of course been established through setting long- to short-term standards for performance during stages 1 through 3 and monitoring performance through stage 4.

managerial incentives

The concept of corporate planning rests upon the premise that managers are motivated and willing to work together in a shared direction toward a long-term strategic position advantageous to the firm. For this to be possible, there must be at least some degree of congruence between the personal goals of each individual key manager and the corporation's goals. Clearly, given that the key managers themselves are instrumental in the formulation of objectives and goals as well as strategic programs, the personal beliefs and business judgments of the management team will to a large extent be congruent with the firm's. However, an individual's objectives might to some extent differ from the firm's, and there might also be organizational subgroups that have different goals. A particularly difficult problem where there might be goal incongruence is the difference in time horizon between the corporate strategy and the individual manager's goals. Because of pressures to show a short-term individual track record to establish oneself for promotions and job autonomy, the individual manager might tend to overemphasize short-term window dressing, and sharp elbow individualism, and consequently see the budget as relatively more important to him than objectives and strategic programs fulfillment. Frequent job transfers make this an even more plausible mode of managerial behavior: One only has a limited amount of time to prove oneself before being transferred; the risk of being caught for executing strategically unsound but in the shorter term interesting decisions is lessened, given that the particular manager does not get stuck with the decision for a long period of time thereafter; the accountability of a manager for strategic management is lessened. Ironically, management incentive schemes as we find them in many companies today tend to reinforce short-term behavior in that bonuses primarily tend to be linked to the annual performance. [12]

Our approach is that the incentives that are under the discretion of the company should be administered in such a way that they ameliorate some of the goal incongruence just discussed. Hence, management incentives are an integral stage of the corporate planning system.

We shall employ a notion of incentives which is broader than managerial bonus payments. In fact we shall identify three classes of managerial incentives: monetary rewards, nonmonetary rewards, and individual feedback. Monetary rewards might be bonuses or stock options. The value of stock options to a large extent will depend on fluctuations in the stock market, so we normally do not favor this incentive payment form since the manager's fortune can be significantly changed due to factors often to a considerable extend outside his control.

Nonmonetary incentives can be of several types and are probably going to be increasingly important, given a growing sense of professionalism among management as well as seemingly a trend toward higher and higher personal marginal taxation. It is therefore important that these often highly effective discretionary items be incorporated into the managerial incentive scheme. Such incentives might be job promotions and job assignments. This is a highly political process in most corporations, at least when it comes to promotions above certain managerial levels. To some extent the promotion process is depoliticized and tied to some sort of formal assessment of how well a manager has performed, a fairer and more professional approach. Another related nonmonetary incentive would be the degree of discretion that a manager is given for managing his business. Managers who perform better do enjoy more freedom in designing and executing their strategies, with fewer modifications imposed during the planning review process. Assuming that it would not jeopardize the corporate portfolio strategy, the more successful managers might be given more discretion over funds management and receive more investment funds as well, in recognition of senior management's confidence in the successful divisions' strategies and programs. Other nonmonetary rewards might be fringe benefits, such as use of cars or paid vacations, and prestige items, such as being assigned a more luxurious office, entitlement to use the company's executive airplane, and so on.

Third, behavioral incentives will consist of individual praise, feedback review, and criticism given to each manager. A systematic review with each manager of his strategic as well as operating performance might be an important motivating device in the hands of an inspiring leader. Similarly, praise and occasionally some criticism during planning and/or monitoring review meetings might be effective.

The key, of course, is that the incentives must be tied to performance as reflected in the achievement of objectives, strategic programs, and budgets. While managerial incentives as just discussed are old and well established in most companies, they may not have been executed in the context of the strategic planning system. Hence, not only might an opportunity to create a more realistic emphasis on planning be lost but, worse, the noncoordinated incentives might actually reinforce non-strategic managerial behavior.

This concludes our discussion of the different stages of the planning process. The major purpose of emphasizing a set of distinctive stages has been to strengthen the focus of the various planning activities. Specifically we have emphasized the need to identify and narrow down strategic options, to achieve both adaptation and integration, through the execution of an objectives-setting stage, a strategic programming stage, and a budgeting stage. We have also stressed the need for the two follow-up stages to reinforce the strategic direction set during the first three stages, namely, monitoring and motivating. This focus on five specific stages for setting strategic direction constitutes the second major dimension of our conceptual scheme for corporate planning. We are now in a position to reconcile this dimension with the other dimension that we previously discussed, namely, the hierarchy of strategic tasks dimension. Together the two dimensions will provide the foundation of a conceptual scheme for planning, the topic to be discussed in the next section.

A Three-by-Five Information Flow Model of Corporate Planning

We have by now identified two of the three major dimensions of our corporate planning conceptual scheme—three levels of strategies and five stages of identifying, narrowing down, and monitoring strategic options. The third dimension of the conceptual scheme, which is to be discussed in this section, emphasizes that there is an important information and communication flow aspect of the planning process that needs specific attention.[13] This will identify a pattern of interaction and iteration among the managers responsible for the various levels of strategy, all contributing toward the development of one overall plan for the company, internally consistent but allowing for the restatement of plans for the various organizational subunits. Exhibit 2-5 gives a flowchart model which indicates how the various levels and stages discussed thus far can be put together. The model specifies a logical sequence of steps that should be carried out in order to make the process come alive within a

EXHIBIT 2-5 Conceptual Model of the Steps in the Information Flow of the Strategic Planning Process

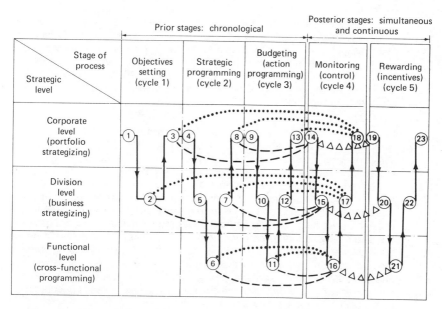

The basic information/communication flow: solid line
The tracking of actual vs. planned performance: broken line
The corrective actions and modifications of plans: dotted line
The comparison of actual vs. planned performance for incentives: triangle line

corporation. We shall briefly discuss each step, following the numbering within the circles of Exhibit 2-5. It should be noted, however, that implementation of these steps may not always be straightforward for two reasons. First, we are dealing with a behavioral process, as already stated above. This means that a step-by-step description of the logical path through the process is likely to be far too simplistic. Even at the risk that the discussion of the sequence of steps in this section therefore probably might smack of being too mechanistic, it is a useful starting point for describing the planning process. Subsequently in this book we shall see how this behavioral process is dominated by feedbacks, negotiation meetings reflecting the powers and roles of executives, revisions, and so on. In addition to recognizing that we are dealing with the implementation of a behavioral decision-making process, we encounter a number of other implementation problems, typically stemming from misconceptions about "technical" aspects of the planning process. In Chapter Four we shall discuss the most common of these implementation issues.

the objectives-setting cycle

STEP 1:

The CEO states his aspirations for the company, in terms of tentative and relatively long-term objectives, and his key assumptions behind the objectives (such as general economic trends and resource constraints on the company). Comparison with the performance patterns of similar companies might play an important role in shaping the CEO's aspirations. Also, of course, the CEO will draw on any experience in the company with planning as well as past performance records.

STEP 2:

Each division manager defines his business charter by identifying the *borderlines* for the product/market/service elements his division is in and by providing a general rationale for being in the business based on its long-term expected attractiveness. He also proposes a set of division objectives in terms of desired competitive strength position, and he elaborates on the rationale and assumptions behind them. The center of the division manager's emphasis in all this is on opportunities and threats he sees in the environment. He finally proposes a tentative resource requirement estimate in accordance with the strategic positioning proposed for the business. (In Chapter Three we shall discuss in detail a way of stating the strategic position of a business in terms of its competitive strength and the attractiveness of its business. We shall see then that the strategic positioning of the business is likely to have strong implications on whether the business will be expected to become a net funds user or a net contributor of funds.)

STEP 3:

The CEO approves the division objectives and strategies. The approval of each division's statements must be assessed within the context of the overall portfolio pattern that emerges from the divisional inputs as well as from potential acquisition opportunities that might exist. He then summarizes the output of the objectives-setting cycle by stating the corporate portfolio strategy as well as specific but tentative corporate and divisional goals, which will serve as the focus for the next cycle.

the strategic programming cycle

STEP 4:

The CEO initiates the strategic programming cycle with a call for division programs to focus on how to achieve the divisional goals.

STEP 5:

Each division manager will state for his functional organization the division's strategy, general objectives, and specific goals, i.e., the division's expected strategic role within the overall strategic pattern developed in the previous cycle. He will then ask his functional organization for alternative strategic programs.

STEP 6:

The functions will identify strategic program alternatives, typically in close cross-functional cooperation. The alternatives may be new ones, such as the development of a new product, or reassessment of existing ones, such as continuing with a mature product. Program alternatives will be analyzed, and the best ones will be recommended to the division general manager. As we have already discussed, carrying out this step tends to be extremely time-consuming and is normally going on all year round. However, at the time when this stage of the planning process is reached each year the status of the ongoing strategic programming activities should be summarized.

STEP 7:

The division manager should at this point make a selection among strategic program alternatives, attempting to come up with a strategic program *package* that fulfills the intended objectives and goals for the division. This strategic program package, including the expected associated funds-flow characteristics, will then be recommended to the CEO.

STEP 8:

The CEO will evaluate each divisional program package input within the overall portfolio context that emerges. He will then make tentative resource allocations to these long-term divisional strategic programs based on their merits in the portfolio and not only in competition with each other internally but also against the allocation of funds for acquisitions. Thus, it is primarily at this stage that the major thrust of the CEO's power to influence the long-term direction of the firm might be applied. This resource allocation pattern marks the culmination of the strategic programming cycle of the planning process.

the budgeting cycle

STEP 9:

The CEO will start out the budgeting cycle by calling for divisional budgets to reflect the near-term actions to be carried out as part of the longer-term strategic thrust.

STEP 10:

The division managers will communicate the division goals and strategic programs to the functional organizations and call for functional or departmental budgets.

STEP 11:

The functional departments will develop and submit for approval their budgets, reflecting their near-term involvement in the execution of the various strategic programs. The strategic programming/budgeting sequence at the functional level, as indicated in step 6 together with the present step, thus follows the two-dimensional format discussed earlier and illustrated in Exhibit 2-4.

STEP 12:

The division manager will coordinate, review, and approve the functional budgets and submit his emerging division budget for corporate approval.

STEP 13:

The CEO will approve the emerging corporate budget which reflects near-term actions to implement the portfolio strategy. This final resource allocation culminates the budgeting planning cycle. It should be noted that the information flow has a segment of discontinuity after this step. The first 13 steps of the information flow, encompassing the three first cycles of the planning process, have been focused around developing a prior set of plans, culminating in the completion of step 13. The remaining steps of the information flow, on the other hand, encompassing the monitoring and reward cycles, are focused around aspects of posterior comparisons of actual performance that had been planned. Exhibit 2-5 should thus be interpreted in such a way that cycles 4 and 5 occur while cycles 1, 2, and 3 for the next year are in progress.

the monitoring cycle

STEP 14:

The CEO states the overall monitoring tasks: to track actual performances against the near-term goals, against the achievement of the strategic programs, and against the fulfillment of the objectives, i.e., against the outputs of planning cycles 3, 2, and 1. He assigns to each of the divisions the task of monitoring its own performance in progressing toward the fulfillment of its objectives, strategic programs, and budgets. Also he assigns to his own offices the task of monitoring progress toward portfolio strategy fulfillment. As part of this, the CEO establishes limits of deviations for actual performance against each of the objectives, strategic programs, and budget standards, attempting to assess when a modification of one or more aspects of the portfolio strategy is needed, either as a result of a deviation induced by one of the internal divisions or because of environmental changes.

STEP 15:

The division manager states the monitoring tasks for his own organization and assigns to his functional managers and to managers appointed to run specific strategic programs the tasks of monitoring progress toward budgets and strategic programs. The division manager also assigns to his own office the monitoring of progress toward his business's strategy fulfillment. Further, he develops standards for when deviations should lead to modification(s) of one or more aspects of his business strategy, either as a result of deviations in strategic program fulfillment or functional budget fulfillment or changes in key environmental factors affecting the objectives of the business.

STEP 16:

The functional managers monitor progress toward their budgets. Similarly, progress toward the strategic programs is being monitored by a functional manager if the program involves his department primarily or by a manager assigned to the task if the program is more heavily cross-functional in nature. Significant deviations are being reported to division management, together with analysis and suggestions of how to react, if at all. Less significant deviations are being responded to directly by the functional or strategic program managers. It should be noted that the monitoring or control cycle consists of two distinctive but interrelated types of tasks: the tracking of actual performance to be compared with the established standards from the plans and the execution of corrective actions resulting in modification of the plans. In Exhibit 2-5 this has been indicated by broken lines for the tracking relationships and by dotted lines for the corrective action relationships.

STEP 17:

The various monitoring inputs from the different aspects of fulfillment of the strategic programs and functional budgets and pertinent changes in the key environmental factors are being reconciled in terms of the effects on the progress of the business as a whole, toward the fulfillment of the business's strategic objectives, toward its strategic programs, and toward its budget. The emerging pattern of progress and deviations is being reacted to through ameliorating actions and revision of plans; however, particularly serious deviations are being communicated to the corporate management.

STEP 18:

The CEO monitors progress toward the long-term portfolio objectives, toward the overall portfolio of strategic programs, and toward near-term budgets, partly as the result of the performance inputs he is receiving from his division and partly based on the inputs received from his own office's monitoring, particularly of key environmental factors. The monitoring at this level, too, is likely to lead to corrective actions if necessary and possible, the initiation of such actions depending on the magnitude of the decision as well as the extent to which a decision might have repercussions on the execution of other strategic elements within the overall portfolio, i.e., whether a particular organizational level possesses the discretionary power to act. The monitoring cycle does not culminate at a particular point in time but is an ongoing process until next year's revised monitoring targets are established through the carrying out of planning cycles 1 to 3 again.

the incentives cycle

STEP 19:

The fifth cycle, management rewards or incentives, also represents a discontinuity in the overall information-flow process from cycle 4. However, this cycle is nevertheless closely related to the other four. It emerges with the CEO's involvement in setting personal achievement goals with his division managers with regard to their expected contribution to the success of the fulfillment of objectives, strategic programs, and near-term budgets. This draws directly on the planned outputs of cycle 1 (step 3), cycle 2 (step 8), and cycle 3 (step 13) and reflects the accountability that the CEO is assigning to the division managers for their performance.

STEP 20:

The division managers set personal achievement goals with their functional managers and strategic program managers, reflecting their expected contribution toward the fulfillment of longer-term strategic programs as well as nearer-term budgets (consistent with the planned outputs of steps 7 and 12).

STEP 21:

The functional managers and strategic program managers report to their division managers the nature of their actual contribution toward their agreed-upon personal targets. This draws upon the information already revealed during the tracking of actual vs. planned performance during cycle 4.

STEP 22:

The division managers report to the CEO the nature of their actual contributions toward their agreed-upon personal targets. This also will be based on the performance tracking information gathered during the monitoring stage.

STEP 23:

The CEO disburses incentives to the various levels of managers based on actual versus intended performance in accordance with the prior and posterior information provided during the previous 22 steps of the planning process. Incentives might be monetary as well as nonmonetary.

This concludes the sequence of steps to be carried out in our proposed conceptual scheme for corporate planning, encompassing the development of a set of plans that feature both adaptive and integrative strengths, that are being monitored in terms of how well they are actually being fulfilled, and that are tied to the performance of specific managers. It should be stressed again that the last ten steps of Exhibit 2-5, being concerned with monitoring and rewards, are simultaneous and continuous in nature, in contrast to the steps of the first three cycles, which *are* chronological (narrowing down). We may make a useful distinction in this respect as to the separation of planning—the first three cycles—from reenforcement—the last two cycles. It is thus important not to confuse the meaning of the combination of the five cycles. Although the steps may seem straightforward enough, most companies will have considerable difficulties in making them work. Most of the remainder of this book, in fact, will discuss how to operationalize the model. At this point, however, it is important to stress again that this model is a behavioral one, its general distinctive characteristics thus being that it is a communication-flow model; it is interactive; it is iterative. Consequently, it is useful to discuss these three characteristics more specifically.

Feedback Characteristics

The task of developing an operational set of coordinated strategic plans for a large, complex corporation is certainly not a trivial one, given that a large number of interrelated elements of plans will have to be created. The task of developing plans is of course particularly complex when we are faced with a highly diversified corporation, where each business plan will have to fit within the overall corporate portfolio strategy context. For this to become feasible it is necessary to develop tight time schedules for what should be developed and reviewed by whom within the corporation. The communication system specifies this; as indicated by the flowchart (or *snake)* of Exhibit 2-5, it is a system with a high degree of interdependence and typically little slack; it is therefore necessary for each unit within the organization to adhere strictly to communication patterns and time schedules.

The system is interactive. This is a reflection of the intent to develop a system which enables the release of the creativity, skills, and insight of individual people across the organization by means of a clear division of labor among managers. This interactive mode follows a highly formalized pattern of *top-down/bottom-up* interfaces within the organization. This two-way process goes on at each of the five stages of the process. Although it therefore will be essential with a two-way interaction when it comes to each of the objectives setting, strategic programming, budgeting, monitoring, as well as management incentives stages, the actual balance between the top-down and bottom-up influences may of course change between the stages, and it will normally also be different from one firm to another. In Chapter Five we shall discuss this.

The system is also iterative, although this may not be directly apparent from Exhibit 2-5, except for the corrective actions that are being initiated as part of the monitoring stage and which may lead to modifications in objectives, strategic programs, and/or budgets. However, with the need to develop complex, coordinated outputs at each stage of the planning process, a lot of trial and error will normally have to take place before a finalized set of plans can be reached. There are two aspects of this. First, during each stage there will typically be considerable *trial and error* or iterations before a gradual, coordinated commitment across the organization's strategic hierarchy will be reached in terms of acceptable objectives, strategic programs, or budgets. Particularly when the planning system is new and/or during periods of major and rapid changes the tentative plans can go up and down several times before senior management reaches consensus with respect to the outputs of a particular planning cycle. These iterations are inevitable, although they might involve time-consuming and perhaps frustrating meetings and revisions. This is a necessary and unavoidable part of planning which underscores a major characteristic of the process: Planning involves rigorous, detailed, and time-consuming work for all; the plans are only as good as their weakest part. In Exhibit 2-6 we have indicated that there might be five different

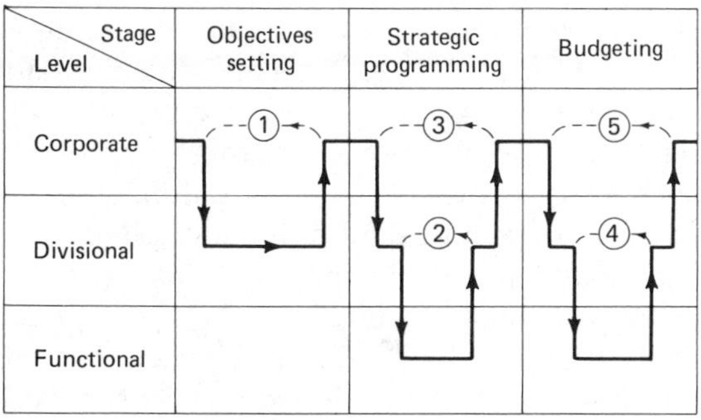

EXHIBIT 2-6 Iterative Loops in the Strategic Planning Process

kinds of iterative loops of this kind within the planning process (encircled numbers 1 through 5 in Exhibit 2-6).

> **LOOP 1:**
> When the CEO receives the divisional inputs indicating where the businesses may be going, he may have to reconcile the emerging portfolio picture with his initial tentative objectives. As a result he may ask one or more of the divisions to revise their inputs, and he may change his original tentative objectives as well. One or more iterations may be necessary before the loop is closed.
>
> **LOOP 2:**
> During the division manager's strategic programming package consolidation he may frequently go back to the functional departments and request revisions of particular programs in order to fit individual programs into a more coherent package from the business strategy viewpoint.
>
> **LOOP 3:**
> When the CEO receives the portfolio of divisional strategic program inputs he may have to cycle one or more of these back for revisions to achieve the desired portfolio strategy.
>
> **LOOP 4:**
> During the budgeting cycle a division manager may have to recycle the functional budget proposals so that the overall budget attains the desired strategic properties, i.e., becomes a near-term reflection of the longer-term strategic program thrust.
>
> **LOOP 5:**
> Similarly, the CEO might want to call for revisions in one or more of the divisional budgets so that the final overall fit is achieved.

The other aspect of iteration relates to revisions that have to be made to a completed stage of the planning process because subsequent analysis at later stages indicates that the decisions taken during that stage were not all that plausible in retrospect. These major iterations may be necessary as a result of entirely unforeseen circumstances. In most instances, however, these iterations might have dysfunctional effects and should therefore be kept to a minimum, because corporate planning as a decision-making process implies that the organization's members should be expected to commit themselves to particular directions and courses of action by the end of each stage. If it is widely accepted that one can get away from these commitments, then an unrealistic atmosphere for planning might be created. Needless to say, too, additional and less useful planning is created through this kind of iteration. It should be stressed that these major iterations refer to modifications of stages before the overall set of action programs or budgets has been completed, i.e., iterations affecting two or more of cycles 1 to 3. These undesirable revisions should not be confused with the desirable revisions of cycles 1, 2, or 3 resulting from actions taken in the monitoring stage.

Summary

In this chapter we have developed a conceptual model for corporate planning based on three general sets of premises. First, it acknowledges that there is an opportunity for division of labor among the various levels of management in an organization, so that three distinctive levels of strategy can be developed, with corporate management to be held primarily accountable for the portfolio strategizing task, division management to focus on business strategizing, and the specialized functional management groups to cooperate on developing strategic programs. We have attempted to demonstrate in our discussion the significant benefits that might accrue to an organization by having an explicit division of labor to carry out the strategic tasks. This will provide for specialization, but within an overall corporate context.

The second premise that the conceptual scheme rests on is that the planning task must accomplish a multifaceted set of purposes, much broader than traditionally recognized. Specifically, relevant opportunities must be identified and choices narrowed down to arrive at the best set of coordinated action programs for the company. This underscores an issue that we have been stressing, namely, that planning is a decision-making process. In line with this it is also necessary to see monitoring and motivating as part of the planning process. We have suggested that a systematic and sequential shift of focus from one key activity to another is useful to facilitate the development of full-bodied plans, which might encompass both adaptive and integrative qualities instead of being partial. Useful cycles are objectives setting, strategic programming, budgeting, monitoring, and management incentives.

A final premise of the conceptual scheme is acknowledgment of the behavioral nature of planning, that it is a framework for interaction among human talents. Thus, the planning process should be seen as an information process and above all should facilitate innovative and creative managerial behavior. To facilitate this the planning scheme that has been developed incorporates explicit patterns of interaction, sets out clear agendas for discussions, assigns explicit patterns of accountability to the various managers, and provides incentives to those managers who contribute toward the firm's strategic success.

Why is it necessary to have such an elaborate conceptual scheme for planning? We shall briefly suggest two interrelated reasons at this point; however, as our discussion proceeds, several other reasons will emerge. First, given that we are proposing that the task of planning should be approached by means of a process model for planning, it becomes essential that the overall logic and rationale of the process be made explicit and understandable to a relatively wide number of managers. To do a good job, both in terms of understanding and motivation, within the much narrower part of the planning process model that he normally will see, it is essential that the manager should have a feeling for the overall approach. Only an explicit process-oriented conceptual corporate planning scheme can facilitate this. Related to this is our second rationale for the necessity of a conceptual scheme: It is unreasonable to expect that planning's many facets will be equally well elaborated and operationalized at once. However, developing a firm's planning system requires a keen understanding of how the various elements fit into an overall scheme, almost like attaching bits and pieces to a skeleton. Many companies, unfortunately, lose track of this and end up with several modules for aspects of planning that cannot easily be reconciled. Consequently, even through considerable efforts have gone into planning, these efforts do not lead to a pattern of evolution toward an overall integrated planning system.

Our conceptual scheme is a general model which should apply to any multidivisional company and also to any single-business firm in a modified version by eliminating the portfolio strategic level. It is clear that the conceptual model as outlined here represents only a first cut at installing a corporate planning system. Further modification is needed to tailor-make the system to respond to the planning needs dictated by the firm's situational setting; we shall discuss this in Chapters Four and Five. Therefore, before seeing how we might build certain desired capabilities into the model we need to discuss how to undertake an analysis of a particular firm's situational setting in order to better identify a firm's particular planning needs. Chapter Three will deal with this, particularly the identification of what needs a firm might have for planning that stem from the strategic setting that the firm finds itself in.

Appendix: Complex Hierarchal Organizational Structures with Dual Strategic/Operating Emphasis

This appendix contains an example which is intended to illustrate the complexity of identifying the relevant levels of strategies in a diversified, multinational organization. The example is intended to underscore the need for careful analysis of a firm's formal organization structure as well as a delineation of its strategic structure in order to determine the division of labor for strategy development within a company. While the example provides an excellent illustration of the complexity of the task of identifying the strategic and operating structures, this company has not yet come up with a definite mode of reconciling these structures. We shall therefore briefly describe the approaches for reconciling a dual strategic/operating mode adopted by two pioneering companies in this field, Texas Instruments and General Electric Company. This will serve as indications of how the complex problem raised in this appendix might be "solved."

The company was a Swedish-based industrial company, working mainly in the fields of pharmaceuticals and chemical products, on a worldwide basis, with world sales of approximately 250 million dollars. The company had five autonomous divisions: pharmaceuticals, industrial anticorrosion chemical specialties, chemical-based consumer products, agricultural feed products, and fish protein products. The company had started out and established itself primarily within the pharmaceutical field; the other divisions were still relatively small. The present operating structure, which is the result of acquisitions as well as internal development efforts, can be seen in Exhibit 2-7, in which the pharmaceutical division, which accounts for 70 percent of sales and most of the profits, is exhibited in considerably more detail than the other four divisions. Within the pharmaceutical division itself there are a number of "divisions," namely, five so-called product companies which are responsible for the development of their own product lines, most of these in fact being larger than any of the nonpharmaceutical divisions. Also, there are a number of market companies responsible for serving the markets in the various geographical territories around the world. An initial potential issue for the strategic management of the company stemming from the organizational operating structure is the potential dysfunctional effect that the extreme diversity-in-size distribution of business divisions might have on strategy development. In terms of developing an overall company portfolio strategy based on the business families as elements, the present organizational setup is potentially less useful in that the smaller divisions might distract senior management from making appropriate portfolio trade-offs and choices, above all between various segments of the pharmaceutical area. By adding relatively small, unfamiliar, and potentially problem-ridden businesses to a company's portfolio, a problem of overloading the strategic system might result, with senior management pulled in too many directions and failing to pay sufficient attention to critical strategic portfolio issues concerning the core businesses. Thus, it seems to be a definite advantage for effective portfolio strategizing that the size distribution among business families be relatively even.

A more fundamental organizational issue within the context we are discussing relates to the complex way the pharmaceutical sector is structured, with at least five different key substructures:

1. In Sweden we have a divisionalized type of organizational structure, with each of the three Swedish product companies operating its own business, with its own R&D capabilities and independent marketing and distribution forces. This implies a considerable duplication of efforts—with three R&D organizations

EXHIBIT 2-7 Formal Organization Structure, Swedish Multinational Company

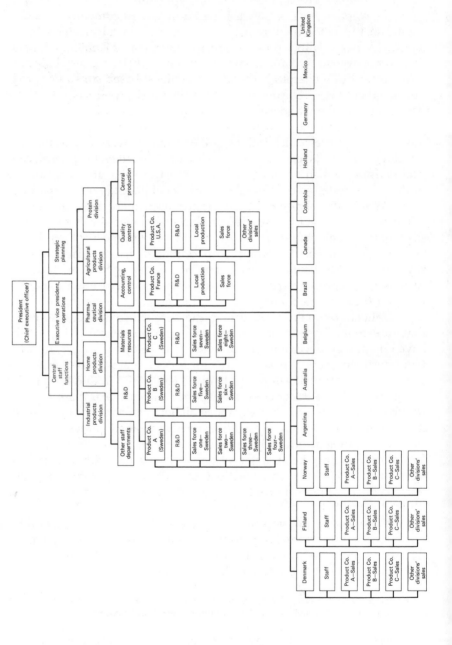

and eight sales force organizations in Sweden. Presumably the activity levels of the product companies are high enough to justify the costs of duplication. There are considerable benefits from having relatively simple and easily identifiable strategic units like these, not the least because people can better associate themselves with such strategic settings. The adaptive planning task for each of the three Swedish product companies will be to identify new and emerging product/market opportunities. The Swedish sales force organizations should be critical in this. Integration, on the other hand, will be a primary responsibility of the functional organizational units. There are, however, potential difficulties that a product company might develop strategies that might "hurt" the other product companies and the company as a whole by adopting marketing campaigns that might create bad will for the others, by focusing on the same customers and thereby causing customer fatigue, by competing for the same personnel resources, and so on. This problem becomes even more difficult due to a high potential for increasing overlap among the three product companies' business segments, stemming primarily from the difficulty of keeping the outputs from pharmaceutical R&D efforts within the interest areas of each product company—not touching upon other product companies' sphere of involvement. It should thus be a planning task to provide strategic coordination across the pharmaceutical businesses in Sweden, i.e., integration planning.

2. Within the rest of the Nordic countries (Norway, Denmark, Finland) each of the product companies has its own marketing and sales organizations. However, all of these (together with the sales organizations of the nonpharmaceutical divisions) are part of a geographical area company. We thus seem to have a sort of matrix organization with the product dimension being the dominating or leading one and the geographical dimension being supplemental or grown. Presumably, then, we might expect that the product organizations should be primarily involved in integration planning, and the area dimension in adaptation planning. Thus, the area viewpoint should be the focus when relating the inputs from these countries to the overall pharmaceutical sector strategy. The issue would be to focus on the strategic opportunities of each country so that the relative involvement can be determined on the basis of relative country attractiveness and not by merely adding up the strategic inputs of each of the product line organizations per country. Hence, the planning system should facilitate the availability of country-wide inputs as a vehicle for adapting to environmental opportunities and/or threats.

3. Within the rest of the world is a total of ten marketing companies that carry out marketing and sales in a given country of all the product companies under a common corporate label; the product companies do not have separate sales forces. What we seem to have here is a different form of a matrix structure, this time with the area dimension as leading and the product dimension as grown. Thus, the integration planning tasks should be heavily focused around the area, and the adaptation planning task around the product/business dimension: Which products/businesses are potentially the most attractive in the years to come given our own strengths and the general business attractiveness trends in this area? Thus, the planning system should provide these inputs about long-term product opportunities from the areas worldwide into the objectives setting of the pharmaceutical sector.

4. The product companies outside Sweden, namely, the United States and France, form yet another strategic setup. These organizational units are chartered with the function of R&D in order to develop their own products

within defined business segments (analogous to the Swedish product companies) as well as to market the products of the other product companies in the United States and France (analogous to the ten marketing companies). Thus, a dual and particularly complex planning role seems to exist for these organizations. One is to provide the same planning inputs as an ordinary marketing company, notably with regard to the long-term product/business opportunities in the United States and France, so that the pharmaceutical sector can take the potentials of these important markets into account when the sector's overall objectives are formulated. Second, there is a planning need to be carried out with respect to the direction of the particular product/business segment of the organization, analogous to the planning tasks of the three Swedish product companies. The organization will have an important need for area opportunity inputs from the ten marketing companies as well as from the Swedish and other Nordic countries to develop meaningful plans for this. In general a clear-cut distinction will have to be drawn with regard to the two planning tasks, so that the overall pharmaceutical sector's global strategy will not be unclear as to the R&D/product roles of the United States and France as well as to the market opportunities in the United States and France for the other (Swedish) pharmaceutical products and R&D.

5. Outside of Sweden, the four nonpharmaceutical divisions seem to rely on the pharmaceutical division's organizational resources. A major argument for this is that the other divisions are still so small that they cannot afford to develop their own separate international organizations. The problem with this, however, is that a lack of realism might develop as to what should be the true strategic opportunities worldwide. Similarly, the accountability for successful strategic fulfillment might easily get diluted. Thus, neither the adaptive nor the integrative planning task inputs from the international side of these businesses will probably be adequately attended to.

In summary, then, we see that the corporate portfolio planning task involves developing a balance between the pharmaceutical division and the other four divisions as to where the emphasis should be. However, it also seems clear that the portfolio strategizing task in this instance is both much simpler and probably also relatively less important than the task of developing a business family plan within the pharmaceutical division. Here the issue is that the five product companies represent different business elements. Thus, a good pharmaceutical division business family plan will have to be based partly on planning inputs from the business elements and partly on an approach which builds on the interrelationships between the business elements. When it comes to the third level of planning, namely, the development of predominantly cross-functional strategic programs, this will also be relatively complicated given the extensive duplication of functional capabilities, particularly when it comes to R&D.

We have seen that the formal organizational structure within the pharmaceutical group is structured in at least four different ways for developing appropriate product/market focus in the diverse settings; we have different operating organizations for Sweden, the rest of the Nordic countries, the United States and France, and the rest of the world. Importantly we have also seen that the nature of the adaptive strategic tasks is different within these four settings; i.e., they need to emphasize different environmental opportunities and/or threats. Even though the company has not yet formally instituted a strategic organizational structure, this should be focused around the adaptive tasks. Thus, such a hypothetical strategic structure would be a very complex one, too, taking on four different forms corresponding to the needs of the different operating organizations. To get better insight into how a strategic structure might be developed and how to delineate the interrelationships between the strategic structure and the operating structure, let us briefly examine the approaches taken by two companies with experience in this field.

At Texas Instruments a corporate-wide dual operating/strategic structure has been developed.[14] The elements of the operating dimension are four in total (the approximate number of management units at each level as of 1971 is shown in parentheses): corporate (1), groups (4), divisions (9), product/customer centers (PCCs) (77). The strategic dimension also has four elements: corporate objective (1), business objectives (8), strategies (50+), tactical action programs (TAPs) (more than 100 launched). Many managers have responsibilities within both dimensions; they are wearing two hats. For instance, a group manager may also be responsible for an objective, although this does not have to be the case. A manager of a PCC is also frequently responsible for a strategy. Exhibit 2-8 illustrates the matrix interrelationship between the two dimensions that thus emerges.

To give an indication of how this dual structure might work, let us consider the role of a manager of a PCC who also has been given the

EXHIBIT 2-8   Texas Instruments' Dual
Strategic/Operating Structure

Source: Texas Instruments Case, in Peter Lorange and Richard F. Vancil, *Strategic Planning Systems* (Englewood Cliffs, N.J.: Prentice-Hall, 1977), p. 347

			Group 1							Group 2
			Division A			Division B				Div. C
O	S	TAP	PCC₁	PCC₂	PCC₃	PCC₄	PCC₅	PCC₆	PCC₇	PCC₈
I	A	1	X							
		2	X							
		3		X						
		4					X			
	B	1			X					
		2	X							

responsibility for a strategy. Qua operating manager, he is concerned with the management of the strategic resources under his control—the deployment of people, funds, and know-how. Partly this will be a function of his response to the requirement to deliver adequate day-to-day operating performance. Partly, too, however, his resources will be deployed in response to what has been identified as needed to carry out strategic tasks. Qua strategic manager, on the other hand, his task will be to operationalize the necessary set of tactical action programs to implement his strategy and, importantly, to identify and secure the necessary strategic resources throughout the organization to be able to carry out his TAPs. For this he will typically have to draw on resources which will be under the control of other PCC managers; a greater or lesser part of these resources may or may not be under his control qua PCC manager. It thus follows that when wearing his PCC manager hat he will typically be providing resource inputs to several strategies other than his own, through being responsible for supporting a diverse set of TAPs.

The General Electric Company in 1978 adapted a dual strategic/operating structure along lines somewhat different from those of Texas Instruments.[15] The operating structure has five levels: corporate (1), sector (6), group (10), division (50), and department (150). For strategic purposes approximately 50 operating units (this can be either a group, a division, or a department) have been identified as strategic business units (SBUs), the primary criterion for being identified as this being that the unit serves a set of outside markets with a family of products which makes it essentially independent of the other SBUs. As such an SBU is analogous to what we have identified as a business family. An SBU manager of an SBU submits his strategic plan to sector and corporate management. Thus, the strategic structure consists of three elements: corporate (1), sector (6), and SBU (50).

The setting of the example of this appendix as well as the two brief company discussions should illustrate the difficulty of developing a meaningful hierarchy of strategic tasks in a highly complex organization as well as underscore the challenge to tie the strategic structure and the operating structure together in a sufficiently explicit and operational manner.

NOTES

1. The conceptual scheme to be presented is an extension of R. F. Vancil and P. Lorange, "Strategic Planning in Diversified Companies," *Harvard Business Review*, 53 (Jan.–Feb. 1975), 81-93. Several authors have presented conceptual frameworks for corporate planning; see, for instance, Frank F. Gilmore and R. G. Brandenberg, "Anatomy of Corporate Planning," *Harvard Business Review*, 40 (Nov.–Dec. 1962), 61-69; Robert F. Stewart, "A Framework for Business Planning," *Report No. 162* (Menlo Park, Calif.: Long Range Planning Service, Stanford Research Institute 1962); Robert N. Anthony, *Planning and Control Systems: A Framework for Analysis* (Boston: Division of Research, Harvard Business School, 1965); John W. Humble, "Corporate Planning and Management by Objectives," *Long Range Planning*, 1, no. 4 (June 1969), 36-43; George A. Steiner, *Top Management Planning* (New York: Macmillan, 1969); Russel L. Ackoff, *A Concept of Corporate Planning* (New York: Wiley-Interscience, 1970); K. A. Ringbakk, "The Corporate Planning Life Cycle—An International Point of View," *Long Range Planning*, 5, no. 3 (Sept. 1972), 10-20; Kalman J. Cohen and Richard M. Cyert, "Strategy: Formulation, Implementation and Monitoring," *Journal of Business*, 46 (July 1973), 349-367; Allan T. Malm, *Strategic Planning Systems: A Framework for Analysis and Design* (Lund, Sweden: Student Litteratur, 1975); Arnoldo C. Hax and Nicholas S. Majluf, "Towards the Formalization of Strategic Planning—A Conceptual Approach," *Technical Report No. 2* (Cambridge, Mass.: Sloan School of Management, M.I.T., 1977); George A. Steiner and John B. Miner, *Management Policy and Strategy* (New York: Macmillan, 1977); Bernard Taylor and John R. Sparkes, eds., *Corporate Strategy and Planning* [New York: Wiley (Halstead Press), 1977]; Hans H. Hinterhuber, *Strategische Unternehmungsführung* (Berlin: Walter de Gruyter, 1977); and William R. King and David I. Cleland, *Strategic Planning and Policy* (New York: Van Nostrand Reinhold, 1978). For a good discussion of the role of *formal* systems in planning, see George A. Steiner, "Comprehensive Managerial Planning," in *Contemporary Management: Issues and Viewpoints*, ed. Joseph McGuire (Englewood Cliffs, N.J.: Prentice-Hall, 1974).

2. We shall not do an extensive survey of the planning literature in this book. Several planning literature surveys exist; see, for instance, David E. Hussey, *Corporate Planning: Theory and Practice* (Elmsford, N.Y.: Pergamon Press, 1974); Charles W. Hofer, "Research on Strategic Planning: A Survey of Past Studies and Suggestions for Future Efforts," *Journal of Economics and Business*, 28 (Summer 1976); 261-286; George A. Steiner and John B. Miner, *Management Policy and Strategy* (New York: Macmillan, 1977); and Peter Lorange, "Formal Planning Systems: Their Role in Strategy Formulation and Implementation," in *Strategic Management: A New View on Business Policy and Planning*, eds. Dan Schendel and Charles W. Hofer (Boston: Little, Brown, 1978). For those who wish to be referred to case studies on corporate planning practices, see, for instance, P. Baynes, *Case Studies in Corporate Planning* (Bath, England: Society for Long-Range Planning, 1973), and Peter Lorange and Richard F. Vancil, *Strategic Planning Systems* (Englewood Cliffs, N.J.: Prentice-Hall, 1977).

3. For discussions of portfolio strategy analysis, see D. R. Ziemer and P. D. Maycock, "A Framework for Strategic Analysis," *Long Range Planning*, 6 (June 1973), 6-17 and H. Igor Anoff and James C. Leontiades, "Strategic Portfolio Management," *Journal of General Management*, 4, no. 1 (Fall 1976), 13-30.

4. There exist several excellent literature discussions on the relevant

aspects of objectives setting; see, for instance, H. A. Simon, "On the Concept of Organizational Goal," *Administrative Science Quarterly*, 4 (June 1964), 1-22; F. J. Aguilar, *Scanning the Business Environment* (New York: Macmillan, 1967); Kenneth R. Andrews, *The Concept of Corporate Strategy* (Homewood, Ill.: Dow Jones-Irving, 1971); William D. Guth, "Formulating Organizational Objectives and Strategy: A Systematic Approach," *Journal of Business Policy* (Autumn 1971); Basil W. Denning, "Strategic Environmental Appraisal," *Long Range Planning*, 6, no. 1 (March 1973), 22-27; Eric Rhenman, *Organization Theory for Long-Range Planning* (New York: Wiley-Interscience, 1973); Edward H. Bowman, "Epistemology, Corporate Strategy, and Academe," *Sloan Management Review*, 15, no. 2 (Winter 1974), 35-50; Frank T. Paine and William Naumes, *Strategy and Policy Formation: An Integrative Approach* (Philadelphia: Saunders, 1974); G. P. Latham and G. A. Yukel, "Review of Research on the Application of Goal Setting in Organizations," *Academy of Management Journal*, 18 (Dec. 1975), 724-740; Richard F. Vancil, "Strategy Formulation in Complex Organizations," *Sloan Management Review*, 17 (Winter 1976), 1-18; James Brian Quinn, "Strategic Goals: Process and Politics," *Sloan Management Review*, 19 (Fall 1977), 21-39; and H. J. Tosi, J. R. Rizzo, and S. J. Carroll, "Setting Goals by Management by Objectives," *California Management Review* (Summer 1977).

5.   The PIMS (Profit Impact of Market Share) project is being administered by the Strategic Planning Institute, a nonprofit organization located in Cambridge, Massachusetts. For a discussion of the PIMS approach, its strengths as well as limitations, see Carl R. Anderson and Frank T. Paine, "PIMS: A Reexamination," *Academy of Management Journal*, forthcoming, and Derek Abell and John S. Hammond, *Strategic Market Planning: Problems and Analytical Approaches* (Englewood Cliffs, N.J.: Prentice-Hall, 1979).

6.   Data Resources Institute (DRI) provides a well-known service of industry-specific as well as larger-sector econometric models. Another well-known model is the Wharton econometric model. See M. D. McCarty, *The Wharton Quarterly Econometric Forecasting Model, Mark III* (Philadelphia: Wharton School of Finance and Commerce, 1974), and V. D. Duggal, L. R. Klein, and M. D. McCarty, "The Wharton Model Mark III: A Modern IS-LM Construct," *International Economic Review* (Oct. 1974). See also Robert S. Pindyck and David L. Rubinfield, *Econometric Models and Economic Forecasts* (New York: McGraw-Hill, 1976), chap. 12.

7.   See Richard F. Vancil, "Better Management of Corporate Development," *Harvard Business Review*, 50 (Sept.–Oct. 1972), 53-62.

8.   The following articles and books discuss in more detail issues brought up in this chapter: Edgar M. Barett, "Conflicting Roles in Budgeting for Operations," *Harvard Business Review*, 55, no. 4 (July-Aug. 1977), 137-159; William H. Sihler, "Towards Better Management Control Systems," *California Management Review*, 10, no. 3 (1971); Robert J. Mockler, *The Management Control Process* (New York: Appleton, 1972); Peter A. Pyhrr, *Zero-Base Budgeting* (New York: Wiley-Interscience, 1973); William H. Newman, *Constructive Control* (Englewood Cliffs, N.J.: Prentice-Hall, 1975); C. F. Bales, "Strategic Control: The President's Paradox," *Business Horizons* (Aug. 1977); E. E. Carter, "Designing the Capital Budgeting Process," in *Prescriptive Models of Organizations*, eds. Paul C. Nystrom and William H. Starbuck (Amsterdam: North-Holland, 1977); and Paul J. Stonich, *Zero-Base Planning and Budgeting* (Homewood, Ill.: Dow Jones-Irwin, 1977).

9.   See Peter Lorange and Richard F. Vancil, "How To Design a Strategic Planning System," *Harvard Business Review*, 54 (Sept.–Oct. 1976), 75-88, Exhibit 2.

10. See Note 8 for a number of references pertinent to monitoring. See also John Child, "Strategies of Control and Organization Behavior," *Administrative Science Quarterly*, 18 (1973), 1-17 and Peter Lorange and Michael S. Scott Morton, "A Framework for Management Control Systems," *Sloan Management Review*, 16 (Fall 1974), 41-56.

11. For overviews of project management techniques, see David I. Cleland and William R. King, *Systems Analysis and Project Management* (New York: McGraw-Hill, 1968), and E. S. Quade, *Systems Analysis Techniques for Planning-Programming-Budgeting*, P-3322 (Santa Monica: RAND Corporation, 1966).

12. For a recent discussion of the strategic roles of incentives, see Alfred Rappaport, "Executive Compensation vs. Corporate Growth," *Harvard Business Review*, 56, no. 4. (July-Aug. 1978), 81-95. Also, see Lyman W. Porter, Edward E. Lawler, III, and J. Richard Hackman, *Behavior in Organizations* (New York: McGraw-Hill, 1975); Richard M. Steers and Lyman W. Porter, *Motivation and Work Behavior* (New York: McGraw-Hill, 1975); K. R. S. Murthy, *Corporate Strategy and Top Executive Compensation* (Cambridge, Mass.: Harvard University Press, 1977); and H. J. Tosi, J. R. Rizzo, and S. J. Carroll, "Setting Goals by Management by Objectives," *California Management Review* (Summer 1977). For a survey of empirical research findings relating to this issue, see Richard A. Guzzo, "Types of Rewards, Cognitions, and Work Motivation," *Academy of Management Review*, 4, no. 1 (Jan. 1979), 75-86.

13. For discussions of several aspects of the planning process as a basis for communication, interaction, and conflict resolution, see Andres L. Delbecq, "The Management of Decision Making Within the Firm: Three Strategies for Three Types of Decision Making," *Academy of Management Journal*, 10 (Dec. 1967), 329-340; Arlyn J. Melcher, and Ronald Beller "Towards a Theory of Organization Communication: Consideration in Channel Selection," *Academy of Management Journal*, 10 (March 1967), 39-52; K. J. Arrow, *The Limits of Organization* (New York: Norton, 1975); C. R. Hinnings and others, "Structural Conditions of Intraorganizational Power," *Administrative Science Quarterly*, 19, no. 1 (1974), 22-45; Victor H. Vroom and Arthur G. Jago, "Decision Making as a Social Process: Normative and Descriptive Models of Leader Behavior," *Decision Sciences*, 5, no. 4 (1974), 743-770; K. J. Arrow, "Vertical Integration and Communication," *The Bell Journal of Economics*, 6 (Spring 1975), 173-184; and J. Hunger and C. Stern, "An Assessment of the Functionality of the Superordinate Goal in Reducing Conflict," *Academy of Management Journal*, 19 (Dec. 1976), 591-605.

14. For a discussion of the strategic systems and processes at Texas Instruments, Inc., see pp. 338-361 in Peter Lorange and Richard F. Vancil, *Strategic Planning Systems* (Englewood Cliffs, N.J.: Prentice-Hall, 1977).

15. For discussions of the General Electric Company planning system, see Richard F. Vancil, *Decentralization: Managing Ambiguity by Design* (New York: Financial Executives Research Foundation, Inc., 1979), p. 5-4; Jacques de la Brie, "General Electric's Approach to Strategic Planning," paper presented at North American Society for Corporate Planning Conference, Hofstra University, May 1978; "G.E.'s Evolving Management System," case study, in Charles W. Hofer and others, eds., *Strategic Management: A Casebook* (St. Paul: West Publishing, 1979); and William K. Hall, "S.B.U.s; Hot, New Topic in the Management of Diversification," *Business Horizons* (Feb. 1978).

Auditing the Company's Strategic Positions: Determining Planning Needs

Introduction

Before implementing a strategic planning system along the conceptual lines presented in Chapter Two, it will be necessary to develop a clear picture of the company's present strategic position. The situational setting of the firm will be a major factor in establishing planning needs; the purpose of this chapter is to propose a framework for assessing the types of needs a company will have. Only after establishing a relatively clear picture of the capabilities that the planning system should be able to provide will we be in a position to tailor-make a system to meet these needs by building the desired capabilities into the conceptual planning scheme. It is thus an essential step to carry out a strategic audit of the firm's situational setting as a prerequisite to a tailor-made approach for implementing a strategic planning system. In this chapter we shall explore approaches to strategic audits and planning needs analyses.

A necessary first step in the strategic audit planning needs analysis will be to assess the issue of identifying the building blocks of the planning system: Which are the divisions (from a strategic relevance point of view)? What is the nature of the corporate portfolio strategizing task? And so on. We touched upon this issue in Chapter Two but shall operationalize further the delineation of a strategic structure here. We shall approach this by first operationalizing the concept of a product/

market element as the smallest general management denominator and business strategizing building block for the planning system. We shall then propose an analytical approach for assessing the strategic position of a product/market element in terms of its market share and the growth of the business it is in. This is, however, based on the relevance of two phenomena that provide the basis for a product/market's business element strategy analysis, the experience curve and the product life-cycle concepts. We shall discuss when these premises seem to be relevant and will identify the situational settings in which they seem less relevant. The product/market element analysis will culminate with the identification of the adaptation and integration-related planning needs stemming from the strategic posture identified.

Having discussed how to assess the strategic posture and planning needs of one product/market element, we shall then approach the issue of how to consolidate this into an analysis of a cluster or family of several product/market elements, typically what one will be faced with to establish the planning needs at the division level of the firm.

A shift in focus will then follow in that the corporate-level strategic portfolio position and planning needs of the firm also will be assessed. We shall discuss two basic aspects of this: First, we shall address relevant ways of assessing the nature of the financial performance pressures that the firm as a whole is under. Prominent factors in this respect will be profitability and stability in earnings patterns. Second, we shall analyze the nature of structural pressures that the firm might be facing, such as being in unattractive business segments or seeing one's competitors making innovative corporate moves to restructure their business mix. Chief among the tools to assess this phenomenon will be funds-flow analysis and comparative portfolio analysis of oneself versus key competitors. At this point we shall also find it useful to address the issue of how to assess the company's overall exposure to environmental risks and the different needs for planning that arise from different environmental exposures. In Appendix I we shall provide an example of how one highly diversified company approaches the task of developing an index of strategic fit within its corporate portfolio for each of its 40 divisions based on an assessment of the situational strategic positioning of each division. Finally, in Appendix II we shall discuss the role of financial statement analysis for indicating the needs for particular portfolio-level strategy modifications.

The Product/Market Element Concept

To analyze the strategic position of a business, it is useful to adopt as a unit of measurement or building block the concept of product/market elements, which, as noted, we have already briefly discussed in Chapter Two. A product/market element can be defined as the smallest organizational unit that performs an identifiable general management business task, i.e., the creation of a specific and distinct product or service that serves a well-defined market, distinguishable from and relatively independent of other product/market combinations.[1]

There are several important implications of this definition of product/market element that need to be raised in order to operationalize this concept further. First, the definition of a product/market element assumes that one is able to define and formulate in writing an operational mission for this entity. Particularly important in this context is the need to identify a well-defined market, including coming up with a clear perception of who one's competitors are. Almost equally important in this respect will be to come up with a clear notion of what product or service the unit is offering. These assessments will have to be specific and far-reaching. Second, it will be critically important that the definition of a product/market element allow management to conceive of and focus on the set of truly unique potentials and risks that will characterize this business. These opportunity and/or threat factors should have a high level of visibility and ought to be clearly identified. Thus, the definition task is a creative one, calling for an imaginative delineation of a product/market element along dimensions which are likely to be critical for the development of a successful competitive strategy. Third, the common thread of products and/or services that run through the product/market element entity must be clearly identified. Thus, the definition of the product/market element must not represent such a high level of abstraction that it will become more or less meaningless. Finally, we probably will have to be reconciled to the fact that although the task to come up with a useful definition of a product/market element and to develop a clearly delineated and useful pattern of product/market elements is a critical requirement for strategic management, this task is a difficult one which probably will have to be classified more as an art than an exact science. This is an important recognition in that it should allow management to approach the product/market definition task in a creative and imaginative manner, without being frustrated by applying overly stringent and inflexible criteria to the task.

To delineate the product/market elements within a division, we might start out by referring to Exhibit 3-1. We see that what might be considered a generic element of analysis would be one consisting of one product in one market, marked as I in the exhibit. In practice, of course, this would normally be too small a unit of analysis to be operational. Thus, we may want to combine several markets being served with one product, II, several products serving one market, III, or ad hoc combina-

EXHIBIT 3-1 Delineation of Product/Market Elements to Be the Basis for Business Element Strategies Within a Division

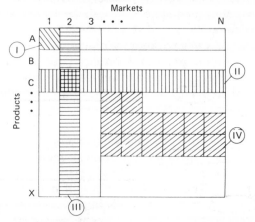

Markets

Products

tions of products and markets, IV, so that a useful set of product/market elements can be delineated as the basis for our planning.

Let us provide a set of questions that might serve as a first checklist for whether we have reasonable delineation of product/market element. If any of the questions below have to be answered in negative terms, then we might have a problem with this particular product/market element delineation.

1. Does the product/market element enjoy a strategic independence from other product/market elements which is operational in the sense that it is feasible to develop a competitive strategy for a particular product/market relatively independently of other product/markets? Another way of phrasing this question is to determine the extent to which the competitive strength of the product/market element is based on other product/market elements and whether an assessment of the attractiveness of the business can be done independently of the other businesses. The last question normally cannot be answered affirmatively unless the product/market element has some degree of control over its own raw materials sources as well as its own finished products markets. If, however, a product/market element does not have a reasonable control over its sources and/or markets, then cost and/or revenue patterns among the product/market elements should be separated by means of a transfer pricing scheme. Needless to say, the criterion of pseudoindependence among product/market elements by means of transfer pricing schemes has to be done carefully; it is often a difficult managerial judgment to draw the line beyond which the arbitrariness of forced independence becomes so great that it would be more natural and beneficial to combine these units into one larger product/market element, pursuing one larger strategy. It should be stressed that although a product/market element normally should enjoy independence from other product/market elements when pursuing its own competitive strategy in a discretionary manner, as just discussed, this does not

necessarily imply that each product/market element should possess its own functional departments. Functional departments might be shared by all or some of the product/market elements within a division, not only as a way of performing a functional task more efficiently but also reflecting the strategic interrelationships among the product/market elements as being part of one business family strategy. A functional department might report directly to the division management or to the product/market element which is drawing most extensively on this particular function.

2. If the product or service that is being created by a product/market element was withdrawn from the marketplace, then a key question is whether or not the company would be out of the competition within this general area of business. If not, we have an indication that the product/market element might not be strategically independent of other product/market elements, and we need to assess the degree to which strategic relationships with other product/market elements exist. In this connection, we should stress that the relevant dependence among product/market elements to assess is along the strategic dimension. Whether or not product/market elements are dependent or not along the operating dimension, too, is not relevant in this context (although of course it is important when it comes to executing the integrative aspects of planning).

3. Is the corporate and/or the divisional management's intent real when it comes to dealing strategically with a product/market element? An important rationale for establishing product/market elements is the benefit from a division of labor among managers within the firm's organizational hierarchy when focusing on various strategic tasks, as discussed in Chapter Two. A manager responsible for a product/market element should be closer to the competitive scene than anyone else in the company and should have sufficient discretionary leverage to act on the basis of this to opportunistically secure competitive advantages for the firm. However, a typical phenomenon among managers is that they prefer decentralization down to their own level in the organization but centralization at the levels below. Hence, it is often difficult to practice the hands-off management style that is needed in order to make the product/market element concept work. At this point it should be noticed that we need to distinguish between the degree of decentralization of operational issues versus strategic issues. For instance, we may often have relatively decentralized operations coupled with relatively centralized strategic management.

4. Does the company have adequate management skills and talent to allow for the functioning of product/market elements as vehicles for defining and implementing strategies? This may often be the most critical issue. What type of experience has the company had with traditional responsibility centers for operating purposes? There are typically three types of responsibility centers relevant to the decentralized management of the line activities of a firm: cost centers, profit centers, and investment centers. (The so-called revenue center can be seen as a hybrid between a profit center and a cost center. A discretionary expense center is relevant primarily in connection with staff department activities.) The sequence in which these are listed is important in that it signifies an increasing degree of decentralization and autonomy to be enjoyed by the management responsible for the performance of the responsibility center: the cost center, with discretionary responsibility for inputs only (costs, expenses); the profit center, with discretionary responsibility for inputs and outputs (revenue); the investment center, with discretionary responsibility for inputs, outputs, and investment base (size of investment that has created a

given net output). We might consider a product/market element as a logical extension of the investment center in the sense that responsibility for long-term strategic performance has been delegated to the management of the responsibility center, in addition to short-term performance responsibility. We might apply a measure of long-term ROI (or residual income) to be optimized by the product/market element. To do this its management must develop and implement a long-term strategy which encompasses the development of the long-term competitive strength of the product/market elements, its strategic base. Thus, a product/market element may be appropriately relabeled a strategy center, which will have discretionary responsibility for inputs, outputs, investment base, and strategic base. We shall use the terms *strategy center* and *product/market element* interchangeably. Since the task of strategizing goes on within many organizational units other than a product/market element (notably at the division and corporate levels), one might argue that it might be misleading to use the term strategy center in this way. However, the argument for it is to underscore the evolution in decentralization when seeing a product/market element as a natural extension of the conventional responsibility concept—from operating decentralization to strategic decentralization.

In an evolutionary sense, the step from managing an operating investment center to managing a strategy center is probably a relatively natural and short one. Thus, a strong investment center tradition is probably an advantage when attempting to develop a decentralized strategic mode of operation. Nevertheless, the change from a short-term performance fulfillment orientation to a long-term strategic orientation can be a formidable problem. Particularly critical is the change in the responsibility center manager's technique from a short-term, fire-fighting, stick-and-carrot game to an orderly planning process of identifying and narrowing down long-term strategic options. The switch in managerial style is of course even greater when one attempts such a strategic mode of operation after a less full-blown traditional mode of decentralized operation, such as going from a profit center or particularly a cost center mode of operation to a strategy center. Such a monumental change in management style seems to be what was called for in the cases of some of the major integrated oil companies when these broke themselves up into strategy centers. (Gulf Oil Corporation, for instance, was reorganized into 7 strategy centers, Sun Oil Company—now Sun Company—was reorganized into 14 product/market elements.) To restructure into a pattern of strategy centers might be particularly difficult in instances where there is a jump by passing one or more of the evolutionary stages in the responsibility center sequence. It might be a real issue whether an organization in fact will be able to mobilize overnight the necessary managerial competence for such an instant switch in mode of operation.

A second and related issue involves the degree of past stability in the operating organizational structure as well as maturity of managerial communication patterns within the organization. If there have been a number of recent reorganizations and/or structure changes due to acquisitions, and/or if the management succession rate has been high, then it might be more difficult to create a meaningful strategy center structure. An essential reason for the strategy center concept is its role as a building block: the focus of strategizing for competitive business success. It assumes that management is in fact intimately familiar with the businesses. It should be stressed that the product/market elements or strategy centers, although representing the strategic structure of the firm, are in fact examples of shadow organization components. They should not be confused with the operating organizational structures.[2]

We see, then, that the issue of identifying a reasonable set of product/market elements is not an easy one, and because it calls for a considerable degree of managerial judgment, this task causes concern among management attempting to undertake a business position strategic assessment the first time. Experience, however, shows that the task does not turn out to be as difficult as anticipated—for three reasons. First, when starting out with the assumption that one's present operating product/market grouping is going to be the basis for the analysis unless compelling reasons for doing otherwise are given, the task becomes one of strategic stratification rather than creating a new operating structure from zero. Second, when we ask what is the market share of a particular strategy center relative to other strategy centers, we might come up with answers that indicate that our definitions of strategy centers are unreasonable. For instance, if for a strategy center we can quite readily identify several market shares, each for different subsegments of the business, then we might have applied a product/market definition that is too aggregated. Or, alternatively, if the market share is 100 percent or close to this, then we should be particularly suspicious about whether a too narrow definition has been made of what would be a relevant product/market segment. Third, when we employ the concept of market growth to several product/market elements and we find that they seem to fall remarkably close together into a pattern which reflects a sound, steady growth, with only a few strategy centers receiving the embryonic high-growth label on the one hand or the mature or decline label on the other, then we have an indication that we might have grouped our strategy centers into units that are too large. Conversely, if there is no dominance of normal growth strategy centers on the middle of the scale, we might have applied a grouping that is too fragmented. In the next section we shall define market share and market growth and discuss why these concepts should be included in our analysis.

The Concepts of the Experience Curve
and the Product Life Cycle as Premises
for Product/Market Business Element Strategic Analysis

Having established the concept of the product/market element as our unit of business element strategic analysis, we shall now develop a way of analyzing its strategic position. It is useful to assess the product/market element or strategy center in terms of the degree of competitive strength that it represents as well as the degree to which it is positioned within an attractive business segment. Market share and business growth rate are often useful proxies for determining such a strategic position. Before we launch our discussion of how to carry out this type of analysis, however, it is necessary to examine the rationale behind the approach. This rests on two premises: the so-called experience curve and the product life-cycle concepts. We shall discuss each of these in turn.

The first premise relates to the experience curve concept.[3] This stems from the learning curve phenomenon of time-and-motion study engineering, which states that when repeating a production task several times, such as building a new airplane, experience in building the first plane will make it easier to build the second plane, and so on. The direct labor and materials cost per plane is therefore expected to go down as a function of the number of planes built. In addition, there will of course be savings per plane due to less overhead burden per plane when the number of units produced goes up; this effect should, however, not be confused with the learning curve effect. The consequence of the learning curve effect which causes lower costs per unit produced is that it opens up a competitive cost advantage if one is able to produce a greater volume of units than one's competitors.

Although traditionally developed in the context of job-shop manufacturing settings, the learning curve functions in continuous process-oriented industries too. In such settings, however, the technological advantages associated with modern and large capital equipment provide the competitive advantage rather than the learning effects experienced by the labor force. Thus, the more capital-intensive the industry, the less important will the learning curve effect be. Instead, plant size and sophistication of equipment might provide an equivalent competitive advantage.

It turns out that the concept of learning curve effects applies to many of the managerial and support functions that are carried out within a firm. This is based on the assumption that a management team which consists of experienced executives and is well coordinated will probably do a job faster and better than a recently assembled team of less experienced executives. Marketing expertise, for instance, is probably one of several managerial factors that accumulates with experience. The marketing organization which enjoys the larger volume of business will accumulate relevant insights and experience to a larger extent than a smaller competitor. Thus, it will be in a better position in terms of marketing value added per unit produced. Given this broader and extended application of the learning curve concept, it has become common to denote this as the experience curve phenomenon, and we shall henceforth use the latter term.

There are, however, several limitations on the experience curve phenomenon. As already discussed, the absolute magnitude of a positive experience curve effect is likely to decrease as volume goes up; after some level of activity there is probably relatively less to be gained in expenditure curve effects. Thus, when two competitors have reached a particular level of size there is probably no longer a very significant competitive advantage to be the larger one. Further, the strength of experience curve effects will differ from industry to industry. It is probably greater in labor-intensive industries and in industries which to a large extent rely on job-shop, product-related manufacturing. The durability of the experience curve advantages is also an unknown; the effect is certainly not permanent due to such factors as job rotations (another reason for management to cut down on unnecessary job rotations) and major job task modifications that in many ways can be compared with starting the experience curve anew. Thus, for companies in industry settings that are encountering a rapid rate of change, such as frequent technological modifications within areas of the electronics industry, positive experience curve effects will be harder to obtain on a more permanent basis.

A final problem with applying the experience curve concept would be within extractive industries where a natural resource is being depleted and further production requires reserves that are more difficult and expensive to reach than the older reserves. Thus, total cost per unit might rise even though unit production costs fall. We can probably find examples of this within the oil and gas exploration industry, where it may become necessary to carry out more expensive deep-water offshore exploration, or in the uranium industry, where deeper mine shafts are needed to reach the only available unexplored deposits. There will of course be opportunities for positive experience curve effects to counteract the negative effect just discussed; at each new stage of more expensive exploration there will be an experience curve effect, say, from drilling holes more efficiently from an offshore semisubmersible rig.

At this point it should be noticed that the experience curve phenomenon, based on the concept of its essentially being a function of accumulated volume of production to date, is different from the well-known concept of economies-of-scales, the latter being a function of the rate of production and thus leading to significant technological process-related savings. These two phenomena should also be distinguished from the calculation of fixed cost per unit, which will be falling with increased volume, given that the overhead costs, say, can be spread over a larger number of units produced. All these effects, however (i.e., experience curve effect, economies-of-scales effect, fixed cost absorption effect), will have performance impact in the same direction for a business. However, the experience curve effect is the only one of the three which can be impacted through planned performance, once the decision to make a resource commitment to a new production facility has been made.

Despite the many questions that can be raised about the exact nature of the experience curve effect, it can be usefully associated with analyzing the benefits from having a high market share. A high market share implies a high-volume activity level. For instance, a market leader will have the highest activity level. This, however, also implies that the leader also has the highest potential experience curve effect benefits. Thus, it seems clear that high market share and volume will yield at least some competitive advantage. Thus, the market share position relative to one's competitors is normally a significant aspect of the strategic audit of a business, and different planning needs will be created depending on relative market share position. If a product/market element enjoys a high share, the task will be to plan so that the experience curve effects can in fact be achieved; they do not come automatically. If in a low market share, the planning task will be to ameliorate some of the potentially negative effects from not having the same experience curve potential as one's competitors.

Let us now turn to the question of the relevance of the experience curve premise as an element in our strategic audit analysis of a business unit. There is strong empirical evidence of a positive relationship between market share and profitability, i.e., that profits are a function of market share, due to experience curve effects.[4] The studies indicate that several other factors, too, are important in predicting the economic performance of a business, but market share clearly seems to be the most significant. It is beyond our purpose to review and discuss these research findings in detail here. However, one large-scale empirical attempt at determining the critical strategic factors that influence the economic performance of a business should be discussed, the so-called PIMS project (Profit Impacts of Marketing Strategies) that is being carried out at the Strategic Planning Institute, a nonprofit institution. Three reasons justify a brief discussion of PIMS at this point, namely, the remarkable detail, scope, and ambitousness of the project; the real-life strategic decision-making orientation of its design; and the wide impact and use that its results have had on actual corporate planning practices.[5]

Over 1,200 businesses analogous to our product/market elements from more than 100 companies are in the PIMS data base. The mission of the project has been to isolate those variables that determine ROI, approaching this by means of a multiple regression model which contains 37 independent variables and predicts 80 percent of the criterion variable. These 37 independent variables have been combined in 9 factor groups, which we shall list in terms of order of impact upon ROI:

1. Investment intensity
2. Productivity
3. Market position
4. Growth of served market
5. Quality of product/service
6. Innovation and differentiation, when supported by market share
7. Vertical integration, when markets are stable, not growing, or growing very rapidly
8. Cost push influence
9. Current strategic thrust; the direction of change of the variables

A company might make use of the PIMS data base to determine what a "normal" ROI should be for a business within a particular industry and with a given set of situational characteristics. This might provide useful inputs, say, for the setting of top-down expectations for various strategy centers. The model might also be used to search for ways to improve a particular strategy center's strategic position.

While the PIMS approach sheds considerable empirical light on the importance of a strategy center's strategic position as the determinant of performance, and while also it might be used by a particular company as one tool in its planning process, it has several limitations. Some of these limitations refer to methodological constraints of the study; it is, however, outside the scope of this book to discuss them. Other limitations refer to the ways the data should be used in the planning process, and these merit brief mention. The major danger is developing an overly mechanistic, extrapolative approach to strategy formulation as a result of the use of the data. It should be stressed that the data are historical and also that they do not measure the quality of strategic insight on behalf of management. It is therefore important not to allow the data to become more or less an unescapable law for how one's business should do. Positive, creative thinking focused around opportunities and threats can facilitate future strategic success, not extrapolations of the past. Another danger, albeit much smaller, is the emphasis on ROI as the criterion for judging the success of a business element strategy. Not only might other financial variables such as net cash flow be more relevant as indicators of the creation of strategic values (PIMS has in fact developed a cash-flow model as an alternative to its ROI model), but, more importantly, strategic performance should probably be judged in terms of variables that emphasize longer-term effects in addition to near-term ROI or cash flow.

Another important general implementation issue which relates to a vast number of tools and techniques used in business strategizing, as elements of the overall planning process, is that one may be creating potential dangers of simplistic, mechanistic, and narrow-minded approaches to planning. We shall come back to this later in this chapter.

Instead we shall turn to the other phenomenon, in addition to the learning curve concept, which is a premise for our product/market element strategic position analysis. This is the so-called product life-cycle concept, based on the observation that products tend to follow a life-cycle pattern of evolution over time.[6] Consider, for instance, the following scenario: A product might start as no more than a set of untried ideas that will have to be refined to go through a first or embryonic stage of commercialization with heavy emphasis on getting a better focus for what the market niche might be, through marketing, ironing out production problems, and so on. Having succeeded through this first stage (most product ideas probably don't), the product, if well conceived, might enter into a period of rapid growth. The emphasis during this growth stage will probably be focused on trying to get the product produced and distributed in order to respond to an unsaturated demand for this product idea, attempting to reap benefits from the fact that prices can probably still be maintained at a reasonably comfortable level for such a novelty product. A major concern of course will be to attempt to reach the market ahead of one's competitors. As a probably inevitable saturation of the market demand for the product sooner or later approaches, another life-cycle stage is reached, the mature stage. The concern here is to make the product available at a lower price, to emphasize experience curve effects and process improvements, attempting to take advantage of efficiency programs in order to come up with a competitive product so that one's own margins can be kept. After some time, however, another period of decline in the demand for the product might set in due to obsolescence in the face of new product developments. The emphasis during such a decline stage will probably be to shift toward retreat, getting as much cash as possible out of the project before it dies out entirely.

From the above example we see that a product might go through several distinctive evolutionary stages in its life cycle. To a large extent the number of distinctive generic stages will be a matter of choice. Our present discussion recognizes four distinctive stages: the embryonic or start-up stage, the growth stage, the leveling off or mature stage, and the decline stage. We might thus say that a product's growth rate will provide a useful insight as to what degree of maturity the product is having. Thus, the growth rate might give an indication about how much more useful time a product is expected to have. Presumably it is more attractive to have a relatively new, high-growth product, which can be expected to be of economic use for a relatively long period to come, than to possess a mature, lower-growth product, which might be expected to be phased out relatively sooner.

From our description of the stages of the product life cycle, it seems natural to examine associated funds-flow considerations. During the embryonic and growth stages the investments in getting the product developed, commercialized, and distributed are likely to outweigh the funds generated from sales. During the later stages, however, income from sales should outweigh the more modest continued expenditures needed for keeping the product alive. The criterion for whether a product is economically viable, then, would be the extent to which the expected accumulated inflows will be larger than the expected accumulated outflows (time-adjusted): A dilemma, of course, is due to the fact that a large share of the outflows will be committed before any significant inflow might be expected.

It should be noted that, as with the experience curve concept, the life-cycle concept does not represent an iron law. There are many products that have grown largely because management was able to handle a continued growth through innovative product modifications, marketing extensions, and so on. There are also examples of companies, however, that took the evolutionary life-cycle movements to be so inevitable that management's actions actually led to an unnecessary shortening of the life of a product through early decline. This is particularly so because the classification of a product/market element as outlined in the preceding paragraphs might become a stifling element in management's thinking. Above all, management may be less prone to address the important issue of potentially *repositioning* a product so as to give it a new start on the product life cycle, or at least slow its evolutionary decaying. Failure to consider this might actually lead to a premature killing of a product. An example might illustrate this. Within most parts of the industrial specialty chemicals business one can observe the product life-cycle phenomenon in its iron-law sense, implying that new product and/or process research will with high likelihood make a product in its present form obsolete within the future, this being more or less distant depending on the type of product. As a consequence, a firm's pricing practices should reflect this—you raise prices when a product is approaching the latter stages of its life cycle so as to milk the most out of it. Given that the product in all likelihood will face a demise anyway, one would not be too concerned about such a price rise policy killing the product off. A particular industrial specialty chemicals company happened to have a product aimed at a consumer market, notably a film for household wrapping purposes. In line with its customary pricing tradition, the price of the consumer product was raised in anticipation of a life-cycle decline, with the effect that its market share dropped drastically. What management failed to see was that they might easily have been able to extend the life cycle of this product through impacting the consumers, i.e., through an advertising campaign coupled with a lowering of prices. Instead of extending the product life cycle, they killed the product prematurely.

Although this is not the proper place to launch a full-blown discussion of how a planning system might facilitate the avoidance of a stifled view on the positioning of a product/market element, let us briefly point out two response aspects to this kind of problem: First, as we shall see, the corporate-level management should play an active role in reviewing the possibilities of repositioning product/market elements. The managers of the strategy centers in question, if left alone, might become so close to the product/market that they fail to see the repositioning opportunities. Second, the monitoring system should play a useful role in this context in focusing on whether key environmental premises are still valid or whether signals come up which would suggest repositioning.

Despite the reservations in the previous paragraphs about becoming too mechanistic, the product life-cycle position is an important and useful concept in our strategic audit analysis; typically product growth is largely outside the discretionary domain of management, in contrast to the market share/experience curve position which can be more under the influence and discretion of management.

A product which is in a high-growth position, then, will have an attractive future, a growing and widening demand not likely to taper off for a long time. A product which has passed the high-growth stage and entered a phase of lower growth, on the other hand, will see its markets cool off and become narrower. Maybe it is even becoming clear that the economic life of such a product is approaching its end. Thus, we may claim that growth rate is a useful surrogate for business attractiveness, given that a high growth rate tends to be associated with a favorable life-cycle position, while a low growth rate tends to be associated with an unfavorable position.

From our discussion thus far in this section, we have seen that the two premises identified for assessing the strategic attractiveness of a strategy center—market share position and growth rate posture—both seem to highlight different aspects of strategic attractiveness. Thus, in fact, it is not possible to make a strategic audit without simultaneously assessing a product/market element on both these dimensions, as we shall now discuss.

The Market Share/Market Growth Grid

The approach of assessing the strategic position of a product/market element on a two-dimensional grid with relative market share and business growth as the two dimensions was spearheaded by the Boston Consulting Group (BCG) under its president Bruce Henderson. This development represents perhaps the most significant contribution to strategic planning over the last two decades. By today this approach, or extensions of it, has come to be very popular and widely used by managers with business strategizing tasks. Exhibit 3-2 illustrates the basic BCG grid. [7]

Before discussing the strategic implications of being positioned at various cells in the grid, let us first define the dimensions of the two axes. At the horizontal axis relative market share is normally defined as the sales of one's own strategy center relative to the sales of the largest competing strategy center. If this measure takes on values larger than 1, then one's own strategy center is the leader in this business; if, for instance, the relative market share is 2, then this strategy center is twice as large as its largest competitor. If the measure is taking on values less than 1, then the strategy center is smaller than the largest competitor; a value of ½, for instance, indicates that the strategy center is half the size of the largest competitor. Relative market share has been chosen instead of absolute market share because it gives a direct indication of one's own experience-curve-derived cost advantage potential relative to the competition.

EXHIBIT 3-2 Strategic Position Grid for a Product/Market Element

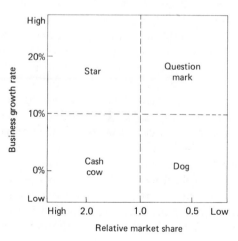

On the vertical axis annual compound growth of the market that the business is in is being measured. Growth rate can be measured in several ways. For instance, in some businesses with highly erratic growth tracks, such as certain parts of the electronics components businesses, it may make sense to measure average growth over a period of several years in order to lessen the effect of such near-term fluctuations around a longer-term growth trend. Similarly, for certain businesses the growth will be highly dependent on general movements in the economy; in such cases one might adjust the growth calculation with some sort of gross national product movements index or another index deemed meaningful as an indicator for general economic movements adjustments. One might also have to compensate for the general inflation rate. The key is to apply a measurement for business growth which is useful in distinguishing between product/market elements that are in a high-growth mode and those which are less so in a particular business. The measurement chosen must of course be consistently applied in the analysis of all the product/market elements of the firm. We shall return to the issue of defining more operational measurements for the two dimensions of Exhibit 3-2 at the end of this section, after having discussed the impact of the strategic positioning of strategy centers located within each of the cells of the matrix.

Discussing the strategic implication of positioning in each of the four cells of Exhibit 3-2, the first cell we shall discuss is the one labeled *star.* This is a very advantageous position, strategically, in that one's own strategy center is dominant in the market place and also in that one's business is in a high-growth area. In terms of funds-flow implications, however, there will be two opposing effects at work: On the one hand, there will be a potential positive effect from the experience curve cost advantage that the strategy center is likely to enjoy relative to its competitors. On the other hand, the presence in a high-growth business is likely to require considerable investment in capacity expansion of production and/or distribution facilities. In total, then, the overall funds-flow balance is likely to be more or less neutral; it is difficult to predict whether the net position will show a small negative or positive value. Maybe more often than not the funds-flow balance may tend to be slightly negative.

The position marked *cash cow* in Exhibit 3-2, with a high market share but low growth, however, is likely to be a net contributor of funds; the competitive experience curve advantage of this strategy center's position is good and the growth rate is low, causing the strategy center to enjoy the positive funds-flow benefits from its cost advantages from its experience curve position. Further, it will no longer have to invest heavily in sustaining an adequate production and/or distribution facility now that growth has fallen off and ample capacity thereby should already exist.

Strategy centers in this position will typically be a cash cow, i.e., provide the backbone of discretionary funds for continued expansion into new product areas. Typically a product/market element in this position was previously in a star position.

New product developments may take on many forms, but it may be useful to dichotomize them into two classes: *original new products*, which will not have yet created a market and a demand (and, consequently, for which we cannot yet meaningfully talk about growth rate and/or market share), and *me too products*, which attempt to latch onto someone else's original new product development. This might thus be classified in the high-growth/low-market share segment. Here the issue will be to invest in new product/market elements which, over time, can build themselves a market base and become stars. For both types of new product developments, the net funds-flow position is of course expected to be heavily negative, reflecting the investment in creating a future market as well as establishing a market share. One issue facing the strategists is concern that such new ventures might fail; hence, we denote this cell with a *question mark*.

Let us finally consider the fourth position: low market share and low product/market element growth. Clearly such a position is strategically undesirable for a product/market element to be in. Neither is the growth such that the strategy center offers much long-term promise, nor is the competitive position strong enough to provide a likely base for competitive advantages. Although it is likely that the funds-flow position will be approximately neutral—neither large cash inflows nor outflows—the strategy center will consume managerial resources and will easily develop into a drag. When a strategy center ends up in this *dog* position (i.e., we have a question mark that failed), the decision is likely to be taken not to pursue this particular product any longer but gradually to phase it out or to withdraw.

As already alluded to, we also face the issue of affecting changes of position within the strategic grid that a strategy center might go through. Ideally a strategy center would start out as a question mark, then build up to a star, and then evolve into a cash cow. Hopefully, we would never allow it to be tapering off as a dog. In Exhibit 3-3 we have indicated this desired evolutionary path for a strategy center with a solid line.

However, there might be several scenarios of a product/market element's evolution that would indicate less of a success. For instance, it is not uncommon that product/market elements reach the dog position from an initial question mark position. This is an indication of a strategic failure; management was unable to establish a solid market position for this product/market element. We have indicated this evolutionary scenario by a broken line in Exhibit 3-3. Another less desirable but not

EXHIBIT 3-3   Evolutionary Paths for a
Product/Market Element's Life
Cycle

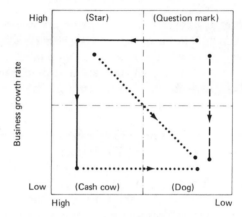

High | (Star) | (Question mark)
Low | (Cash cow) | (Dog)
High | | Low

Business growth rate

Relative market share

*The solid line represents a desirable path;
the dotted and broken lines represent less
desirable paths.*

uncommon pattern of evolution is when a strategy center reaches the dog
position directly from a star position. This too is an indication of a
strategic failure; management has been unable to take advantage of the
favorable funds-flow potential which would have resulted if it had been
able to maintain its market share. This is indicated by a dotted line in the
exhibit.

In line with this, we can identify four major strategic alternatives for
managing a product/market element within this analytical context. We
might adopt a strategy which attempts to *build* market share through
relatively heavy investments in strategic programs. Typically we find this
for strategy centers in the question mark sector but with reasonable
prospects for being moved into the star category. Second, we might
follow a *hold* strategy, which implies that enough must be invested in
strategic programs to maintain the market share. A strategy center in a
star position or a cash-cow position might fall into this category. *Harvest*
will be a third alternative for a product/market element, implying that the
market share is being allowed to diminish. A product/market element in a
cash-cow position might be a candidate for such a strategy but only after it
is evident that the product life-cycle position indicates a relatively short
and finite remaining usefulness. Finally, a *withdraw* strategy might be
appropriate when a strategy center offers little or no potential for further

strategic benefits. A dog position should be a basis for this strategy. We might add a fifth strategic option, *explore* (or wait, hold), which would apply to entirely new product developments at the preliminary precommercialization stage, before having decided to embark on a build strategy, or, alternatively, to cancel the project at this early stage.

The approach just outlined in the preceding paragraphs is a simple and powerful one. It provides a clear picture of the strategic position of a strategy center, and it has an intuitive logic that should appeal to most executives. At this point in our discussion we need to recall, however, that the purpose of our strategic position analysis is to determine the needs for planning that a particular strategy center will face in terms of adaptation as well as integration. We recall that only after having determined these needs will we be able to tailor-make the planning system in such ways that it will be provided with capabilities to meet the needs. It should also be pointed out at this point that the basic product/market element strategic position analysis just discussed often might need to be modified in important ways, now and then extensively, in order to become operational.

A basic problem is that market share and market growth might not always be the only useful measures for determining a product/market element's strategic position. To illustrate this we need to raise the following fundamental question: What do we really attempt to capture by means of our measurements of market share and market growth? Market share is really, as we have seen, a proxy for an indication of the strategy center's competitive strength. Thus, we need to ask whether there might be other measures of competitive strength that could be equally-or more relevant. In particular, we might want to explore alternative measures of competitive strength in cases where we do not expect that the experience curve phenomenon will fully apply.

One such area might be within certain segments of high-technology industries where new product development is critical. In such instances R&D capability, for instance, might be a more relevant measure of competitive strength than market share. This implies that some measure would have to be developed to assess a strategy center's strength along this dimension relative to one's competitors. Another and related aspect of competitive strength might be one's ability to come up with unique patent protection in one's R&D efforts—also a phenomenon that one would need to measure relative to one's competitors. Further, with a rapidly changing business environment vis-à-vis such factors as the labor force, government relations, etc., it becomes an important competitive strength for firms to be able to maintain good and flexible labor relations, including having located themselves in such a way that labor costs can be kept at a competitive level. Similarly, good government relations might be a competitive advantage. This would probably be particularly true for labor-intensive and/or highly regulated industries, such as shipyards. Finally, given the raw materials shortages that businesses now and then seem to be facing, for instance, within the energy area, it might be a competitive strength to be able to carry out as energy-efficient a business as possible. Within high energy consuming industries such as in the cement or the airline businesses, a measure of energy efficiency relative to competition might be a highly relevant indicator of competitive strength. What we see emerging from these examples is a necessity to evaluate in each case for a particular product/market element how its competitive strength should be measured. In some instances we may have to make use of alternative measures to market share; in other cases, we may have to develop a composite measure of competitive strength based on market share as well as on other measures.

Let us now take a closer look at the other dimension in the product/ market element strategic position matrix, namely, the growth dimension, and ask whether this is a unique proxy for business attractiveness. Although growth used to be the panacea, many questions are being raised as to whether this is the only attractive aspect of a business. Again, we might find instances where other attractive factors are prominent within areas where the underlying premise, the product life-cycle concept, does not hold. One example of an important additional business attractiveness issue is to attempt to avoid businesses with a heavy element of induced obsolescence. A fairly stable and not too rapid rate of technological change is therefore probably one increasingly important additional factor of business attractiveness. Another potentially important aspect of this is the nature of competition itself. For instance, with an industry which enjoys a relatively healthy competitive structure, there is less likelihood of the competitive pressure inducing exceedingly rapid and expensive changes into the evolution of the product life cycle. The nature of the competition may, for instance, also be excessively fragmented, with a significant number of smaller, relatively weak, and marginal competitors. Frequently such competitors may have to take drastic short-term actions just to survive, say, cutting prices to move one's inventory to meet payroll. The constant havoc in settings of this kind makes such businesses less attractive. Barriers to entry, such as large investment hurdles due to the cost of new plants, similarly should increase the business attractiveness. In all these instances it is necessary to measure business attractiveness in a different way from merely growth.

The examples of alternative measures of business attractiveness and competitive strength are not meant to be exhaustive. Instead they are merely meant to illustrate that the two dimensions need to be measured in such a way that they realistically reflect the underlying phenomena in each instance. As already alluded to, a likely development might be to devise indexes for business attractiveness and competitive strength that incorporate several factors and which employ some reasonable weighting of the factors.

Thus, we need to delineate the situations in which the approach is valid as outlined versus those situations in which modifications are necessary. Consequently, in the next two sections we shall discuss these issues, starting with an extension of the strategic position analysis so that the planning needs that would follow can be deduced and followed by a discussion of useful avenues of modification of the basic approach.

Adaptation and Integration Needs of a Strategy Center

Let us reconsider the two basic dimensions of our product/market element strategic position analysis, namely, the business attractiveness factor and the competitive strength factor, and let us for the moment assume that the growth rate of the business and the relative market share are meaningful surrogates for these two dimensions. A strategy center which is facing a rapid growth rate in its industry will be confronted with a number of planning issues which will be primarily adaptation-oriented in their nature: how to capture a position in the market by developing more effective competitive strategies than other companies, how to reposition oneself to new consumer tastes, how to expand into another geographic market, and so on. It seems as if a major share of the planning needs of product/market elements that are facing a high industry growth rate will be predominantly the following: Reassess and adapt to environmental opportunities and/or threats so as to establish an effective strategic direction. These needs will thus manifest themselves partly in terms of having to reexamine the objectives of a strategy center, given rapidly evolving new opportunities and threats. Also, however, there will be a need to develop new strategic programs and make significant modifications in existing ones in order to be able to implement such a rapidly evolving business element strategy. More generally, taking advantage of a rapid growth situation which offers high business attractiveness creates high adaptation planning needs.

Let us now consider the planning needs that might stem from the other dimension, namely, relative market share. As we recall, a high relative market share might yield significant competitive advantages stemming from experience curve effects, thus allowing the market leader to enjoy lower costs per unit produced, higher margins, and more flexibility in competitive pricing decisions. We also pointed out, however, that positive experience curve effects do not necessarily occur automatically.

To take competitive advantage of a strong market share position, action would have to be taken to enable the experience curve effects to take place, for instance, more efficient planning of the activities of the various functions such as production, scheduling of distribution, more efficient planning of the interactions and interdependencies of the various functions, development of more raw-material- and/or energy-efficient production processes, providing for improvements in quality and/or design of one's products, and so on. Thus, we see that the planning needs of a strategy center which enjoys a high relative market share position manifest themselves partly as needs for developing strategic programs for making increased efficiency take place. In general, we see that a strong competitive strength position will create what primarily seems to be a high need for integration planning.

At this point, it is easy to extend the initial grid analysis of strategic positioning of product/market elements to incorporate the adaptive and integrative planning needs. Given that adaptation needs will be a function of business growth primarily and that integration needs will depend primarily on the relative market share position, we can easily see the combined adaptive and integrative needs that a strategy center will face when it is located in a particular strategic position. Specifically, we have four different combinations of planning needs for a strategy center, depending on what type of strategy center we are dealing with, as illustrated in Exhibit 3-4.

We see from Exhibit 3-4 that a quite diverse pattern of planning is emerging:

EXHIBIT 3-4 Adaptive and Integrative Planning
Needs of a Strategy Center

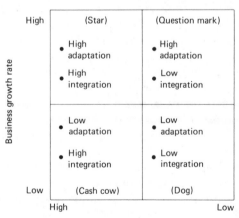

- For a strategy center which is in the star position, we see that there is a relatively high need for both adaptation and integration planning. Reflecting on this for a moment, we see that it is a particulary demanding task to manage product/market elements strategically in this position.
- For a cash-cow type of strategy center, there will be a relatively lower need for adaptation planning but the same relatively high need for integration planning as in the case of a star. Thus, we see that the needs focus primarily on integration and that the task of managing a cash cow should be somewhat simpler than that of managing a star, given this unidimensional need pattern.
- For question mark strategy centers, we see that there will be a relatively high need for adaptation planning but a relatively low need for integration planning. Again, the task of building up a new business is a unidimensional one, where a clear adaptive focus must be kept. But surely this is a hard and risky management task. Even though the task of running a star has more dimensions, it is frequently still the easier of the two.
- Finally, for strategy centers of the dog type, there will be relatively low needs for both adaptation and integration planning. This is a reflection of the relatively uninteresting strategic prospects that such a product/market setting represents for a company. Consequently there should not be a willingness to make a long-term commitment to strategic developments of such a strategy center. Hence, we see relatively low adaptive as well as integrative needs.

It is worthwhile to notice a relatively even balance between adaptation and integration planning needs for the two product/market strategic position typologies where there is approximate funds-flow balance—the star and dog positions. The absolute level of both types of planning needs is, however, much higher in the case of a star than a dog. For the product/market types where major funds-flow imbalances can be expected, however, there will be an imbalance between the adaptive and integrative relative planning needs: The net funds-generating strategy centers (cash cows) will have a relatively much higher integration planning need than adaptation planning need; the net funds-consuming strategy centers (question marks) will have a relatively much higher adaptation planning need than integration planning need. In general, funds generation creates integration planning needs; funds utilization creates adaptation planning needs. As we shall see later, this is a particularly useful concept to utilize when it comes to portfolio-level planning.

It is important to notice the effects in terms of changes in the planning needs of a strategy center when the strategy center evolves from one strategic state to another. Given that one task of planning is to help facilitate a desired evolution of a strategy center's strategic posture, as indicated in Exhibit 3-3, for instance, it is important to anticipate the changes in planning needs such an evolutionary pattern should lead to. For instance, when investing in a product/market element to influence a change in its strategic position from a question mark to a star, there will be a need, as an anticipative move, to strengthen integration planning above all, since integration planning needs will be expected to become relatively more important. In our experience, failure to recognize such a relative shift in needs toward a more even balance between adaptation and integration is a major problem in many new, initially successful strategy centers. With highly entrepreneurial aptitudes, the management teams of such strategy centers often find it particularly hard to recognize or understand this change in planning needs.

Considering now a strategy center which is evolving from a star position to a cash-cow position, we might anticipate a relative decrease in adaptation needs. Again, in our experience, it is frequently a problem to have the management team of a strategy center realize this shift, the result often being that the cash cow's funds generation task is hampered by unnecessary adaptive attempts.

It should be pointed out that for expository purposes we have intentionally created a highly dichotomized picture of how a strategy center's planning needs might change in terms of shifts in relative emphasis between adaptation and integration. In actual settings, we are of course dealing with gradual changes in emphasis. The key, however, is to recognize the different planning need pressures that apply in the various strategic positions and to be able to distinguish clearly between shifts in the relative and absolute need balance between adaptation and integration.

Modifications of the Product/Market Element Strategic Position Matrix

Let us now turn to several problems that might arise when attempting to make use of the product/market element strategic position analysis outlined so far.[8]

Let us bring up two more technical issues relating to the development of the two scales of measurement of the business growth/market share grid. The first relates to the way which is commonly proposed for measurement of relative market share, namely, to measure a product/ market element's market share relative to the largest competitor. This measure does not, however, take into account the degree of competitive concentration within the business. For instance, in one setting we might have a business which is dominated entirely by two companies approximately equal in market share, and, thus, the two strategy centers in question might each have a relative market share of approximately 1. In another situation a strategy center might face a handful of competitors relatively equal in size, again producing a relative market share of approximately 1 for each, although the nature of competition in all likelihood would be quite different in the duopoly setting of the first case than in the oligopoly setting of the second. In a third situation, a strategy center might find itself within a highly fragmented industry with more than 50 identifiable competitors. A strategy center may be one of the approximately two dozen largest participants in the business, none, however, being significantly larger than the others. Again, the relative market share will be approximately 1. Here, however, we have close to atomistic competition. Thus, in all three instances, the competitive strength position appears to be the same when in fact the basis for competition is entirely different: duopoly versus oligopoly versus close to perfect competition. Consequently, it is important to keep the nature of the competition in mind when interpreting the relative market share measure, particularly when making policy decisions such as resource allocation trade-offs within a company which involve comparisons between product/market elements that enjoy such different competitive positions. To be aware of this potential source of bias is usually sufficient, however, so that qualitative modifications can be made in interpretation and evaluation. It is usually of little benefit to modify the measure directly, say by measuring a strategy center's market share relative to its largest competitor versus the average of, say, the three largest competitors—the smaller the difference, the larger the degree of concentration.

Let us now raise a final issue with regard to the measurement of the strategic position of a product/market element: how to come up with an appropriate market growth rate level to draw the borderline between stars and cash cows (and between question marks and dogs as well). It is important to make this distinction in such a way that a reasonably meaningful discrimination can be made between net funds contributors and net funds users, so that relatively realistic funds-flow implications can be drawn from the positionings of the various businesses for portfolio planning purposes. In practice it will of course be difficult to come up with an exact growth rate that will constitute such a borderline. Instead, we are dealing with degrees of shifts along a continuous vertical dimension. Thus, any product/market element should be interpreted relative to the others in terms of growth characteristics and expected funds-flow pattern. It might, however, be practical to consider a particular growth rate range to represent the borderlines of a band that more or less distinguishes the stars from the cash cows. This band is probably associated with higher growth rates when it comes to service-related and/or labor-intensive industries that do not require large follow-up investments and with lower growth rates when it comes to capital-intensive industries that might require massive investments on a more or less continuous basis in order to maintain one's business strength position. Thus, it seems important to determine for each particular industry of concern a reasonable growth rate to distinguish between net funds use versus net funds generation. It might, for instance, be justified to handle a highly capital-intensive integrated aluminum producing strategy center which is enjoying only an 8 percent industry growth rate as a star, while a low capital-intensive service-oriented strategy center for specialized production of precision castings might be considered a cash cow, even though its industry growth rate may be 25 percent.

The issue of interpreting meaningful growth rates in an industry-specific way is of course particularly important when within a given company one is faced with making policy trade-offs between product/market elements from entirely different industries, as exemplified in the previous paragraph. Let us stress again, however, that growth rate refers to a market and not to our particular business entity in this market. Net funds generation for us, therefore, depends on our strategy in that market. This is, however, only one of several important considerations when developing a strategic assessment of a cluster of product/market elements. We shall therefore now turn to a discussion of the aggregation of product/market elements into a larger strategic picture as we typically would find it when a multiproduct (and multistrategy center) division develops a business family strategic picture based on several business element strategies.

Consolidation of Several Strategy Centers

A division will typically have several strategy centers under its discretion. The pattern of strategic positions of these product/market elements might be positioned on a grid as indicated in Exhibit 3-5. This will give an indication of the overall cumulative nature of the businesses of the division, whether it is heavily based in the star segment—it is then a typical growth division—or whether it is concentrated in the cash-cow segment—it is then a more mature division. It is likely that a division will have some strategy centers in positions different from the major thrust of its business family. For instance, a predominantly mature division might have one or a few strategy centers in the question mark or star areas. This might represent an indication of the future direction that the division wants to follow in that funds might be channeled from the mature product/market elements and into such new developments. The arrow in Exhibit 3-5 indicates the natural flow of funds within a division that attempts to keep renewing itself. A division's pursuance of perpetuated growth based on internally devleoped new product/market elements is, however, a critical strategic decision that should be taken only in the context of overall portfolio considerations for the whole firm. The issue is

EXHIBIT 3-5 Transfer of Funds Among Strategy Centers Within a Division

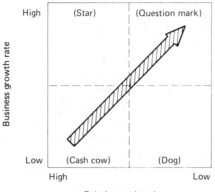

whether from a corporate portfolio strategy point of view it would make sense to allocate discretionary strategic funds for new product/market elements within the same business or somewhere else within the firm where the growth potential might be even better, where the risk can be diminished, and so on.

When the strategy centers of a division are scattered all over in terms of strategic positionings, this might be interpreted as a lack of strategic focus for the division. It would then be hard to classify a division in terms of whether it should be a growth division or a division chartered with becoming a net contributor of funds within a corporate portfolio strategy. It should be stressed that from a corporate portfolio strategy point of view a business will have strategic value only if strategic resources—above all, funds—eventually can become freed for reemployment. If we assume that a company is managed in accordance with such an explicit corporate strategy, we expect that each division's plans will provide for more clearly clustered strategic focus. If, on the other hand, we assume that there is no articulated corporate portfolio strategy concept in existence and, instead, that the company's growth is a function of what each division is able to grow, in a more or less laissez-faire fashion, then we expect the strategic positioning of a division's product/market elements to be widely scattered. The latter situation is probably a quite accurate reflection of reality in many cases.

A critical issue will be the amount of strategic resources such as funds a company will be able to free from product/market elements in cash-cow positions for reemployment in high-growth product/market elements. It is important to keep in mind in this context that even reasonably mature strategy centers might require considerable funds to maintain their position. This is particularly so during periods of inflation. It should also be remembered that some funds will have to be paid out as capital rent to the parties that have financed the firm—interest and dividends. Thus, what emerges is a realization that there will be a maximum sustainable rate of growth. To improve on this will require infusion of additional capital from outside, one source of which might be the trimming of dividend payments.

Let us now turn to another area of concern when it comes to considering several strategy centers in context. This relates to the nature of interdependence among strategy centers.[9] A major criterion in our definition of a strategy center stressed that it be substantially independent of other strategy centers. In many instances, however, it is neither feasible nor desirable to make a strategy center entirely independent. First, since the strategy centers that are part of the same division typically will be operating within quite related business areas, it might be natural to pursue the question of to what extent it might be advantageous to consolidate strategy center activities in selected areas. There might be considerable savings in having a joint sales force or in sharing manufacturing facilities. Such integrative moves might be essential in providing the division with a viable position of strength in the market place. Thus, there is in fact a need for an additional dimension in our strategic business assessment analysis; we need to analyze the consolidation effect on the strategy centers beyond merely assessing whether the overall sum of the strategy centers' funds flow is a positive or negative figure. We shall call this the consolidation dimension. As alluded to above, the planning needs stemming from this dimension will be primarily of the integration type. To recognize and develop this dimension is of course central in the development of a sound business family strategy.

Several factors might go into this consolidation dimension. First, there might be aspects to the evaluation of the cash-flow pattern from the strategy centers other than focusing solely on the funds generation/ utilization balance. For instance, how does the cash flow of a strategy center fit in with other cash flows in terms of covariance? Common underlying cyclical patterns would of course normally not be an advantage. The size of the cash flow of one strategy center relative to the others would be another issue: Is there one main cash-flow source, or is there a more even distribution among the strategy centers? The latter would presumably be more advantageous because of less reliance on one source. Finally, it is necessary to assess whether a particular level of planned cash flow will accrue. Such an evaluation should be carried out for the strategy center in absolute terms as well as relative to the risks associated with the reliability of the cash flows of the other strategy centers. The issue of doing a meaningful assessment of the risk associated with a strategy center's funds flow is a difficult one. We shall return to this later in the chapter when we discuss the corporate portfolio strategy evaluation of the set of business divisions, at which point the robustness of the various funds-flow components will be critical.

Another set of factors that should be brought to bear on the analysis of the consolidation dimension is the so-called operating synergy effects. These accrue when a division's functional departments are able to serve all or a substantial number of the strategy centers, thus avoiding duplication of efforts. For instance, as already alluded to, within the manufacturing function there might be ample opportunity for many of the operations activities to be carried out in a coordinated fashion within the scope of the division as a whole, as an alternative to a greater degree of independent manufacturing for each strategy center. It is therefore an important secondary divisional strategizing issue to facilitate a strategy center pattern which will encourage development of an overall synergy in manufacturing. Similarly, in marketing there might also be opportunities for synergy in that joint strategy center sales forces might be developed. Within R&D, too, such synergy might be important.

During our discussion of the significance of a strategy center's growth posture earlier in this chapter, we pointed out that the life-cycle position of one product/market element relative to the others will be an important aspect of the analysis of the business elements' strategic positions, because of the funds-flow implications. There is an additional problem which arises from this and which might create integration planning needs. This stems from the recognition that the strategic management task is likely to differ between product/market elements positioned differently within the product life cycle in terms of management style to be encouraged through planning, balance of product versus process emphasis in the strategic programs, the nature of incentive schemes, and so on. To develop a management team within a division to manage such a diverse set of strategy centers and also to cope with changes in the balance of the business family strategy over time might call for considerable planning along the management development dimension. This is yet another consolidation planning need. We shall return to this in more detail in Chapter Five.

It is important to recognize, however, that added size/complexity of a division, manifested by an increase in the number of product/market elements, leads to a relative increase in integration planning needs, stemming from the requirements of the consolidation attractiveness dimension. Thus, diversity in the business family normally leads to relatively more integration planning.

It is also important to recognize the potential effect of organizational learning in this respect. One might expect that learning will cut down the formal work load needed for planning. Whenever reorganizations in a division are made, such as redefining product/market elements, reassigning product/market elements from one division to another, or acquiring/divesting a product/market element, then the integration planning need is likely to go up. Similarly, management job rotations, if done frequently, might increase the integration planning need.

There are two concerns that should be raised at this point, both relating to the fact that integration planning might tend to suppress adaptation planning. When the complexity of a business increases, causing an increase in integration planning needs, then one might become overwhelmed by the work load implied by the integration planning need of the business family and, by default, pay insufficient attention to the adaptation planning needs. This seems to be a true danger in large and complex businesses; integration planning might easily consume so much attention that adaptation planning is likely to suffer. The typically relatively stronger formality and numbers orientation of the integration aspect of planning tends to reinforce this danger.

Similarly, when a division goes down the learning curve and its management becomes more and more comfortable with (integration) planning, a natural and desirable reduction of effort spent on integration planning should follow. However, this may also be accompanied by a similar reduction in adaptation planning, i.e., a reduction of planning emphasis altogether. This scenario for the degeneration of planning is not uncommon, particularly in mature business settings. A false sense that one is mastering planning as a whole is allowed to develop because of the organization's improved abilities to be on top of the more structured integration planning aspects.

We have now completed our discussion of how to assess the strategic positioning of those organizational units within a company which pursue its business strategies. We have come up with a way of determining the needs for planning at the business level in terms of adaptation as well as integration. We saw that these planning needs in part stemmed from the positioning of each product/market element on the business attractiveness/competitive strength matrix. In particular, we saw that market share position seemed to influence primarily integration planning needs, while market growth characteristics seemed to affect the adaptation needs above all. We also saw that the planning needs at the division level were partly a function of the aggregated pattern of the strategy center positions in question but also partly a function of the consolidation requirements facing the division. The latter factor would lead to integration needs above all. In total, we thus saw how to determine the particular needs for business element strategizing for each strategy center as well as how to determine the business family strategizing needs for a division as a whole. Having now completed the need assessments at the business family strategic level, we shall have to pursue the need assessment at the corporate portfolio level. This will be the focus of our discussion in the rest of this chapter.

Corporate Strategic Planning Need Assessment: Financial Position

We shall now turn our attention to the assessment of needs for planning at the corporate portfolio level. In this instance, too, our approach will be to identify critical sources of strategic pressures that would give rise to needs for various strategic planning approaches. The factors that will be important for identifying planning needs at the portfolio level will of course differ from the factors for identifying the planning needs of a strategy center or division. In those instances, we focused on the business attractiveness, competitive strength, and consolidation attractiveness positions for determining planning needs, as we recall from our discussion in the first part of this chapter. When it comes to assessing the needs at the corporate level, we shall propose that the needs for planning tend to be established as a function of various kinds of pressures facing the corporation, particularly two major classes of factors of key relevance, corporate financial pressures and structural portfolio pressures. Financial pressures as a source for creating corporate-level planning needs will be discussed in this section. In the next section we shall discuss the role of pressures on the corporation to change its basic structure, creating another set of planning needs. It should be noted that these sources of pressures, too, will create adaptive as well as integrative planning needs. The specific nature of these needs will, however, be different.

Proceeding with our discussion of the relevance of the financial position of a firm, a first distinction might be to determine to what extent the financial position of the company as a whole might be characterized as strong or weak. It is of course difficult to define exactly a strong or weak financial position, and for our purpose an exact definition is not needed. What is needed, however, is to focus on the following two interrelated issues: first, to carry out an evaluation of the financial strength of the firm relative to what would be normal for companies of approximately this size and pattern of diversity. Unused debt capacity is probably a particularly important element in such an assessment. The debt/equity ratio, of course, correlates highly with unused debt capacity and might be used as a proxy for measuring unused debt capacity. Several more elaborate schemes for determining unused debt capacity also exist. [10]

Another important aspect for judging the financial position of the firm will be near-term overall financial performance. This is the first derivative of the factor discussed in the previous paragraph in that it will influence the strength of the financial position. Near-term reported corporate performance factors such as quarterly or yearly profits, return on investment, earnings per share, and growth in sales might be important indicators of this. Also related will be the stability of short-term financial indicators over time.

These financial position factors in creating planning needs will have effects primarily on integration. For instance, a weak basic financial position should create a high need for integration planning at the portfolio level, because the relatively modest unused debt capacity cannot provide a basis for a more aggressive expansion. Thus, a weak financial position should call for a strong emphasis on integration planning to consolidate the present position; the reality of the financial situation does not allow for aggressive adaptive strategic moves. It is important to recognize this added need for integration that a weak overall financial position creates. A better integrative capability is probably the best way for such a company to protect its position and to cope with this competitive disadvantage. Unfortunately, despite a weak financial position, a few near-term successes might lead some companies to a false sense of comfort, overlooking the need for a continued aggressive integrative thrust.

Let us now turn to the near-term financial performance aspects. As indicated, these should also influence the needs for portfolio planning. If the near-term financial position is worsening, then too there is an indication that there is a growing integration planning need; there is not enough internal efficiency in the way the firm is operating. What is needed in such a situation is to improve on the efficiency of the internal operation.

We see from the discussion thus far that a weak corporate financial position primarily is causing the use of integrative needs and that many of these pressures may be relatively near-term in nature. In fact, some of these effects, such as attempting to maintain a highly stable reported corporate earnings flow, might be seen by some as antistrategic. In other words, there might be reason for some to interpret the corporate financial pressures as near-term deterrents to strategic planning, so that consequently the strategic planning should be designed to counteract these pressures, not to comply with them. We do not share this view, however, for two reasons. First, we feel that the financial performance pressures at the corporate portfolio level are real, particularly as seen by the CEO. Consequently, we should let the actual needs determine the design of the planning system. A system diverging significantly from what the users perceive to be the relevant tasks will in all likelihood simply not work. Second, we shall see that the structural need that will be raised in the next section generally will add a more long-term strategic focus to planning at the corporate portfolio level. Our aim will be to show that a balance between the recognition of the financial and structural needs will lead to a better portfolio-level planning approach.

A natural question at this point may be to ask: What would be the effect of a strong financial position? It turns out that we cannot meaningfully talk about a positive effect per se—only that a strong integrative pressure has ceased to exist. The added flexibility implied by this is of course a positive potential opportunity.

Before concluding this section on the financial pressures' roles in creating more near-term integrative planning needs, let us elaborate on why these pressures should be carefully observed in the context of developing a strategic planning system.

Except for the CEO, all line executives within a corporation will have a boss within the organizational hierarchy. Thus, they will be accountable primarily to other executives within the firm for strategic as well as near-term performance fulfillment. The CEO, on the other hand, is not accountable to anyone within the firm itself for his performance fulfillment. Rather he is accountable to the board of directors and to the stockholders at large. For a number of reasons, not the least because of lack of enough time to be thoroughly familiar with and comfortable with the major strategic issues, it will be difficult for these outside parties to pass extensive judgment on the strategic performance. Near-term financial performance, however, can more easily be judged by an outsider. It is therefore to be expected that the CEO is facing near-term performance accountability issues to a greater extent than are many of his subordinates.

A significant source of near-term external pressure for corporate performance probably comes from financial analysts. They can spark considerable upward or downward momentum in a company's stock prices and can also influence the image and respectability of the company as a whole as well as its CEO. A major parameter in the judgment of most financial analysts about a particular firm's performance potential will be the short-term profits picture, in terms of size, stability, and growth. This parameter is particularly relevant to the owners, even though as an individual a shareholder would probably not pay such unilateral attention to this in his own strategic decision making.

Given the prevalence of short-term pressures on corporate management, however, it will become exceedingly important that relatively near-term planning considerations should not be allowed to blur more long-term concern about coming up with viable strategies for improving the firm's portfolio. Thus, strategic resource allocations should be taken within a context which provides a balance between short-term and long-term strategic considerations and not be dictated by short-term profits pressure only. In the next section we shall discuss further why it will be necessary also to take a longer-term perspective, and we shall see the nature of these structural planning needs.

Corporate Strategic Planning Need Assessment: Structural Position

At the outset of this section, let us clarify what we mean by using a firm's structural position as a source for determining the planning needs at the portfolio level of a company. We mean an assessment of the structure of the portfolio of business activities that the firm is in. Is this a healthy portfolio, or could it be improved? Will the funds-flow projections that are the consequence of this particular portfolio yield acceptable financial results? Are environmental opportunities to modify the portfolio structure being pursued, particularly in terms of changes in the firm's own portfolio relative to changes in the portfolios of major competitors? Is the risk that the company seems to be facing with a particular business portfolio acceptable, or should top management modify the portfolio to decrease or increase the overall corporate risk posture? In line with the above examples we shall distinguish between these different but highly interrelated sources of pressures that will be part of the portfolio planning need assessment. These are the pressures stemming from internally developed funds-flow considerations, from comparative strategic analysis, and from top management's perception of the overall corporate risk posture. We shall discuss the first two topics in this section, putting off the discussion of risk until later, given that the last aspect will be treated in the broader context of relating it to strategy center and divisional risk position assessment in addition to portfolio-level considerations.[11]

As a first step in judging the long-term attractiveness of a particular corporation's portfolio, we shall discuss how to carry out a corporate funds-flow analysis as an extension of the pattern of funds-flow sources and uses that we have developed from analyzing the strategy centers and the divisions. This corporate funds-flow analysis consists of developing a picture of the firm's overall funds-flow pattern stemming from its structure, as evidenced by the pattern of the various organizational units of the firm. This enables management to judge the funds-flow implications of different strategic choices and to see whether a particular strategic choice in fact is feasible from a funds-flow point of view. The data for such funds-flow analysis for the assessment of the portfolio normally are available or can quite readily be made so. There often seems to be insufficient recognition of the funds-flow analysis tool as an element in the portfolio-level strategic planning need analysis.

To provide a funds-flow analysis which is capable of shedding light on the strategic properties of the portfolio, two requirements must be met: The funds flows need to be broken down in such a way that they are associated with each strategic unit, and they need to be broken down into components which indicate those funds-flow elements that are discretionary versus those that are committed, that is, that cannot easily be altered. This is an important step in the analysis of the company's strategic position, highlighting such issues as the amount of funds which are generated from which operations and from which businesses, how much of the funds are used by expanding and/or contracting the businesses, and what might be the needs for new external financing. In Appendix II to this chapter, we shall give an example of how the funds-flow assessment might be carried out, showing useful steps in the analysis. Presently, however, we still need to be discussing several potential pitfalls and difficulties frequently associated with portfolio structure funds-flow analysis.

There are a number of less self-evident issues that might be significant when interpreting the structural portfolio planning pressures stemming from a corporate funds-flow analysis. The first issue relates to the reasons for potential increases in the divisions' needs for working capital during periods of inflation; at such times there will be an automatic increase in the need for working capital. It is important to separate this source of pressure from the strategic consideration, i.e., from what is needed to maintain and/or expand the operation of the portfolio. Inflation might have two additional effects on the interpretation of the cash-flow analysis. Fixed assets might have to be replaced at costs greater than depreciation. Also, the de facto unused debt capacity might be increased, given the replacement value of equity due to the inflation. Both of these might have an effect on the firm's ability and willingness to restructure its portfolio. Thus, particularly in periods with heavy inflationary pressure it is important to separate inflationary impacts on the funds-flow analysis from real growth impacts.

There is, however, a more fundamental problem associated with analyzing a particular portfolio strategy path by means of a funds-flow analysis approach in the way discussed in the previous paragraphs and in Appendix II, because the analysis is based on historical data, generated through the internal accounting process. From a strategic decision-making viewpoint we should be more interested in expected funds-flow patterns based on long-term planned performance of the firm. Most companies undertake long-range planning to avoid relying heavily on historical data. It will therefore be necessary to develop statements of future expected funds-flow consequences from various potential strategic paths that the company might pursue. The starting point here should be to extrapolate what the funds-flow consequences might be from continuing to pursue more or less the same portfolio strategy. Such an extrapolation might highlight the needs for portfolio shifts and thus structural measures. Funds-flow projections of the alternative portfolio strategies then will have to be made.

The extrapolation of funds-flow activities in this instance, as just discussed, in no way conflicts with our strong advocacy for an open-ended, nonextrapolative assessment of opportunities and threats in planning. This is what needs to take place when developing actual alternative portfolio strategies. The funds-flow analyses merely project an aspect of the consequences of these portfolio strategy alternatives, thereby providing an indication of the structural soundness of this portfolio alternative.

Let us now turn to another aspect of analyzing the longer-term structural pressures on a portfolio strategy, namely, by direct assessment of selected critical changes in one's own portfolio relative to one's major competitors. This analysis might serve as a valuable complement to the funds-flow analysis.

The major purpose of an assessment of a company's portfolio in the context we shall use here is to determine the extent to which one's own portfolio seems to change favorably or unfavorably over time relative to one's major competitors. It will of course be virtually impossible to develop exact patterns of change for one's key competitors' portfolio strategies; it is equally difficult to pinpoint exact shifts of portfolio directions. However, even though comparative strategic portfolio structure analysis therefore will have to be relatively crude in terms of degree of specificity, the development of an approximate picture of major comparative strategic portfolio shifts should suffice to highlight whether one's own top management should be increasingly concerned with changes in its own portfolio.

The first step in a comparative corporate strategic analysis should be to identify a set of relevant companies with which to compare oneself. If a company is primarily in one well-defined business segment, the logical choice of companies will probably be other ones within approximately the same business. For relatively diversified companies it might be less easy to single out other companies for comparison. In such instances one might choose companies that seem to be relatively similar in terms of past performance patterns, size diversity, nature of businesses that they are in, and so on. Other companies might be singled out for comparison because one's senior management considers them to be superbly performing firms. Maybe firms that are generally felt to be weak performers should be included as well. In these cases too, however, it is important that the companies be at least moderately similar in structure to one's own.

A simple approach to a comparative structural analysis might be to collect such commonly available external performance indicators as profits, sales, or rank position, say, from *Fortune's 500* list, preferably over a relatively broad time span. As discussed in the previous section, such factors will be closely associated with what we have denoted as financial pressures and will be rather near-term in nature. Thus, there will still be a need for a more in-depth comparative assessment of the longer-term trends in shifts among companies' portfolios in order to understand the pressures one's own company is facing from the long-term portfolio strategy moves of one's competitors.

As discussed, the critical strategic decision facing corporate management is how to allocate its strategic resources among its various businesses. We have also pointed out that it is useful to define what should be a strategic resource in a somewhat broader way than merely focusing on capital investments. Notably, allocation patterns for discretionary expenditures, particularly into R&D, as well as for assigning key personnel, will also be important. Thus, ideally we would want to measure comparative changes in the allocation patterns of all these factors. However, it might become exceedingly difficult to gather the necessary data for this.

We shall therefore propose that the investment intensity in strategic programs be used as a measurement device for the comparative analysis. This will have two components. First, it will be useful to measure the absolute level of investment in strategic programs relative to the competitors. This would give an indication of relative investment aggressiveness among the firms. Capital investments as well as strategic expenditures should go into this figure. It is often particularly difficult to determine the relevant strategic expenditure spendings. On the other hand, in some industries the most significant fraction of the strategic expenditures might be available from public sources, such as R&D expenditures for pharmaceutical companies, advertising expenditures for tobacco companies, or exploration expenditures for integrated oil companies. A useful way of measuring relative investment aggressiveness, or relative strategic programming emphasis, would be to calculate the total investment (capital plus strategic expenditures) as a fraction of total assets and to see how this fraction changes over time for all the firms being studied.

Second, it will be useful to investigate for what uses the strategic investments are being allocated for the various firms being compared. For instance, for an integrated oil company, what is the fraction of investment in upstream (exploration, production) versus downstream (refining, marketing) activities? For a tobacco company, what is the fraction of investments in low-tar brands? Thus, a way of measuring the nature of the strategic program spending pattern is to calculate the fraction of a particular type of strategic investment relative to the total for the various companies studied and to compare shifts in the strategic program patterns over time.

Through this type of analysis we might detect, at least partially, an emerging pattern that will show the broad direction the various competitors seem to be going in allocating their strategic funds. Several important questions should be addressed at this point. Is one's own portfolio planning effort indeed resulting in a more desirable portfolio business mix when evaluated within the context of the competitors' moves? Is the degree of aggressiveness in pursuing a portfolio strategy adequate to keep up with the competition; i.e., is the structural pressure being kept under control?

The emerging picture of the evolution of one's own portfolio strategy relative to the competitors, seen as functions of strategic spending patterns over time, might thus yield another indication of the nature of the structural portfolio pressures that a particular senior management group is facing. It should be noted that these more long-term strategic pressures are just as real as the shorter-term financial portfolio pressures that might face senior management, as discussed in the previous section. However, it is probably realistic to recognize that it might largely be a function of a CEO's aspirations and sense of devotion and professionalism whether he in fact will be paying sufficient attention to the structural portfolio needs. Given that his own self-generated pressure rather than pressure from outside will have to be a prime motivator of the CEO in his assessment of the structural needs, there will always be a danger that the more visible, short-term financial needs might become too dominant. The CEO's incentive-and-compensation-scheme will play a particularly challenging role in counterbalancing such an effect.

Portfolio-Level Planning Needs: Synthesis

Having identified in the previous two sections two broad classes of factors that seem to create different sets of planning needs at the corporate portfolio level, let us in this section attempt to synthesize the emerging combined pattern of adaptation and integration planning tasks for the corporation.

We recall that the financial pressures were relatively short-term in nature, striving to achieve relatively stable, predictable financial performance. As already discussed, the emphasis should be on integrative planning, above all at the corporate level, to facilitate this. Near-term coordination of expenditure patterns, of trimming costs, and of monitoring inventory efficiency levels will be important at the corporate level to achieve this. When it comes to the structural pressures, on the other hand, we recall that these will be more long-term in nature, and these pressures will create a need for adaptation at the corporate level, above all. The ability to identify new long-term business opportunities, the insight to develop strategic programs to make shifts happen, the foresight to shift one's emphasis in time, and so on are all critical adaptation planning needs. [12] We see, then, that while at the corporate level integrative planning needs are primarily a function of the financial position, adaptive planning needs above all will be a function of the structural properties of the firm's portfolio. We are now in the position to indicate the mixes of adaptive and integrative planning needs that might be found at the corporate level as a function of different financial and structure pressures.

In Exhibit 3-6 we have indicated how this adaptive/integrative planning needs pattern might look at the corporate level. We see from this exhibit that we have four different archetypes of planning needs positions, just as was the case in the product/market element planning needs analysis discussed in the first part of this chapter. Although seemingly

EXHIBIT 3-6 Portfolio-Level Adaptation and
Integration Planning Needs

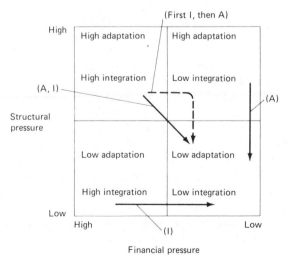

Financial pressure

similar at a first glance to Exhibit 3-4, which summarized the adaptation and integration needs for the product/market elements level, the two are of course fundamentally different. It should be kept in mind that the two sources of planning pressure at the corporate level do indeed signify that there might be lack of stability or disequilibrium in the corporate portfolio. For instance, a financial pressure would indicate that corporate management is facing the task of modifying the portfolio to eliminate the pressure. Thus, when a corporation's strategic situational setting is such that it is located in the bottom-right square of Exhibit 3-6, it indicates a lack of planning pressures, i.e., a healthy portfolio. The planning emphasis will be largely to maintain this position, and there will be relatively little pressure to plan major changes at the portfolio level. However, if the company is located in one of the other three cells, there is pressure to plan for a change in the portfolio to ameliorate a particular pressure. Thus, any portfolio setting which falls into any of these three cells is in a state of strategic disequilibrium.

It follows from this that there are three major types of strategic disequilibrium at the portfolio level and that each of these will create different planning needs in order to move toward the preferred bottom-right stable position. The solid arrows of Exhibit 3-6 indicate the derived direction to emphasize. For a company which finds itself in the upper-right strategic portfolio need position of Exhibit 3-6 the challenge will be to face the needs for adaptive planning so as to upgrade the structure of the corporate portfolio over the longer run while there still is time, i.e., relatively little short-term financial pressure. This is signified by the vertical arrow and the adaptation (A) focus connotation. For a company which is located in the bottom-left cell of Exhibit 3-6, the need will be to plan for relatively short-term financial improvements of the corporate portfolio—hence, the horizontal arrow integration (I) connotation. The basic structure of the portfolio will be healthy and should not be changed significantly. The third disequilibrium position will be for a company which finds itself in the upper-left position of Exhibit 3-6. This is a serious portfolio disequilibrium position in that it indicates pressures to plan both for financial performance improvements and for upgrading the longer-term health of the structure of the corporate portfolio. Serious corporate-level planning needs exist in this case. This is indicated in Exhibit 3-6 by the solid arrow going from the upper left to the lower right, signaling that there will be both strong adaptive and integrative (A,I) needs. In practice, however, it may be extremely difficult to attempt to ameliorate both kinds of pressures simultaneously. Experience has shown that a more operational approach is to first attack the integrative problems, to get the financial problems more under control, then to emphasize the adaptive, structural pressures. The broken-line arrow of Exhibit 3-6 indicated this. Contrasting this situation with the ideal bottom-right stable position of Exhibit 3-6, we see that while in the former there will be a major pressure on the corporate level to plan for changes in the firm's portfolio, there will be little such pressure in the latter case. Thus, while corporate-level planning activities might be expected to be intensive and result in far-reaching substantive changes in the former case, the planning activities will probably be more low-key and focused on monitoring the maintenance of the strong portfolio position.

We now see that we cannot consider the corporate portfolio level's strategic planning needs as evolving over time in a manner analogous to the planning needs of a typical product/market element changing in accordance with a planned sequence of stages (question mark, star, cash cow, dog). For the corporate level the needs will be to maintain a stable and healthy portfolio balance; as soon as imbalances occur the pressures will be to restore the equilibrium. Thus, while we are facing both adaptation and integration needs for planning at the business and corporate levels, the planning responses to these needs will be entirely different, reflecting the different levels of strategy. At the business segment and family strategy level, there must be acceptance of changes over time in the absolute levels of planning needs for adaptation as well as integration and also in the relative balance between adaptation and integration. At the corporate portfolio strategy level a low absolute need for adaptation and integration as well as an even relative balance between adaptation and integration will always be the ideal.

An important interrelationship between the planning and assessments of the portfolio and business strategic levels should be noted. As alluded to in the previous paragraphs, when the corporate level is facing a portfolio planning pressure several types of corporate-level actions might be expected to be initiated in order to instill the appropriate adaptation or/and integration reemphasis required in this situation. However, another set of actions is also likely to be taken by the corporate level, namely, to impose a corresponding sense of modification on the business element and family strategies so as to bring them in line with the corporation's overall needs. In Chapter Five we shall discuss ways that this is being done. At this point we should, however, notice that the effect on planning needs at the business level will be to dampen or magnify the specific need patterns found for each product/market element and/or division. For instance, let us assume that at the corporate portfolio level relatively strong financial pressure is being felt; thus a strong corporate-level integrative planning need exists. For simplicity, let us assume that the company consists of two strategy centers only, one in the question mark stage and thus with high adaptive and low integrative planning needs and the other in the cash-cow stage, with high integrative and low adaptive needs. The effects on the strategy centers' needs due to the corporate integrative pressure will be that their adaptive needs will be deemphasized, affecting the question mark strategy center above all, while their integrative needs will be amplified.

We have now completed our discussion of the significance of a firm's particular strategic setting as a determinant of the particular needs for planning that the firm is facing in terms of adaptation as well as integration and at the business as well as the corporate strategic levels. An analysis of the planning needs along these lines will serve as the takeoff point for developing a corporate planning system with capabilities for meeting these needs. Before initiating our discussion of situational design of strategic planning systems, our topic in the next three chapters, it is necessary to discuss one additional issue which is important when assessing the planning needs at the business as well as the corporate levels, namely, to determine the nature of the risk associated with any of these strategic positions. This will serve as a device to magnify the importance of the needs for planning in those situations where the strategic position is highly risky. We shall emphasize the riskiness of a strategy as a function of its exposure to environmental factors, applicable in corporate- as well as business-level strategies. Hence, we shall discuss the risk assessment concept in one separate section, thereby avoiding duplication of the discussion by covering it as part of both the business and corporate strategy need assessment analyses.

Assessment of Risk Exposure of Strategic Positions

From a corporate point of view a key issue in a strategic audit is whether the portfolio pattern of business activities represents a satisfactory blend in terms of exposure to environmental threats and/or opportunities. The key concern is whether the risk/return pattern deriving from one's particular business portfolio is acceptable. Thus, our task in this section will be to carry out a risk/return analysis. Such an analysis must apply to the business element and family strategy level, and it must also lend itself to aggregation into an overall picture of the portfolio risk exposure. A major requirement is that our analysis be meaningful from a senior management point of view. This seems to call for an analysis different from classical statistical measurement of risk in that a senior executive must be able to relate his own perception of risk preference to the measure. We shall propose a measure of strategic risk exposure with two foci: the firm's exposure to environmental events which can be predicted with varying degrees of certainty and the degree of managerial flexibility that is available in responding to a particular event. Such a predictability/response concept is particularly useful for senior management in assessing business as well as portfolio strategy risks in that it closely resembles managers' cognitive structuring of their analysis of such problems.[13]

A first step in such a risk assessment analysis would be for each of the strategy centers to develop a list of environmental factors that might significantly change the projected funds flows from the strategy centers and thus the likelihood of achieving the product/market element strategies. These factors might represent major environmental threats to a strategy center, or they might represent potentially major positive environmental developments. The emphasis should be to develop a reasonably short list of critical environment exposure factors. One should focus only on those factors that are judged to be truly critical. The list should be developed as a collaboration among the strategy center involved, the division involved, and the corporate level. A product/market element manager should normally be able to identify relatively easily the few environmental factors that truly represent a potentially significant challenge to his business. If the manager has not already developed such a list for himself, the question can be raised as to whether he is worth his salt. This initial input from a strategy center manager will then be refined and improved on through discussions first with the relevant division manager and then with the corporate level. Under all circumstances it will be critical that both the strategy center, division, and corporate managements be involved in the development of such a list in order to increase its credibility and impose a stronger sense of accountability for it.

Some of the key factors identified might turn out to be so general that they relate to most of the businesses as a whole, for instance, in that they may affect all of a division's strategy centers. However, some factors might be more specifically related to one or a few of the strategy centers. Thus, while a division manager will have a list of critical environmental factors which captures the exposure of all strategy centers reporting to him, this list will be shorter than the sum of the strategy centers' factors. However, he might have to include other additional critical environmental factors that apply to his division's business family strategy but not to any of the business element strategies. Similarly, at the corporate level the environmental factor list will be less than the sum of the divisional factors, except if the general factor list relating to the corporate portfolio strategy as a whole is larger than the divisional factor duplication/reduction effort.

It will of course be impossible to identify all potentially relevant factors. This is particularly so since nobody is able to outguess the future. However, given that all realize that no list of factors can ever be perfect but that a serious effort has gone into developing the list, it should be acceptable to base the analysis on what information management can perceive. Further, all environmental factors will not be equally important, and a weighting of the factors might be necessary—potentially a complicating, subjective step. Let us briefly discuss each of these issues.

It is of course a critical problem to be unable to come up with a list which captures a significant share of the relevant factors. Even the most sophisticated and insightful management will be unable to develop a complete view of the future. However, an analysis which is based on a reasonable set of assumptions is far better than no analysis; within the area of strategic planning just as within any other area of management analysis we must utilize the information we can get and not allow ourselves to abandon analysis because we conclude that the information is incomplete.

The problem of ranking the environmental factors as to their importance should be approached as follows. First, the factors should be sorted into two subgroups: those that might have potentially positive effects and those that might have potentially negative effects on the strategic success of the business. In each of these subgroups one should identify the most important factor, if one such factor stands out; otherwise one should identify the two or three most important factors. It should be considered whether the rest of the factors within each of the two sub-groups are indeed important supporting environmental factors. If not, these factors should be stricken from the list. The question should always be raised whether too many factors have been included. Often this is the case; the marginal factors will not matter much after all compared with other factors on the list. The issue of ranking and eliminating factors becomes particularly important as we consolidate the factors at the divisional and at the corporate levels in order to maintain a reasonable focus for the managers.

Having developed the lists of critical positive as well as negative environmental factors for each product/market element and division and at the corporate level, the next question is to assess, for each factor on the lists, to what extent each environmental phenomenon can be predicted or foreseen. Each strategy center should develop a sense of predictability for its own list of factors. Similarly, each division as well as the corporate level should determine how to predict each of the factors on its list.

There are two approaches that should be explored, in combination if possible, in order to come up with a factor prediction. One approach might be to make use of time series of historical data in order to come up with a prediction of future developments based on past experience. This approach will almost never be perfectly applicable in that there typically will be a lack of relevant historical data for many of the environmental factors that are strategically significant. Also, many of the critical phenomena take place as discrete unexpected events, such as crises, and thus cannot easily be detected by analyzing trends of the past. Most critical as a potential problem with this approach, however, might be its tendency to rely too much on historical trends regarding strength and weakness factors for developing a picture of the future.

A second approach to assisting in the factor forecasting is to identify so-called lead indicators—developments which relate to environmental activities that might be seen as indicators of the factor's likely development. Here, too, ingenuity and deductive insight are probably important factors. Lead indicators that are too obvious tend to give warning signals too close in time to be useful. Several lead indicators might often be combined into some sort of scenario. Again, it is critical that such a scenario not be developed through a process of mental extrapolation but rather as the result of a more unconstrained effort.

Despite all the rigor that one might attempt to apply to develop forecasts for a particular environmental phenomenon, it may happen that for some factors few or no meaningful forecasts can be achieved. For other phenomena at least some useful forecasting support might be the result. Often to management's surprise and delight several environmental phenomena lend themselves quite well to forecasting when subjected to hard and rigorous analysis. The result of the forecasting analysis efforts is that we can get a feel for each of the environmental phenomena in terms of whether it has a relatively high versus a relatively low degree of predictability potential.

Let us now turn to a third step in our analysis, namely, to explore potential managerial response options to a particular environmental phenomenon. For each critical factor we might ask whether there is anything we can do to take advantage of a potentially positive development in the environment or, alternatively, to ameliorate a potentially negative environmental development. Thus, for each of the environmental factors a specific evaluation should be made of potential response approaches. This should allow management to come up with a better understanding of whether the firm actually can respond at all, and if so, to what extent the response can be expected to have any effect. It will probably be concluded that when it comes to some environmental factors there is little de facto response potential, while for other factors there might be quite some flexibility, with several realistic response possibilities and a reasonable chance of ameliorating or taking advantage of an environmental event. For some of the environmental phenomena the degree of response potential might be higher than management had expected before it put systematic efforts into formal analysis of how to respond. When summarizing the efforts to determine the discretionary response potential to critical environmental factors, the factors can be ordered along a continuum in terms of degree of discretionary response potential, just as was the case when it came to degree of predictability.

To integrate the three assessment phases that we have just been making into an overall concept of strategic risk exposure, the predictability assessment and the discretionary response assessment for each key environmental factor relating to a strategy center should be plotted on what might be termed this strategy center's strategic risk exposure chart, as illustrated in Exhibit 3-7.

Exhibit 3-7 should be interpreted as follows. On the horizontal axis we have plotted the degree of predictability from high to low. On the vertical axis we have plotted the degree of discretionary response potential from low to high. Let us, for instance, assume that the most important environmental risk factor falls into the upper-left quadrant of Exhibit 3-7, so that we can predict this factor reasonably well and also enjoy a relatively high response potential. This would mean that should an adverse environmental factor develop there will be a fair chance that we might become aware of this development in time and respond so that we can ameliorate some of the adverse effects. Assuming that the other environmental factors that might have a negative effect also generally fall within the general area of the upper-left quadrant of the exhibit, we might conclude that the environmental risk exposure of the business element strategy of this strategy center is relatively low. If on the other hand our assessment locates a critical environmental factor in the lower-right-hand

EXHIBIT 3-7 Positioning of the Predictability/Response Characteristics of the Major Environmental Factors that Determine a Strategy Center's Risk Exposure

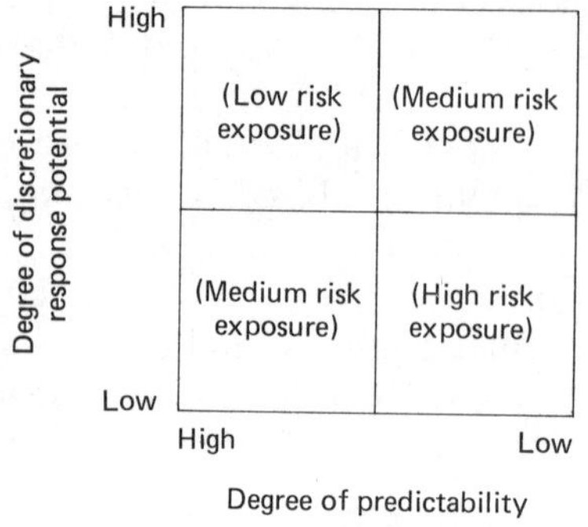

Degree of discretionary response potential (vertical axis, Low to High)

	High predictability	Low predictability
High	(Low risk exposure)	(Medium risk exposure)
Low	(Medium risk exposure)	(High risk exposure)

Degree of predictability

corner of Exhibit 3-7, we are then facing a situation where we have little possibility to predict the development of an environmental factor or to make any responsive move. In this situation we have to conclude that the strategy center is faced with a highly risky environmental exposure. The two remaining positions at the upper-right and lower-left areas of Exhibit 3-7 represent environmental risk exposure positions that fall between the low- and high-risk positions just discussed. If a key environmental factor falls within the upper-right-hand area of the chart, then there will be little predictability but still significant response potential; if it falls in the lower-left-hand area, there is high predictability but low response potential. In such a case we can at least minimize the risk by getting out of the business in time when we expect an adverse development.

To minimize environmental strategic risk exposure is of course not an objective in itself. Risk exposure should be seen in relation to the particular opportunity at hand; if the potential payoff of a product/market element's strategy is high, then it might merit taking the risk. To assess the potential of a business element strategy we must therefore not only consider its risk exposure but also the absolute level of the funds flow expected to result from the strategy. This will give us a perception of the attractiveness of the strategy. In addition to this, however, we must also consider the potential from benefits resulting from *positive* developments among our other environmental factors. Again, if the key potential positive environmental effect is assessed to lie within the upper-left-hand corner and the other positive environmental factors also tend to fall within this sector, then there is high potential for favorable gain as a result of environmental factors.

By completing each strategy center's risk exposure analysis we shall also have the data to carry out the divisional and the corporate portfolio environmental risk exposure analysis. From a corporate point of view the nature of the fit in terms of risk exposure characteristics between the divisions must be considered. One question is whether there seems to be too much risk exposure in general, which might jeopardize prudent management. An alternative question is whether there might be too little overall corporate risk taking. This would mean that the company would be unable to reemploy generated funds in an aggressive enough way. Beyond these critical questions about overall corporate environmental risk exposure two less obvious issues must be raised. First, is there inconsistency in risk taking among the divisions? Second, what potential modifications might be made in the portfolio strategy of a corporation in order for the environmental risk exposure to be changed in a desired direction?

The issue of whether there is consistency in risk taking among the divisions might be explored by comparing the divisions in terms of risk exposure relative to attractiveness of their *base plans* and also by considering the potential for gain from positive environmental developments. It may turn out that some businesses offer far too much risk exposure without providing a reasonable upswing performance potential. It may also be that the risk is very low for some businesses but that the return potential is inadequate too. The key would be to develop a sense of the risk/return configuration for each business element in the corporate portfolio. It will ultimately depend on senior management's attitude toward risk what risk/return level will be acceptable. Each business should ideally fall on the "efficient" risk/return trade-off line given this senior management's risk preference; a higher risk/return would be too speculative to be acceptable and a lower risk/return would be unnecessarily conservative. The issue of achieving consistency in environmental risk exposure among the divisions does not imply that each division should be exposed to the same level of environmental risk but rather that the risk/return of all the divisions should be efficient.

Regarding the issue of carrying out modifications of the portfolio strategy in order to modify the overall environmental risk exposure there are two considerations that should be raised. First, when it comes to decisions such as acquisitions and/or divestitures or whether to scale up or down some of the businesses' activity levels, it is important to include in one's evaluation whether this incremental portfolio change will lead to a better risk/return fit. Second, it should be made explicit what kinds of modifications should be attempted in terms of initiating new strategic programs or even modifying the entire strategy of a business in order to reduce its risk posture. The assessment of risk exposure and how to improve on this should be a key element in the interaction and review between the corporate level and each of the divisions as part of the planning process.

We have now completed the discussion of how one might approach the issue of how to assess the nature of a strategy's exposure to environmental factors. This is an integral part of the assessment of a corporation's strategic position. Such an overall assessment of the risk exposure is a critical ingredient for understanding what types of planning are needed, both at the product/market element level, at the division level, and at the corporate strategic level.

Summary

In this chapter we have discussed how to determine the needs for planning that different companies might have. The underlying premise for the rationale of our approach is that all companies in fact are unique and will therefore have different needs for planning. Hence, it becomes necessary to go beyond the general planning concepts that were developed in Chapter Two, namely, to tailor-make a planning system to the unique needs at hand. It follows that an explicit determination of a firm's planning needs is the first step in this direction. The purpose of the present chapter has been to discuss how these needs might be determined.

We have advocated a strategic position audit approach for determining the needs for strategic planning facing the corporation. This consists of a set of analytical steps to be carried out before developing the planning system in order to focus on the overall situational context for planning. This strategic position assessment approach involves assessment of a firm's strategic position at three organizational levels.

First, within each division a set of product/market elements should be identified as the building blocks for strategic planning. An assessment should be made of the position of each product/market element in terms of its competitive strength within the business as well as the general attractiveness of the business. We concluded that a product/market element's adaptation-related planning needs would be primarily a function of the general business attractiveness dimension, while the integration-related planning needs would be a function of one's competitive strength. In line with this a pattern of different planning needs emerged for strategy centers that were in different positions on the two dimensions just mentioned in terms of absolute as well as relative differences in adaptation and integration planning needs. A strategy center in a so-called question mark strategic position would have relatively high need for adaptation and relatively low need for integration; a star strategy center would face high needs for both adaptation and integration; a strategy center in the cash-cow position will have relatively high needs for integration and relatively low needs for adaptation; and, finally a so-called dog will have a low need for both adaptation and integration planning. Also, given that the strategic position of a strategy center typically might change over time because of plans as well as evolutionary pressures, say, from being a star to becoming a cash cow, it becomes important to recognize the dynamics of changing strategy center planning needs.

Second, the consolidation attractiveness of carrying out the related business activities of the strategy centers within one division were analyzed. We pointed out that heavy consolidation challenges would lead to an increased need for integration planning above all, so that a business family strategy might emerge which would tie together the business element strategies.

Third, we proposed a corporate-level planning needs analysis which also was based on two dimensions. A financial analysis would emphasize the more near-term pressures to show stable overall performance associated with a particular corporate strategic setting. This would provide a picture of the needs for integrative planning at the corporate level, above all. In addition, the corporate-level assessment should include an analysis of the longer-term structural portfolio pressures that the company is facing, as seen when extrapolating the funds-flow patterns as well as when undertaking a comparative analysis of several companies' changes in portfolio structure. These longer-term structural pressure challenges would lead to increased adaptation planning needs at the corporate level.

In addition to the analysis of the planning needs stemming from the strategic position at the various organizational levels we advocated the need for assessing the environmental risk associated with a strategy. We outlined how such a risk/return analysis should be carried out—by relating the return potentials of a business, including those that might come through favorable environmental developments, to the risks resulting from potentially unfavorable developments in the environment. The intention is to come up with an assessment of the overall pattern of business elements of the corporate portfolio which indicates whether the risk/return configuration associated with each product/market element is consistent with the others and in accordance with management's attitude toward risk taking.

In Appendix I we have included an example which illustrates how one large, diversified corporation approaches the analysis of the attractiveness of its portfolio of businesses in order to come up with a more focused picture of the various planning needs it is facing. In Appendix II we have included an example which shows how the financial statements might be analyzed in order to shed light on some structural pressures which might be created on the corporate portfolio.

Appendix I: A Portfolio Attractiveness Index: An Example

The issue of getting an overview of the portfolio planning needs of one's company is particularly difficult to grapple with in a highly diversified corporation, partly because of corporate management's heavy reliance on a large number of subordinate managers' inputs to the planning process as well as on the managers' ability to implement the plans. Given the almost impossible task for corporate management to develop an in-depth feel for all of the businesses, it will be hard to understand the relative attractiveness of one business versus another. One highly diversified corporation with annual sales around 1.5 billion dollars and with more than 40 operating divisions has attempted to comprehend its portfolio planning needs by developing an index for business attractiveness based on data collected from the planning output of each division. This is primarily intended as an aid in evaluating the merits of each business to set better investment priorities within its portfolio. The attractiveness index was developed from a composite measure of the attractiveness of each business, based on 14 factors falling within three major areas. Five market-related factors form a composite measure of each business's competitive strength, five factors relating to underlying aspects of the competition form a composite measure of the attractiveness of the competitive climate, and, finally, a composite measure of the riskiness of the business is developed based on four underlying risk factor measurements. A relative weighing scheme was devised so that index value scores could be derived for each business. The businesses were then ranked in terms of their attractiveness.

The elements of the index and the weightings of these factors were developed as follows.

1. *Market attractiveness (40% weight)*
   a. Market size; dollar value of overall industry sales within the market segments served by this strategy center of the company (10% weight).
   b. Market growth; average annual expected compound growth rate of sales within the market segments served (10% weight).
   c. Market maturity; an assessment of this strategy center's positioning along the product life cycle based on recency of product developments, general availability of relevant technology, degree of stability and direction of purchase patterns, and demographic/socioeconomic trends of customer profiles (10% weight).
   d. Buyer fragmentation; an assessment based on estimating the number of immediate customers who account for 50% of the total industry revenue within this market. A high number signifies less vulnerability to a single demand or a few customers' demand (5% weight).
   e. Frequency of purchase; an assessment of how often immediate customers buy the product. A high purchase frequency signifies less vulnerability to potential cuts in the consumer's expenditure budget (5% weight).
2. *Competitive strength (35% weight)*
   a. Market concentration; the percentage of overall sales within the relevant market segment accounted for by the four largest competitors in the industry. The higher the concentration, the easier it might be to make the competitive skills of a large company to bear (10% weight).
   b. Relative market share; the company's market share within the relevant market segment divided by the combined share of the three largest competitors. If possible, the company prefers to measure market share in terms of physical units rather than dollars, because it finds the former more reliable (10% weight).
   c. Consumer/customer industry recognition strength and recognition of brand names within the relevant market (5% weight).

    d. Technology/innovation leadership; an assessment of the company's relative standing within the relevant market in terms of technology leadership and product innovation (5% weight).

    e. Quality; an assessment of the company's relative standing within the relevant market in terms of its products' quality (5% weight).

3. *Risk (25% weight)*

    a. Profit variability; a statistical measure of the variation around a trend in pretax profits performance over the last five years (10% weight).

    b. Operating leverage; the ratio of total fixed costs and expenses to total variable costs—the lower the break-even point, the better, as indicated by this ratio (5% weight).

    c. Net asset intensity; the ratio of net assets employed to revenues—the lower the ratio, the better (5% weight). (Note that this ratio, in order to provide a basis for meaningful ranking among divisions, assumes that the age distribution of a division's assets is relatively similar for all divisions. Otherwise, a division with relatively older assets would automatically receive a higher score than a division with relatively newer assets.)

    d. Price leadership; an assessment of the pattern of price change initiation—the more control by the company, the better (5% weight).

The company makes use of this index to rank the attractiveness of its businesses. The businesses were clustered into three major groups, each with different planning needs. The highly attractive businesses need planning which will enable them to receive corporate funds to the extent that they are able to expand and actively pursue opportunities. The somewhat attractive businesses need planning to maintain their present competitive strength position, to receive corporate funds to pursue selected strategic programs to solidify their present position and improve their attractiveness position. Finally, the unattractive businesses will have planning needs primarily within the area of improving their efficiency and carrying out cost reduction strategic programs. These businesses will also have a planning need for maintaining or improving attractiveness as divestiture candidates, thereby providing the basis for an even larger net funds contribution than through continued operation. In total, corporate management makes use of this ranking scheme in sharpening its perception of the planning needs of each of the businesses, in interacting with the businesses, and ultimately in allocating resources within what it considers a more focused overall portfolio context. Thus, it explicitly recognizes that providing for a clearer statement of the strategic setting of each business will allow each business to focus on what should be its particular major strategic issues and will provide a basis for how the various businesses should fit together into a portfolio strategy pattern. Thereby corporate management will have created a setting in which resource allocation can be exploited to influence the company's strategic posture.

Appendix II: Funds-Flow Analysis to Highlight Portfolio Strategy Structural Pressures

A corporate funds-flow analysis for strategic purposes might be approached as illustrated in the following simplified example of a company with two existing divisions, the rapidly growing division A, which is pursuing businesses that generally are located at the early stages of the product life cycle, and division B, which is growing much more slowly and finds most of its business in the more mature end of the product life cycle. Further, one division, C, has been divested during the year, while another division, D, has been acquired. Division C's businesses were so mature that they offered little prospect for long-term business viability; division D, however, is involved in entirely new business areas that may or may not eventually become a significant commercial success. There are three major steps of analysis, as indicated by the three segments of the example below: determination of funds flows generated by existing operations, funds used in expanding the business, and new external financing. The figures of the analysis for our imaginary example are as follows:

1. Funds generated by existing operations
   a. Sources of funds
      —Profits before taxes

Division A	20.0	
Division B	14.0	34.0

   —Depreciation

Division A	4.5	
Division B	7.5	12.0
—Divestiture of division C		2.0
		48.0

   b. Uses of funds
      —Replacement of fixed assets

Division A	5.5	
Division B	6.5	12.0

   —Increase in working capital

Division A	7.5	
Division B	2.0	9.5

   —Taxes paid

Division A	7.0	
Division B	3.0	10.0
—Dividends paid		4.0
		35.5

   Funds generated by existing operations:
   48.0 − 35.5 = 12.5

Alternatively calculated:

Division A (20 + 4.5 − 5.5 − 7.5 − 7)	=	4.5
Division B (14 + 7.5 − 6.5 − 2 − 3)	=	10.0
Divestiture, division C		2.0
Dividends		4.0
Generated from existing operations		12.5

2. Funds used in expanding the business

Fixed assets purchased, division A	7.0
Acquisition, division D	15.0
Total use of funds for expansion	22.0

   Total outflow before new external financing:
   22.0 − 12.5 = 9.5

3. New external financing

   a. Movement in issued equity and long-term debt

—Equity issued	1.0
—Increase, long-term debt	8.0
	9.0

   b. Movement in short-term funds

—Increase in short-term debt	0.5
Total inflow from new external financing	9.5

Interpreting these figures, we can immediately see the relevance of this type of analysis for the assessment of the corporate-level portfolio strategic position. We see that division A, which is expanding rapidly, is not generating enough funds to cover its own expansion; corporate management has reallocated 7.0 − 4.5 = 2.5 of corporate resources as a net investment for the continued operation of this expansive business. Division B, on the other hand, has contributed a net total of 10.0 in funds, which corporate management has elected not to have reinvested in this mature business. Instead corporate management has invested in a new business, division D, which presumably can provide an additional basis for corporate growth during years to come. These modifications in the corporation's portfolio have been financed partly by another portfolio strategy modification, namely, the sale of the lackluster-performing division C, and partly through external financing in order to cover the needs beyond what was made available through the internally generated funds. Thus, the above example points out several significant changes in the firm's portfolio: a relative increase in emphasis on the business of division A, a relative decrease in emphasis on division B's business, exit from an old business through the divestiture of division C, and entry into a new business through the acquisition of division D. Further, the unused debt capacity of the company has been reduced by 9.5, which is significant in terms of corporate management's future flexibility in carrying out externally financed additional portfolio modifications.

NOTES

1. One of the first to emphasize product/market relationships as building blocks in a company's strategic plans was Ansoff; see H. Igor Ansoff, *Corporate Strategy* (New York: McGraw-Hill, 1965). The definite discussion of how to define product/market business elements has been provided by Derek F. Abell, "Strategic Windows," *Journal of Marketing*, 42, no. 3 (July 1978), 21-26 and Derek F. Abell, "Business Definition as an Element of the Strategic Decision," in A. Shocker, ed., *Analytic Frameworks for Product and Market Planning*, Cambridge, Mass.: Marketing Science Institute, forthcoming. See also George S. Day and Allan D. Shocker, *Identifying Competitive Product-Market Boundaries: Strategic and Analytical Issues* (Cambridge, Mass.: Marketing Science Institute, 1976), and William E. Rothschild, *Putting It All Together* (New York: Amacom, 1976).

2. Two important and much discussed examples of companies which have made explicit distinctions between their operating structure and their strategic structure are Texas Instruments and General Electric Company, see Footnote 15 of Chapter Two for references. For a good, recent discussion of the interrelationship between operating structure and strategy, which also reviews the empirical studies on strategy and structure, see Jay R. Galbraith and Daniel A. Nathanson, *Strategy Implementation: The Role of Structure and Process* (St. Paul: West Publishing, 1978).

3. For discussions of the experience curve and its impact on business strategizing, see W. B. Hirschmann, "Profit from the Learning Curve," *Harvard Business Review*, 42, no. 1 (Jan.–Feb. 1964), 125-139; Patrick Conley, "Experience Curves as a Planning Tool," *IEEE Spectrum* (June 1970); Bruce D. Henderson, "The Experience Curve Reviewed: The Growth-Share Matrix of the Product Portfolio," in *Perspectives* (Boston: Boston Consulting Group, 1973); and W. J. Abernathy and K. Wayne, "Limits to the Learning Curve," *Harvard Business Review* (Sept.–Oct. 1975).

4. See, for instance, Sidney Schoeffler, Robert D. Buzzell, and Donald F. Heany, "Impact of Strategic Planning on Profit Performance," *Harvard Business Review* (March–April 1974); and Robert D. Buzzell, Bradley T. Gale, and Ralph G. M. Sultan, "Market Share—A Key to Profitability," *Harvard Business Review* (Jan.–Feb. 1975).

5. For a discussion of the PIMS approach, its strengths as well as limitations, see Carl R. Anderson and Frank T. Paine, "PIMS: A Reexamination," *Academy of Management Journal*, forthcoming, and Derek Abell and John S. Hammond, *Strategic Market Planning: Problems and Analytical Approaches* (Englewood Cliffs, N.J.: Prentice-Hall, 1979).

6. A vast body of literature has been developed around the causes of innovation and its role as a *triggering mechanism* for product life-cycle development. For a summary of the earlier literature, see Richard R. Nelson, *The Rate and Direction of Inventive Activity: Economic and Social Factors* (Princeton, N.J.: Princeton University Press, 1962). See also Theodore Leavitt, "Exploit the Product Life-Cycle," *Harvard Business Review*, 43, no. 6 (Nov.–Dec. 1965), 81-94; William E. Cox, Jr., "Product Life-Cycles as Marketing Models," *Journal of Business*, 40 (Oct. 1967), 375-384; Bonald K. Clifford, Jr., "Managing the Product Life Cycle," *European Business* (July 1969); Rolando Polli and Victor Cook, "Validity of the Product Life Cycle," *Journal of Business*, 42 (Oct. 1969); Louis T. Wells, Jr., "The Product Life Cycle Approach," in *The Product Life Cycle and International Trade*, ed. Louis T.

Wells (Boston: Division of Research, Harvard Business School, 1972); and C. R. Wasson, *Dynamic Competitive Strategy and Product Life Cycles* (St. Charles, Mo.: Challenge Books, 1974). For discussions of the role of technology and its impacts on the product life cycle through innovations, see Thomas J. Allen, *Managing the Flow of Technology* (Cambridge, Mass.: M.I.T. Press, 1977), and Alan R. Fusfeld, "How to Put Technology into Corporate Planning," *Technology Review*, 80, no. 6 (May 1978), 51-55.

7.   See Bruce D. Henderson, "The Product Portfolio," in *Perspectives* (Boston: Boston Consulting Group, 1970); Bruce D. Henderson, "Cash Traps," in *Perspectives* (Boston: Boston Consulting Group, 1970); Louis V. Gerstner, Jr., "Can Strategic Planning Pay Off?," *Business Horizons*, 15, no. 6 (Dec. 1972), 5-16; *A System for Managing Diversity* (Cambridge, Mass.: Arthur D. Little, Inc., 1974); and Arnoldo C. Hax and Nicolas S. Majluf, "A Methodological Approach for the Developing of Strategic Planning in Diversified Corporations," *Technical Report No. 3* (Cambridge, Mass.: Sloan School of Management, M.I.T., 1977).

8.   For discussions of several of the problems raised in Chapter Three, see William E. Fruhan, "Pyrrhic Victories in Fights for Market Share," *Harvard Business Review* (Sept.–Oct. 1972); Yoram Wind and Henry J. Claycamp, "Planning Product Line Strategy: A Matrix Approach," *Journal of Marketing*, 40, no. 1 (Jan. 1976), 2-9; George S. Day, "Diagnosing the Product Portfolio," *Journal of Marketing*, 41, no. 2 (April 1977), 29-38; and R. G. Hammermesh, M. J. Anderson, Jr., and J. E. Harris, "Strategies for Low Market Share Businesses," *Harvard Business Review*, 56, no. 3 (May–June 1978), 95-102.

9.   See Peter Lorange, "Divisional Planning: Setting Effective Direction," *Sloan Management Review*, 17, no. 1 (Fall 1975), 77-92.

10.   See, for instance, Gordon Donaldson, *Strategy for Financial Mobility* (Boston: Division of Research, Harvard Business School, 1969), and Robin C. Marris, "An Introduction to Theories of Corporate Growth," in *The Corporate Economy: Growth, Competition and Innovative Potential*, eds. R. C. Marris and A. Wood (New York: Macmillan, 1971).

11.   For several works that might be interpreted so as to underscore the existence of a set of structural planning needs, see William J. Baumol, *Business Behavior, Value and Growth* (New York: Harcourt Brace Jovanovich, 1967); Robin C. Marris, *The Economic Theory of Managerial Capitalism* (New York: Macmillan, 1968); George A. Steiner, *Top Management Planning* (New York: Macmillan, 1969); and Harvey Leibenstein, *Beyond Economic Man: A New Foundation for Microeconomics* (Cambridge, Mass.: Harvard University Press, 1976).

12.   See Howard H. Stevenson, "Defining Corporate Strengths and Weaknesses," *Sloan Management Review*, 17, no. 3 (Spring 1976), 51-68.

13.   For several articles and books relevant in operationalizing the concept of environmental risk exposure and identification and monitoring of critical environmental factors, see F. J. Aguilar, *Scanning the Business Environment* (New York: Macmillan, 1967); R. B. Duncan, "Characteristics of Organizational Environments and Perceived Environmental Uncertainty," *Administrative Science Quarterly*, 17 (1972), 313-327; Basil W. Denning, "Strategic Environmental Appraisal," *Long Range Planning*, 6, no. 1 (March 1973), 22-27; Eric Rhenman, *Organization Theory for Long-Range Planning* (New York: Wiley-Interscience, 1973); H. K. Downey, D. Hellriegel, and J. W. Slocum, Jr., "Environmental Uncertainty: The Construct and Its Application," *Administrative Science Quarterly*, 20 (1975), 613-629; H. K. Downey and J. W. Slocum, Jr., "Uncertainty Measures, Research,

and Sources of Variation," *Academy of Management Journal*, 18 (1975), 562-578; Les Metcalfe and Will McQuillan, "Managing Turbulence," in *Prescriptive Models of Organizations*, eds. Paul C. Nystrom and William H. Starbuck (Amsterdam: North-Holland, 1977), pp. 7-25; Jerry Dermer, *Management Planning and Control Systems: Advanced Concepts and Cases* (Homewood, Ill.: Irwin, 1977), pp. 41-54; Kynng-Il Ghymn, "Strategic Intelligence Systems for Multinational Corporations: An Exploratory Study" (unpublished Ph.D. thesis, University of Pittsburgh, 1974); Harold E. Klein, "Incorporating Environmental Examination into the Corporate Strategic Planning Process" (unpublished Ph.D. thesis, Columbia University, 1973); and K. S. Radford, *Information Systems for Strategic Decisions* (Reston, Va.: Reston, 1978).

chapter four

Implementation of Corporate Planning Systems: General Pitfalls and Problems

Introduction

In this chapter as well as in the following two chapters, we shall address the issue of implementing effective corporate planning systems. We recall that a general conceptual scheme for corporate planning was developed in Chapter Two. It was stressed, however, that in order to become useful in actual corporate settings, the planning scheme would have to be modified in such a way that capabilities were built into the system to correspond with a given firm's particular planning needs. Accordingly, in Chapter Three we discussed how to determine a firm's planning needs, stemming from its stragetic situational setting. The general thrust of the task of implementing a corporate planning system, then, will be to tailor-make the system in such a way that it will be capable of meeting the needs identified. However, this turns out to be such a complex task that we shall find it useful to break down the discussion of it into three parts.

As a first step in this chapter[1] we shall discuss a number of more general pitfalls and problems that we have found to be typical when attempting to install a corporate planning system of the conceptual type developed in Chapter Two. This step will facilitate the elimination of problems that otherwise would have become obstacles during the subsequent sharpening of the focus for the planning system's capabilities. In

Chapter Five this will allow us to, in turn, discuss how to tailor-make the system to meet the pressing needs for planning in a given corporate setting. In Chapter Six our discussion of implementation will focus on a third aspect of the implementation process, namely, on how to manage the evolution of the planning system so that it might continue to be useful over time as a firm's needs for planning change.

We shall address 14 commonly found general implementation problems and issues in this chapter and shall discuss them as they relate to the implementation of each of the five cycles of the conceptual scheme for planning developed in Chapter Two.

Implementation Pitfalls and Problems During the Objectives-Setting Stage

There are five types of potential implementation problems and pitfalls that we have found to be particularly pertinent to the initial cycle of the corporate planning process—the objectives-setting stage. These are the need for the CEO's full involvement, the assessment of new opportunities in the business environment by the divisions, the nature of the portfolio approach toward corporate review of inputs from the rest of the organization, the informal nature of the involvement by the specialized functional departments at this initial stage, and the need for a feedback/ iterative mechanism for reexamining and revising parts of the planning outputs so that overall consistency might be reached among the many elements that will constitute the output of the objectives-setting cycle. We shall discuss each of these issues in turn.

the CEO should initiate the process

When it comes to the first issue, the nature of the CEO's involvement, it is particularly important that top management be fully involved. This would mean more than a general endorsement of planning by the CEO, some general urging that the organization go out and plan. What is needed is that the CEO actually start the process: He should signal his own aspirations, intentions, and performance requirements to the division heads as the first step of the annual planning process. He should be as specific as he feels he can realistically be but stress that his ideas are tentative at this stage. The CEO's inputs should give a useful and stimulating context to planning; it will still be natural and desirable that revisions, modifications, and improvements are likely to result from the planning process itself.[2]

Corporate assumptions with regard to interest, inflation, wage, and currency levels should also be communicated at this stage. These, too, should be tentative in that if a given business has a particular reason for not following the common assumptions as a result of unusual circumstances in its setting, then the management of this business should be encouraged to state this. Each business should be convinced that the general corporate assumptions are valid in their own setting; if not, it should be up to the division itself to raise the issue.

In our experience, it often happens that the CEO does not come out with an adequate statement of involvement at the outset of the planning process. This has detrimental effects on the subsequent planning effort for several reasons. First, the CEO might not feel really committed to the planning process yet in that he has not put his own thought on the block. This implies that time will be wasted on unrealistic planning exercises until he commits himself. Second, the key line executives will hesitate to put efforts into the process because they feel that the process is unreal without the CEO's involvement. Many may hold back on their own positions until they get a better feel for where the CEO stands and what direction he prefers. Third, lack of realism and focus at the objectives-setting stage will at best imply that much more time will have to be spent before a meaningful decision-making focus can be instilled; at worst, it means that corporate planning as a strategic decision-making process is dead, given the lack of realism and the ambivalence about what might be a useful strategic direction of the firm. If the CEO is unwilling to commit himself to the planning system as a viable strategic decision-making tool, the one who will lose is above all himself. He is depriving himself of a management tool which can significantly increase his discretionary ability to manage the firm strategically, or, stated differently, shift the power balance of the firm more toward himself. (This shift toward relatively more top-down emphasis might be a strong reason for the line to resist planning in many companies; their bottom-up influence might seem to be threatened.)

Let us illustrate further the importance of the CEO's involvement in initiating the process by means of two examples. The first example refers to a consumer products food company with annual sales of approximately half a billion dollars. An elaborate set of corporate assumptions is being disseminated to the divisions by the corporate planning department at the outset of the first planning cycle. These fall into three categories, summarized in a condensed version below:

1. General assumptions: No unforeseen major environmental event that would dramatically change the company's environment should be planned for.
2. Managerial assumptions: No fundamental change in organizational structure should be assumed; rapid changes in society and business will call for a need

to review current competitive situations and reevaluate future business plans; capital will continue to be in short supply; consequently, return on investment concepts will be emphasized.

3. Environmental trend assumptions: A general economic environment analysis indicates an expected overall economic trend as well as expected developments for monetary conditions, labor, consumer spending, prices, and raw materials supply patterns; a consumer attitudes analysis indicates trend shifts in life-styles, changes in consumer attitudes and awareness, and expected implications of these consumer attitudes and trends; finally, a demographics analysis spells out the population characteristics of the United States for the next five years.

The above set of corporate assumptions is stated with more thoroughness and spelled out in more detail than in many companies. Nevertheless, for two related reasons, it falls short as a necessary starting requirement for initiating the planning process. First, given that the corporate assumptions have been prepared by the corporate planning group, with the assistance of other corporate staff groups as well as some outside environmental trend service organizations, but with no apparent involvement of the senior line management, the line was reluctant to accept several of the key implications stemming from the corporate assumptions. Thus, it is important to give the corporate assumptions credibility by stating them as the CEO's assumptions. At minimum they should go out over his signature. Preferably, he should also be actively involved during the review of these assumptions so that he can make the substantive impacts he might want. Needless to say, the staff should undertake most of the burden of preparation, for reasons of availability of time as well as specialized competencies. Second, the corporate assumptions do not go far enough in that they do not directly signal the CEO's aspirations and tentative objectives. The indirect inferences that the line might draw about the CEO's intentions may even be conflicting. For instance, under the section of managerial assumptions it is stated, on the one hand, that rapid environmental changes will call for a high planning responsiveness, i.e., a strong adaptive thrust. On the other hand, the shortage of capital and the emphasis on strict return on investment measures are also stated, i.e., a strongly integrative thrust. Thus, it seems necessary that the CEO reveal his aspirations about the general direction in which he wants the firm to go, in addition to the statement of corporate background assumptions. Further, one should avoid stating so many corporate assumptions that they become apparently conflicting and, thus, more or less meaningless unless careful priorities are introduced among the assumptions.

The second example refers to the European-based diversified corporation discussed in the appendix to Chapter Two. The major business involvements of this company fall within the pharmaceutical area. Corporate management has stated that the emphasis in the future should be shifted relatively more toward internal growth and away from the predominant mode of growth through acquisitions of the past. It will be important to encourage a heavy involvement by the businesses in order to capitalize on their familiarity with and understanding of their businesses when identifying internal growth opportunities. However, a seemingly almost total lack of top-down initial input into the planning process on behalf of the CEO causes concern and anxiety among line managers about the role of the planning system as a vehicle for pursuing the internal growth strategy. Above all, this seems to cause each of the businesses to develop its plans in a vacuum and with a lot of caution. The emerging plans generally seem to be uninspiring and conservative. The CEO has not been able to instill much of a sense of what reasonable strategies are from his point of view. By forgoing the opportunity to give the organization clear signals about his ambitions and desires about where he hopes to take the company as well as by not indicating his belief in planning by making clear his readiness to participate at this logical point in time, the CEO leaves the planning process in a state of ambivalence and degradation. The potential seriousness of this deficiency can be seen from examining decisions related to the company's entry into new business areas, which, as we have pointed out in the past, have been largely facilitated by means of acquisitions and primarily within the divisions themselves. The Home Products Division was still active, however, in continuing to acquire a relatively large number of companies over a quite diverse area of activities. Such diversification by subunits might be seen as an indication of a potentially serious lack of corporate top-down portfolio direction. The undesirable implications of this are particularly apparent when it comes to the company's risk taking. A particular division is likely to evaluate a given diversification proposal from the point of view of the activity level of its own business, i.e., more or less whether the acquisition makes sense in terms of risk as if the division were an independent company. The company as a whole, however, is in a position to take far larger selected risks, simply by benefiting from being larger and depending on a wider number of sources of funds flows than a single division. Consequently, it may seem right at the corporate level to acquire one or a few relatively large companies, moves that never would have been taken by a division on its own. Thus, delegation of the acquisition aspect of portfolio planning implies that creation of an overly fragmented and conservative acquisition pattern, with too many small entities, will be likely. One of the few advantages of being a relatively large company is thereby not being pursued. Thus, lack of a clear statement of the CEO's aspirations, including the nature of risk taking that he might want to involve the company in, seems to have led to a breakdown of top-down corporate leadership of the firm's direction setting in this case. A mushrooming, overly conservative bottom-up diversification drive seems to be the result.

In summary, then, it is critical that the CEO initiate the planning process. In our experience problems with effective planning systems can quite commonly be traced back to a lack of top management involvement at the outset. As we have seen, several dysfunctional effects from this are likely to occur, leading to significantly less useful planning in most cases.

assessment of business opportunities and threats

A second implementation problem relates to each division's business opportunity assessment as part of its development of objectives and goals statements for where it wants to go with its respective businesses, responding to the initiation of planning that has come from the CEO.[3] It is critical that each division management team, being the closest to a particular business environment, skillfully and imaginatively assess the major opportunities and threats that are facing its business. These managers should not only have the best insight into the opportunities their business environment can offer, they should also be in the best position to perceive how to take advantage of these opportunities by modifying the objectives and goals of their businesses. It is of critical importance that a creative element of environmental awareness and gutsy business entrepreneurialism to opportunistically pursue new, unconventional leads be captured in the corporate planning process at this step.

Unfortunately, for many companies such an open-minded, environmental opportunity orientation of the planning efforts at this stage may be next to nonexistent. Division management often tends to treat the environmental outlook and the assessment of business opportunities and threats as an exercise that can be taken quite lightly. A common feeling might be that next year the business will continue to be more or less the same as the business in the past. Such a mental extrapolation of the past into the future might suit a manager quite well, not only because it will be comfortable to continue pursuing what he more or less already has been doing but even more so because it avoids threatening the vested interests that a manager typically might have in his present organization. Thus, there is a natural tendency among many managers to wish that there will be no major environmental changes affecting their business so that they can keep on doing business in the future the way they have done it before. Thus, managers' resistance to facing needs for change might add to the problem of taking too lightly the task of assuring one's business opportunities. There will easily be a temptation for the division manager to address the critical task of business opportunity and threat identifica-

tion by merely doing a brief editing a.1d updating of last year's statement.
This might of course be particularly difficult for senior management
to detect, given that one would normally expect relatively little change
from year to year for many of the businesses. The critical issue, however,
is that such a conclusion, that only small changes in one's business will be
necessary to incorporate new business opportunities and/or threats, has
been made after a thorough assessment of the business environment.

It is thus important that the analysis focus on issues in the business's
environment, not inward on the problems of business-as-usual. The
focus should be on the strategic effectiveness of the business, not on
strategic efficiency: "Are we in the right business?," not "Are we doing
this business right?" The approach developed in Chapter Three for risk/
return assessment of businesses faced with potential positive or negative
impacts from environmental factors might be used by a division manager
as a basis for assessment of his opportunities. The issue for him is to
assess the positive and negative factors as well as his own response
potential. He might also follow a set of leading questions in order to detect
pertinent environmental changes: Are there any differences in the attractiveness of the business, in our own competitive strength? New opportunities should be discussed in terms of potential impact on the business's
strategic position in a more narrow sense as well as in the sense of the
broader issue of risk/return impacts on the corporate portfolio.

A major problem in many cases thus might be that explicit or implicit
extrapolative thinking on the part of the business managers might prevent a more meaningful assessment of the strategic opportunities and
threats of the business. The result is often a conspicuous lack of new and
innovative ideas in the plans; the planning steps will be more or less
meaningless too, i.e., the well-known garbage in–garbage out syndrome.
Many companies experienced this during the first wave to undertake
long-range planning, during the mid-to-late-1960s. These planning efforts were often heavily numbers-oriented, which does not necessarily
have to be bad, except when the numbers have been developed primarily
through extrapolation, providing a more or less useless picture of the
strategic opportunities of the future. When we have such a highly
numbers-oriented planning emphasis, the temptation for extrapolation
replacing real and hard thinking seems to be particularly strong. Needless
to say, however, even without a heavy numbers emphasis, we might still
have a verbal extrapolation in the planning exercise, again just as useless.

The failure to have innovative and highly involved divisional
future-oriented opportunity assessment, unconstrained by one's present
business situation, represents a serious obstacle to realistic planning,
particularly so for companies that base themselves primarily on an internally generated corporate growth thrust. Especially for a company in

rapidly changing environments this might be a very serious limitation to effective planning.

portfolio focus in corporate level's reviews

A third implementation problem deals with the mode the CEO and his corporate office follow in reviewing planning inputs generated further down in the organization and giving feedback to the divisions. We shall discuss this issue in relation to the objectives-setting stage since it might first surface as an implementation problem here. However, an appropriate mode of corporate review and interaction with the divisions might be a serious implementation problem at any of the stages of the planning process. We shall discuss two aspects of the issue of implementing a proper mode of corporate-level planning reviews, namely, the need to follow a so-called portfolio review approach as opposed to what might be called a sequential review approach and the need to instill a degree of procedural discipline among the parties in the review process. Let us first turn to the portfolio review issue.

The corporate level's strategic task is responsible for the development of a corporate portfolio strategy, as we have discussed. This, however, implies that any review and evaluation of a particular planning input from a business should be assessed in terms of its relevance within the context of the overall portfolio pattern of the company. Thus, the merit of each business plan should be judged in relation to the other business plans.

Unfortunately, however, corporate reviews of divisional planning inputs often do not follow the portfolio mode that we have just described. Instead, corporate management often tends to review divisions one at a time, in a sequential fashion. This, of course, will not facilitate the development of a corporate portfolio strategy, given that it will be more or less coincidental what the approved business inputs might add up to as a corporate portfolio pattern. To underscore this, when a sequential corporate review mode is followed, it will probably matter for a particular business *when* it is being reviewed relative to the others. For instance, the first businesses to be reviewed might receive encouraging corporate responses for expansion policies, implying commitment of significant funds, but the later businesses reviewed might be penalized by a shortage of discretionary corporate funds, accompanied by a tightening up of resource allocation criteria and tougher corporate review. While this example is perhaps exaggerated, it is nevertheless clear that a sequential corporate review makes it virtually impossible to apply a consistent risk/return criterion for approval of the divisional planning input proposals, given that the portfolio interdependence of the business inputs will have been overlooked. It is also clear that the corporate review process in principle cannot be separated into reviews of smaller clusters of businesses, say within a group, for subsequent corporate review of the aggregate outputs from the groups. Here, too, the overall comparability between the risk/returns of the businesses gets lost. When it comes to ameliorating in practice the problem of groups becoming strategic filters in the review process, this might be very hard within a large, diversified firm, leading the CEO to conclude that he might have an impossible task dealing with the complete overall portfolio of businesses directly. We shall not discuss how to approach this problem here but will postpone it until Chapter Six.

Let us reiterate how a corporate review approach has to be carried out in order to facilitate proper corporate portfolio strategizing: First, all of the divisions must provide corporate headquarters with their business planning inputs. This will provide the corporate level with a complete set of data to carry out the next step, namely, to review what seems to be the emerging pattern when seeing all the business inputs within a single context. Only then, as a third step, should feedback be made to a particu- lar business about potential modifications that it should carry out to provide for this business's fit within the portfolio.

Unfortunately, we have seen frequent examples of corporate plans being developed through a stepwise corporate review process and also by a simple notion of stepwise aggregation. A division manager might develop his plan by reviewing the strategy centers reporting to his division, group plans might then be developed by aggregating and reviewing the plans of each group's divisions, and the corporate plan might come about by "adding" the group plans. Even in companies where corporate management recognizes the need to be closer to the grass roots by having a closer understanding of the nature of each business, making great efforts to give attention to each business, a sequential pattern of review might still prevail, preventing an appropriate risk/return trade-off among the businesses.

Let us now turn to the other aspect of the issue of implementing proper corporate review practices. Needless to say, a proper corporate review procedure requires considerable discipline from the various organizational units involved. For each of the divisions, there will be a requirement that planning outputs be relatively comparable. They have to rest on a common set of consistent premises in terms of data inputs, definitions, and analytical approaches. Further, each division must deliver its output on time; if one division fails to come up with its plan, then the entire corporate review process will have to be delayed because of the impossibility of establishing an overall corporate portfolio context until all business elements are available. The role of the planning calendar is therefore critical—much more so, of course, for companies which recognize the nature of corporate portfolio reviews than for companies that follow a corporate sequential review. Thus, standardization of the format of business planning as well as cutting down on the flexibility of each business conforming to the deadlines of the planning calendar should be seen as necessary conditions for portfolio planning. This is a consideration often overlooked by executives who might be criticizing such a relatively rigorous planning system, blaming it for being too much of a straitjacket on the creative drive of the businesses. We shall discuss the issue of setting useful planning calendars further in Chapter Five.

For the corporate level there will also be a need for discipline. Senior corporate management of a company might be under constant pressure from the operating divisions to give its okay for various new projects. However, it will not be enough for senior management merely to convince itself about the soundness of a project, even though it might be evaluated as part of the strategic programs that the division is in the process of carrying out in order to implement its business objectives. Many projects, of course, are not even tested in terms of strategic program fit; all that matters is that the project's projected return on assets is satisfactory. It will be necessary for corporate management to view the project in a portfolio context. Does the company benefit more from investing in this business than in other businesses?

It should be extremely difficult for senior management to approve major projects that are not part of the corporate planning process. As we recall, the planning system is intended precisely as a decision-making tool for strategic resource allocation decisions. Corporate management which approves major projects outside the context of the planning cycle will thereby jeopardize the future effectiveness of corporate planning. There might be obvious dysfunctional motivational effects among division line managers if they perceive that they can break the discipline of the orderly resource allocation process and succeed in securing funds on an ad hoc basis. An even more serious and fundamentally unfavorable effect for corporate management is the potential for distorting the overall balance of the corporate portfolio strategy. Thus, there is a heavy demand for discipline on the part of corporate management as part of managing the company in a strategic mode; the corporate planning process in fact ties corporate and divisional management together in a contract.

We saw the corporate-divisional discipline problem as a major obstacle to progress on strategic planning in a European-based corporation which was engaged in several businesses within the building materials and construction fields. This example is quite revealing in terms of shedding light on the general nature of this problem and merits a brief discussion. One of the smaller divisions of this company manufactured ready-mixed concrete from a relatively large number of small plants which had to be located near their end-use markets. This division was, however, considerably larger than any competitor in the business. There were a large number of small independent local producers, many representing tempting takeover opportunities for the concrete division. The division manager capitalized on this by stressing the unique ad hoc strategic opportunity to take over a competitor and prevent anybody else from doing this when he approached corporate management for funds to carry out an acquisition move. These acquisitions, however, were entirely out of context with his agreed-upon strategy, which stated that he should concentrate cocentrically around the largest market. After several extraordinary resource allocations, the other divisions, too, started to bring up extraordinary requests. Only strong reinforcement of a portfolio approach restored the necessary strategic discipline.

Needless to say, a company must act on an opportunity when it arrives and cannot foresee or plan for such an exact happening. However, the strategies should have been developed before the opportunity arrives, so that the decision can be taken within a strategic context. An acquisition, for example, then becomes merely another strategic program for how to achieve a particular strategy, not a random shift (and shock) for the corporation. Thus, while corporate management as well as division managers might urge that strategic decisions be taken when they arise, given that it will be undesirable or not feasible to delay a critical decision until next year's planning cycle, this line of reasoning tends to be a straw man argument in that having to take critical decisions outside of the ordinary planning cycle fortunately seldom happens.

Ideally, what the planning system should provide is enough curtailing of decision-making flexibility to be rigorous but rarely so much curtailing as to foster indecisiveness. Line management should understand that it will be rare that an entirely new strategic alternative suddenly emerges; in those instances the significant additional, analytical work load to carry out a proper portfolio strategy reassessment should be met. On the other hand, there might be a danger that willingness and ability to reach a decision get lost in an abundance of analysis and future revisions. The decision-making focus on strategic planning must therefore always be kept in mind.

functional departments' involvement in objectives setting

A fourth implementation issue in connection with the objectives-setting stage has to do with the formal involvement of the managers at levels lower in the organization than the divisional managers and the strategy center managers. It should be pointed out that the nature of the planning process during the objectives-setting stage is different from the nature of the process during subsequent stages in that a general management point of view should be dominant. The issue is to decide on the general strategic direction of the firm in order to achieve a better corporate portfolio balance, i.e.: Which business activities should be expanded? Should growth of present business operations be curtailed in order to acquire new businesses? Should some of the present business activities be divested in order to free funds for reemployment in one's other businesses or in acquisitions? Clearly, a predominantly general management point of view is needed in order to address these critical issues. We shall give three reasons for this.

First, it seems reasonable to assume that corporate management will be in the best position to have a sufficiently broad overview of the relevant corporate-wide information. Presumably, also, corporate-level managers are likely to be in a better position to exercise more of a healthy emotional detachment from a particular business than the division managers involved, so that they might better see what relative business involvement balance will be the best for the company as a whole. The general managers of the divisions as well as strategy center managers should, however, be able to appreciate the general nature of evaluating a business problem with its broader portfolio context. By grasping the significance of this, they should be able to contribute to the development of a portfolio-based set of corporate objectives in a disciplined manner, despite the obvious belief that each division manager should favor his own business. Even after having attempted to do his utmost to convince corporate management about the viability of his business as part of the corporation's portfolio, having been given ample opportunity to bring up his viewpoints and to be heard by corporate management, if it still turns out that other divisions can provide better business opportunities from a portfolio viewpoint, the division manager should agree that the entire corporate family is better off this way. The long-term opportunities of a manager of a business that is being curtailed are probably better served this way too in that the corporation will be able to create more new resources and long-term opportunities for all.

When it comes to the rest of the management within a division, such as functional managers or area managers, one should not expect a general management point of view to prevail. In fact, a parochial commitment to one's special task is the key ingredient for managerial success at this level. Thus, the inputs from these managers will reflect their commitment to their existing functional or area organizations. As such they will tend to preserve a status quo. Thus, when it comes to opportunistic, environmental adaptation, the functional inputs typically will not be central to the general direction-setting decisions of the objectives-setting cycle.

Consequently, special task managers within the divisions should not be formally involved in the planning process at this stage. We have of course assumed that the general manager of the division is intimately familiar with his business, its opportunities and threats, its capabilities and limitations, and its strengths and weaknesses. To the extent that he needs to strengthen his understanding of the business, he should of course be in intimate contact with his specialized line managers on issues that will help him formulate his general management judgments. As such, the special task managers within the divisions are informally involved in the planning process during the objectives-setting cycle as part of the management teams of the division general managers.

A second reason for the specialized managers within the divisions to have only a limited involvement during the objectives-setting stage of the planning process relates to a latent and potentially serious dysfunctional motivational effect. By formally soliciting the function and/or area managers' viewpoints on objectives, goals, and strategies but then having to disregard or modify these contributions in order to satisfy a general management viewpoint to fit within a portfolio strategy, there might be a loss of morale. The divisional general manager's role will also become difficult if he has to interact with corporate management backed up with explicit statements about policy suggestions from his own subordinates; he will, so to speak, find himself between the bark and the wood. Emphasis on ad hoc informal planning activity within the divisions should ameliorate many of these problems.

Finally, the time constraint issue should be kept in mind. A frequent objection to planning has been that it seems to require large amounts of time. At the extreme, a manager might find himself spending his day preparing materials for the planning documents, attending planning meetings, and reviewing planning reports; no time is left for running the business. Therefore, there should be a general requirement not to involve management in planning activities where they are not essentially needed. Particularly given the central, elaborate, and time-consuming involvement of function and area managers in the strategic programming stage of the corporate planning process, it is desirable to keep the involvement of these managers to a minimum during the objectives-setting stage.

In one company which we examined, the issue of the functional management's involvement seemed to become confused due to a strong desire among top management to involve management several levels down in the organizational hierarchy in order to enhance strategic thinking and achieve relevant strategic changes through planning. When calling for the organization's participation senior management seemed, however, to make little distinction between objectives setting and strategic programming. While its desire to solicit the organization's ideas and creativity seemed to have a lot of merit in the strategic programming stage, which by design would be heavily bottom-up through the critical role played by the functions in developing program alternatives, top management did not fully realize the typically more top-down general management nature of the preceding objectives-setting cycle. The task of setting objectives was thus just not satisfactorily achieved; the functional inputs did not add up to generic strategic statements of direction. By involving a large segment of managers it turned out not to be possible for the management teams of each division to reach consensus on a set of operational objectives. Organizational ability to change and adapt became hampered by an overabundance of viewpoints which proved impossible to reconcile. The effect was that next to no adaptation took place.

In this instance, as well as in many other cases when it comes to the design of a planning system, it is beneficial to ask whether the way a particular aspect of planning is executed makes sense, given the nature of the aspect of the planning task one attempts to achieve. An extreme bottom-up approach to a task which is essentially more top-down in its nature should thus not be expected to work.

the iterative feedback loop   " *Close The Planning Gap* "

During our discussion of the conceptual model for corporate planning in Chapter Two, we pointed out that our model places heavy reliance on its iterative properties, the assumption being that good plans are most likely to be developed as a result of an interplay—back and forth—among managers with different strategic outlooks and responsibilities. Such an interplay, however, might easily end up hampering the planning process unless it is spelled out in some detail. Thus, we need to establish a set of rules to guide the feedback process. We shall discuss this implementation phenomenon at this point because it first appears during the objectives-setting stage; however, just as was the case for the corporate portfolio-type review requirement, this issue is of relevance during all of the stages of the planning process.

We recall that during the objectives-setting stage there were three distinct steps of the planning process (see Exhibit 2-5), namely, an initial statement of tentative objectives and expectations by the CEO, an assessment of the business opportunities by each of the divisions, and a corporate portfolio consolidation of these business objectives. The pattern of organization interaction is thus clear: a top-down initiation and a bottom-up response. However, there is an additional element of closing the loop; when the CEO compares the consolidated output of the third step of the process with his initial expectation stated in the first step, there might be a discrepancy; in fact, this would probably be the norm.[4] We recall from Chapter Two that we have called such a discrepancy a planning gap. The way such a planning gap is established, analyzed in terms of options for closing it, and finally closed before proceeding to the next cycle of the planning process comprise a critical implementation issue for the effectiveness of the planning process.

During the objectives-setting stage the planning gap will be defined by comparing the risk/return characteristics of the expected funds-flow pattern that emerges from the portfolio strategy of where the company wants to go (step 3, Exhibit 2-5) with the initially stated expectations of the CEO (step 1). If there is a discrepancy, i.e., a planning gap, then this will have to be closed in accordance with one or more of the following four approaches:

CLOSING THE PLANNING GAP

- A lowering of the CEO's initial expectations, i.e., a realization that the initial push just seemed to be too ambitious. A downward revision of his aspirations will then be needed in order to obtain a more realistic focus for the subsequent planning.
- A corporate demand on one or more of the divisions to develop more aggressive business plans. To some extent this option might be available because of slack in the business organizations; in fact, some of the more publicized benefits from planning have been with respect to how the CEO has used the planning system in pushing for more aggressive, achievement-oriented divisional performance.
- A corporate decision to shift the relative emphasis among the businesses. The CEO would then attempt to reallocate discretionary resources away from some businesses and in the direction of other businesses, so that the commitment to businesses with higher future prospects are increased and less attractive businesses are de-emphasized. This change of emphasis in the balance among the divisions requires an ability on the part of the CEO to make strategic priorities and a willingness to reallocate resources accordingly. This is the essence of corporate portfolio management, and an overriding purpose of strategic planning is to act as the tool in facilitating these decisions.
- A realization that the portfolio balance should be changed through acquisition and/or divestiture in order to achieve more rapidly the intended properties of the strategic portfolio. Above all, potential saving of time is an important factor in achieving strategic changes through acquisitions/divestitures. Internal developments of new businesses of enough substance to have a meaningful impact on changing the corporate portfolio balance typically take a longer time and are often risky efforts.

It is important that a planning gap be closed before the planning process is allowed to proceed to its next stage, and there are two reasons for this. First, the closing of the loop reinforces the decision-making nature of strategic planning. Specifically, top management will have to make some strategic choices. Conversely, proceeding to the next stage of planning without resolving the issues of strategic choices that have surfaced, as sticky and as complicated as they might be, will weaken the decision-making realism of the planning process. Management will be prone to relax its intellectual commitment and become less accountable to such a process. It is significant that it will require a top-down decision-making initiative to close a planning gap. The pressure is thus primarily on upper management to clear the way for the resolution of closing a planning gap. A common implementation problem is often found here, unfortunately, in that upper management fails to demonstrate a willingness to commit itself to specific strategic choice decisions.

A second reason for closing a planning gap is the desirability to provide a gradual sharpening of the focus of the strategic direction as the planning process proceeds. Resolution of strategic decisions with respect to how to fill a planning gap will provide a necessary requirement for more targeted and relevant analysis at the remaining steps of the planning process. If, for instance, ambiguity still exists with respect to strategic choices that have been left unresolved during the objectives-setting stage by not closing the planning gap, then the subsequent strategic programming task will have to be carried out with a much wider and less defined focus. A likely result will be that the quality of the programming process might suffer.

We recall from Exhibit 2-6 that the corporate level will be faced with the challenge of closing of three distinctive planning gaps, namely, at the objectives-setting stage, the strategic programming stage, and the budgeting stage. The specific focus of the strategic decisions to be taken in closing each of these gaps will of course be difficult. The general nature of these decisions will, however, be fundamentally the same in that they all affect the corporate portfolio strategy and in that each planning gap will have to close in accordance with one or a combination of the four approaches just outlined.

At the business level, the division manager will be faced with closing only two planning gaps, as we can see from Exhibit 2-6. The task of closing these planning gaps will be fundamentally different from the closing of the corporate gaps in that the strategic decisions that need to be taken will affect a particular business strategy. There will be only two ways of closing the planning gaps at the business strategic planning level, in contrast to the four alternatives that apply to the corporate portfolio level:

- One will relate to the extent to which investments will be made in building a position of competitive strength for a particular product/market element. Resources may be put into a product in order to build a particular business strength or, to a lesser extent, to hold a particular business position. Resources might on the other hand be released from a product which is allowed to slip in competitive strength position—a harvest posture. The transfer of strategic resources among product/market elements that have products at different stages of the product life cycle and in such a way that each of the products is managed along a deliberate evolutionary sequence of strategic

positions, as indicated by the solid line in Exhibit 3-3, is critical to a good closing of the planning gap at the division level.
- The development of new products, in the question mark category, which can provide the basis for future growth and development of positions of future strength. For this, funds need to be transferred from product/market elements that are presently in the mature product stage to new product development, as indicated by the arrow in Exhibit 3-5.

For the planning gaps at the business planning level it is just as critical that they are closed before planning proceeds to the next cycle for the two reasons already indicated, enforcement of strategic decision-making emphasis and a sharpening of strategic focus.

We have now completed our discussion of five implementation issues that tend to occur during the execution of the objectives-setting planning stage, and we shall proceed to a discussion of implementational issues at the next stage—strategic programming. Several of the implementation issues discussed within the objectives-setting context also apply when it comes to other planning stages; notably the requirement for a portfolio mode of corporate review as well as the need for the closing of planning gaps apply at all of the three first stages.

Implementation Pitfalls and Problems During the Strategic Programming Stage

During the second stage of the strategic planning process, strategic programming, we shall discuss two fairly common implementation problems. These relate to how to enhance a predominantly cross-functional nature of strategic programming to avoid functional compartmentalization and the issue of aggregating strategic programs into packages that are consistent with the business strategy that the programs are intended to enhance. Let us discuss each of these issues in turn.

cross-functional nature of strategic programming

The strategic programming activity is critical for a meaningful corporate planning system in that it is primarily during this stage that the foundation will have to be laid for implementing a particular set of objectives and goals. Specialized management functions within a division will be called on to provide specialized functional skills such as manufacturing, marketing, or R&D. These resources are critical for execution of the strategic programs; strong specialized competence within each of the organizational subunits involved is essential to good strategic programming. A high level of professionalism on the part of each of the components that go into the programming process is paramount.[5]

A difficult implementation problem, however, often tends to arise when we are attempting to blend the inputs of strong organizational functions into an overall cross-functional program. The nature of a strategic program is predominantly interfunctional; the specialized functions will have to cooperate in the execution of a particular program. Even the best functional inputs cannot ensure successful strategic programming if coordination among the various specialized activities is lacking. Specialized organizational subunits' attempts to take an overly independent stance may lead overly narrow professionalism to thrive while creating barriers to the implementation of the strategic direction.

There are several ways to counteract this tendency of organizational subunit compartmentalization. Above all, the resource allocation process implicit in the strategic planning framework which has been developed in this book implies that resources are being allocated to strategic programs within the context of the objectives and goals. This is in contrast to the traditional allocation of resources to specific investment projects and to the organizational subunits' expenditure budgets. Thus, the various functions will have to develop program proposals together, be jointly subjected to the division head's general management review of strategic programs, and share the responsibility for subsequent execution of these programs. Thus, the nature of the programming task itself might reinforce the need for interfunctional cooperation.

An additional precaution that might be followed in order to strengthen the cross-functional flair is for the division manager to encourage the establishment of a milestone summary of each strategic program proposal that is accepted. This is a way of summarizing what should be achieved at given times and who should be responsible. Such a summary helps pinpoint the interdependence of the organizational subunits in a project's development. Above all, it might create a stronger sense of shared responsibility among the functions; although at one stage of development one particular function might be most directly involved, another function will have to carry on when a particular point of progress has been reached.

A step related to this is to specify in considerable detail as part of a strategic program proposal the nature of the *interaction points* between the functions. For instance, a strategic program for developing a new pharmaceutical product from research into full commercialization might be planned in such a way that when a particular function has completed its task and is scheduled to pass the project on to the next function, a review of the program's progress would be made with the participation of all remaining functions which are expected to be involved in the program. Thus, what might seem to be a satisfactory completion of a particular function's input to a strategic program from a narrow point of view might turn out not to be satisfactory from the viewpoint of other functions. It is important that the functions will have a chance to jointly review the progress at a very early stage so that desirable modifications can be defined in a broad enough context to improve the chances of a final commercial success.

Typically, many division managers will feel that there might be a need for development and analysis of separate functional plans. Such plans should, however, not fail to assess the extent to which the function is tuned in with and contributes to the strategic programming activities of the firm to ameliorate apparent dysfunctional activities and to strengthen the strategic focus of each function. Thus, it seems most practical to develop such functional plans as a sequel to the strategic programs, as a summary of the roles that each given function would be expected to play in the overall package of programs to be pursued. Many companies, unfortunately, start out the strategic programming process in reverse order, first developing functional plans and then (maybe) attempting to reconcile them in terms of the strategic program activities they imply. Unfortunately, the strategic programs that emerge from such a sequence of events easily end up being the results of compromises between functional positions. Vitally important, imaginatively developed strategic programs that are based on a more unconstrained outlook of opportunities and/or threats will probably not emerge.

consolidation of strategic programs

Let us now move to another implementation problem that commonly occurs during the strategic programming stage, namely, the issue of achieving appropriate choices among strategic program alternatives so that they add up to the best program package for progressing toward the stated goals and objectives of a particular business.[6] There are two aspects of this that we shall discuss: how to avoid inconsistency between the anticipated impact from a strategic program package that has been chosen and the previously decided-upon strategies and implicitly anticipated funds-flow patterns for the business, and how to carry out the aggregation of the strategic programs—a so-called zero-based approach.

While the objectives-setting stage established a frame for where to go, the purpose of the strategic programming stage is to operationalize how to get there. It follows from this that the strategic program efforts should result in a directional thrust which is consistent with the objectives and goals previously agreed upon. A common implementation problem, however, seems to be to be inconsistent with respect to this. At worst, programming may result in a directional thrust which is in sharp contrast to the intended strategic context. For instance, one particular division might have been arguing for an expansionary role for its business during the objectives-setting stage, resulting in the decision to let this division be designated as one of the major internal growth vehicles within the firm's business portfolio in the years to come. This strategic role of course has not been arrived at in a vacuum but as a pattern of interdependencies with the other businesses, where each has been designated a role as net contributor or net user of funds within the overall portfolio. If, during the subsequent strategic programming stage, it turns out that the division does not come up with a package of programs that provides the strategic direction assumed in the previous stage, then this will represent a potentially serious weakening of the corporate portfolio objectives. The lack of proper implementation of direction that emerges thus affects not only the business strategy of the division itself but may also hold up the implementation of the corporate portfolio strategy as well as potentially causing a need for modification of other businesses' strategic programs, thereby frustrating the implementation of direction here too.

There might be at least three reasons why such lack of consistency might emerge. One reason might be lack of emphasis or the crucial interdependence between the two cycles. The organizational units may simply never be challenged to come up with programs that are consistent with the strategic objectives. An important implication of this is that the objectives-setting cycle can be seen as reduced to a brainstorming exercise with the realistic decision-making emphasis gone. Subsequent strategic programs will be developed without benefiting from adequate strategic context.

Another reason might be that a division lacks critical strategic resources in the forms of functional professionalism and capabilities that will be needed to deliver an adequate set of strategic programs. Typically there will be one or a few functions that turn out to be the bottleneck. In line with this there might also be certain functions that are very strong but are not utilized to their full potential. In a sense this represents an opportunity loss in that the division's management might have misjudged what capabilities it needs to execute a particular set of strategic programs as well as what capabilities it possesses. An unrealistically large gap between needs and capabilities for specialized functional skills might cause serious implementation problems for the strategic programming efforts. Although to some extent the internal functional resources can be made available through ad hoc actions, it takes time to develop internal functional professional capabilities. Hence, a plan should be made to bring the functional capabilities up to the standards needed to fulfill the expected requirements that the execution of the strategic programs will pose. To the extent that this does not seem reasonably feasible within a given period of time the strategic programs themselves become unworkable and must be modified.

We are in fact faced here with a dilemma in our planning approach. We recall that a major premise for the conceptual framework that we have developed is the emphasis on searching for new environmental opportunities and/or threats as the driving force for dictating the firm's direction. We also stressed the sharp contrast between this approach and extrapolation based on one's present strengths and/or weaknesses. However, the pursuance of new opportunities and/or threats cannot be carried out without taking into account the internal strengths and/or weaknesses as constraints. Thus, a reconciliation will have to take place between what would seem to be a more open-ended determination of what opportunities and/or threats to follow, as determined in cycle one, with what would actually be feasible given one's own internal strengths and/or weaknesses surfacing during the strategic programming stage. This important modification activity is an essential part of the strategic program consolidation. The challenge, of course, is to take maximum advantage of internal strengths and attempt to ameliorate the effects from internal weaknesses as much as possible. In this way the strategic programming process can solidify and boost the intended strategic direction set during the objectives-setting stage, not dampen the pursuance of creative and opportunistic direction setting.

This brings us to a related issue with respect to the problem of setting directional congruence between strategic programs and objectives, namely, that of dealing with unrealistic (too optimistic or too pessimistic) managerial judgments. For instance, a set of objectives may be so far off base and ill-conceived that executing a strategic thrust through concrete programs might not be feasible. In such instances, if the deviations and unrealism are great enough, it might be necessary to redo the entire objectives-setting cycle, not only for the division in question but, because of their portfolio interdependencies, for all the business plans. It is of course equally undesirable, and quite common, that some divisions understretch their business potential during the objectives-setting cycle, so that there is little challenge to attain what might be seen as safe strategic programming tasks during the next stage.

The potential problem of lack of consistency between the strategic thrusts of the objectives-setting and the strategic programming cycles might to a considerable extent be ameliorated through emphasizing an important consequence of the decision-making nature of the planning process, namely, that every manager will be expected to live with that to which he has committed his organization unit and himself. Realism, when it comes to objectives setting as well as strategic programming, is thus essential. The key is to hit a reasonable balance between the consideration of opportunities and threats and of strengths and weakness. Useful in this respect will be the linking of managerial performance toward the fulfillment of each planning cycle to the managerial incentive schemes, thus reinforcing managerial credibility for delivering what has been promised.

The problem of incongruence between the planning cycles might partly also stem from procedural shortcomings in the way that program alternatives are being evaluated, chosen, and aggregated into an overall business strategic program package for a division. The so-called zero-base approach might be useful here. A first step in this approach, often labeled zero-base budgeting, assuming that the objectives and strategic tasks have been translated to each function beforehand, is to identify alternative ways of fulfilling the tasks that have been assigned to a particular function. The various alternatives for achieving a particular task are then ranked, and the most cost/beneficial alternative is chosen. After this all the tasks are ranked, again in terms of cost/benefits. A cutoff point is established, and all tasks above this will be passed up to the next level of management. At this level the tasks from all this manager's subordinates will be consolidated and ranked again and so on.

Due to the interfunctional nature of most strategic program alternatives, it will be a general management task to rank these alternatives. Thus, while alternative ways of executing each function's part of a particular task should be explored by the function, a function would be unable to pass in isolation a strategic judgment as to which specific tasks should be done. This can only be done by considering the inputs from the various functions when forming a total strategic program. Thus, ranking of strategic programs must be done from the general management point of view, i.e., by the division head, and not be left in the hands of each function. It follows from this that the strategic direction determined for a business during the objectives-setting stage is particularly useful for the general manager in putting a necessary focus to strategic programming. Without this a straightforward zero-base bottom-up aggregation/ranking approach would not necessarily lead to an appropriate strategic direction.

Implementation Pitfalls and Problems During the Budgeting Stage

Let us now turn to implementation pitfalls and problems that tend to appear during the budgeting stage. There are at least three concerns that commonly might be raised in this respect: difficulty in allocating the necessary strategic resources to the strategic programs because of conflicts with traditional resource allocation mechanisms in the firm which tend to put strong pressures on allocation to departments and/or investment proposals; inadequate recognition of the need for building the budget around key variables, of the dollar as well as nondollar types; and failure to provide a mechanism for personalizing elements of the budget by the various relevant managers throughout the organizational hierarchy. We shall discuss each of these three issues in turn.

resource allocation to strategic programs, not project or expenditure proposals

As already discussed, the advent of a corporate planning approach brings an important implication in terms of a shift in the resource allocation mode.[7] Major strategic resource allocations will be decided on during the strategic programming cycle as a reflection of how to achieve the objectives and strategies of the first planning cycle. This calls for a revised and scaled-down role for traditional capital budgeting and expenditure analysis in the resource allocation process.

In companies with no corporate planning procedures in place as a strategic decision-making tool the resource allocation process will be heavily focused around the capital budgeting process and the approval of expenditure budgets. Capital budgeting's role in such a situation would be as the central vehicle for the allocation of funds to investments in plants and machinery. The core unit to be evaluated would be each capital request proposal, say a project which involves a new plant or a new machine. Traditional analytical tools from the capital budgeting body of knowledge would be brought to bear in order to judge the desirability of the project. Prominent techniques include time-adjusted hurdle rates of return on investment such as net present value or internal rate of return as well as the simpler pay-back method. These ratings may be further adjusted for the riskiness of the project. They may also be classified in terms of size, i.e., whether they exceed the limits of managerial discretion associated with the manager who is deciding on the project. Finally, an investment which, for instance, is an essential replacement part in a large piece of continuous process machinery might be treated differently from an investment which falls within an entirely new area.

The expenditure budget's role in a situation with no strategic planning would be to provide certain limits for the levels of discretionary expenditures of various kinds that each department might spend each year. A vast number of more or less elaborate techniques exist for the development of expenditure budgets too. Typically, however, less analytical efforts tend to go into the resource allocations of discretionary expenditures than what is the typical case for capital budgeting decisions.

Without elaborating further, it is clear that there exists a well-established and widely accepted body of traditional methods for aiding in the resource allocation decisions within the firm.

With the advent of strategic resource allocation's role as corporate management's major device for influencing and reshaping the strategic direction of the firm, we have argued that the roles of capital budgeting and the expense budget should be seen in a different light. However, even though a company may have adopted corporate planning and in principle is allocating resources to major strategic programs, it may be easier said than done to modify accordingly the traditional well-established systems for allocating capital investments and discretionary expenditures. Thus, it is conceivable that a strategic program which has been approved through the planning process might be frustrated or even halted in its implementation due to delays in the appropriation of particular projects which are vital parts of the strategic program but which do not yield the necessary hurdle rate when taken out of strategic context for appropriation according to the classical procedures. Similarly, necessary allocations to some functions' capital expenditure budgets may be insufficient for the functions to carry out their intended strategic roles. Needless to say, serious disturbances in the implementation of strategic direction might result from the phenomenon that elements of a strategic program, be it expense elements or capital investments, are being evaluated separately and according to nonstrategic criteria.

There might be several reasons for this, two of which we shall discuss here. The most nasty problem exists when friction between a strategic resource allocation mode and a classical resource allocation mode can be largely attributed to a power struggle between different groups of management, often associated with changes in generations of managers. Typically some executives, for instance, the board of directors and/or the staff executive heading the office evaluating capital requests (usually the controller or the financial vice president), have retained considerable power as a result of their heavy involvement in the capital budgeting process. Similarly the staff executive heading up the analysis of the expense budgets (for instance, the controller) would have considerable power over the allocations of discretionary expenditures. These groups might implicitly or explicitly resist redefinition of their roles in the resource allocation process, particularly if they feel that a new group of managers has increasing influence.

Another source of friction might simply be due to lack of appreciation of and attention to this as a problem. It is easier to add routines to the management system than it is to dismantle or modify administrative routines. This is a reflection of the common lack of attention for managing the evolutionary direction of the management system so that its various elements continue to be consistent although noticeable changes or additions may have been made to parts of the system over time. (We shall discuss an approach toward managing the evolution of systems in Chapter Six.) One difficult issue in managing the management system is how to run the old and the new resource allocation systems in parallel until the new system has been debugged and is functioning with a reasonable reliability. A second issue is determining exactly what the modified role of the old resource allocation system should be. Both issues merit some further discussion.

It is clearly a complicated and far-reaching decision to implement a corporate planning system. Such a system cannot be expected to function overnight. Not only will there be a large number of formats, routines, and communication channels that will have to be developed. A heavy burden might also fall on the operating managers in learning and internalizing how to work within such a system. It is not likely that every aspect of the system can be operationalized at once or that all managers involved will know how to use the system immediately. Thus, a period of learning and fine tuning will be normal. There will also be considerable learning associated with the gradually increased recognition of the strategic position of the company and its parts; going through the planning exercise will probably heighten the strategic understanding and allow it to be stated in more explicit operational terms. Given these considerations it seems necessary to maintain the traditional resource allocation system in its original form for some time in parallel with the strategic planning system. Efforts should be made, however, during the execution of capital budgeting to reconcile the emerging resource allocation decisions with the strategic programming efforts. If, for instance, a capital budgeting project is proposed which is not part of a strategic program at all, then this should be resolved on an ad hoc basis. Similarly, if the necessary capital for an investment which is an integral element of a strategic program is turned down through the capital budgeting process, then this should also be resolved on an ad hoc basis. An analogous argument can be made with regard to the allocation of discretionary expenditures. The critical issue is to force reconciliation between the old and the new resource allocation procedures, so that the importance of corporate planning is underscored early. Even though planning might still be in its infancy, every attempt should be made to stress that it is going to have effects on how strategic resources are being used within the company.

The modified roles of the capital budgeting system and the discretionary expenditure budget should be seen as vehicles for fine-tuning the major resource allocation thrusts decided upon in principle during the strategic programming stage. Subsequent to this, the resolution of many smaller resource allocation issues typically will remain. Another important role would be as a safety mechanism to detect unrealistic assumptions behind strategic program decisions. Modifications and reassessment of a strategic program might be appropriate if it turns out through the subsequent more detailed capital budgeting process that, for instance, the assumed general level for the cost estimate does not hold. Needless to say, with the modified roles of the capital budgeting and the discretionary expenditure budget, senior management's time involvement with these tasks should diminish substantially and instead shift toward the strategic programming decision-making process as this becomes the major resource allocation vehicle, replacing the traditional procedures.

choice of key variables in budget

Let us now turn to a second implementation issue during the budgeting stage, namely, choosing appropriate and relevant variables for developing budgets, so-called key variables. Such a set of variables might easily be quite different from the traditional all-dollar set of variables commonly found in budgets.[8]

An operating budget will typically be broken down for each department. It will be advantageous for control purposes to structure the budget according to this breakdown. Dollar variables will predominate in such budgets, now and then supplemented by nondollar variables which measure the physical activity levels that provide the basis for the budget. It will, however, also be useful to reconcile the departmental budgets into program budgets, reflecting the nature of the strategic program pattern which the operating budgets are supposed to represent (see Exhibit 2-4). This will enable management to identify the function of each department's activity intended for each of the strategic programs. It is therefore important to be able to break down the budgetary data according to such definitions so that reconciliation with strategic programs becomes possible. All departmental operating budget items will of course not be reconcilable as part of strategic programs, since a significant proportion of the funds will be nondiscretionary, i.e., be in the operating budgets only.

Another set of nondollar variables also becomes important, however. This is related to developing milestones for the progress toward particular strategic programs and for determining whether the progress is satisfactory given the level of resources spent. Not only will this call for the development of a set of operational milestone variables, such as measurement of deadlines, attainment of certain product or process qualities, development of a distribution network, and so on. It will also be necessary to measure not only the rate of use of funds as a strategic resource but probably even more critically the utilization of one's critical managers on strategic programs. In our experience this critical issue is often overlooked, and strategic programs are delayed as well as more expensive to carry out as a result. In line with this there should finally be a measure of whether funds for each category of strategic resources are being spent on a particular strategic project as assumed and not, say, on overspending to bail out another project or on short-term performance boosting. Thus, physical measures are needed to ensure that the timing of the spending on each project is in line and that there is neither overspending nor underspending.

Let us finally discuss how the operating budget might also be utilized as a shorter-term indicator of one's progress toward objectives and goals. Let us, as an example, consider a particular business division. For the division management it would be necessary to consider and interpret financial data in the light of what is happening with the strategic position of the business. For instance, a particular set of operating budget figures might be reasonable enough when the business attractiveness level for this business is assumed to stay the same. However, if the business attractiveness can be assumed to increase significantly, say, as the result of a general increased growth in sales of the products of this business, then the operating budget figures might be interpreted in a less favorable light. Or, alternatively, if the general growth rate is expected to slow down, then the operating budget might be seen as quite favorable, given these adverse circumstances. Thus, it is necessary to interpret budgetary performance figures according to changes in the levels of business attractiveness. Hence, a relevant measure of business attractiveness should be part of the budget. One such measure might be the rate of growth of the business; if one assumes a certain growth rate, then the operating budget should be expected to take on certain values.

Similarly, the competitive strength of the business itself should be specified in order to state a meaningful set of expected budget performance levels. For instance, the market share of one's own business might be increased in an effort to improve one's own competitive strength. This might be reflected in a reasonably moderate budgeting operating result. If one's market share is allowed to fall, on the other hand, then the operating budget should be interpreted in this light, with an expected relatively strong near-term budgeted performance. Figures for changes in one's own business's competitive strength should therefore be part of the budget in order to peg the budget to a particular level of competitive strength position. Nondollar measures of competitive strength level other than market share might of course be relevant, such as productivity measures (again relative to particular competitors, however).

Finally, the budget of a business should be judged relative to changes in the relationships with other organizational units, so that it can be determined whether the level of consolidation attractiveness that the business is enjoying is the same or changing. If, for instance, overhead burden significantly changes as a result of large changes in the activity levels of other business units, then this should be reflected in the budget.

Some businesses include adjustments for inflation and currency changes in their budgets. From a strategic management point of view this has two aspects. First, there is the issue of comparability over time. When such comparability is needed for the development of strategic plans, then the adjustments should be made; this is normally not a major issue when it comes to corporate planning. However, when inflation and/or currency changes have strategic effects, then these should be included. For instance, devaluation of an export-oriented company's home currency might significantly improve the competitive position of the company. We shall discuss further the issue of modifying the planning system to encompass a multinational situational setting in Chapter Six.

In summary, an important implementation problem seems to be that the operating budget often is built up exclusively around traditional internally oriented variables, excluding nondollar variables for activity-level measurements, and that nondollar variables for relating spending to the progress of strategic programs and for normalizing the operating budget for changes in business attractiveness position, competitive strength, and consolidation attractiveness changes are missing. The budget's role is the tip of the iceberg in terms of what can be done to implement the strategic programs during the coming year to proceed toward achieving one's objectives and goals. As such, the budget's role is primarily to facilitate integration and coordination of the organizational activities with a clear internal focus. However, the variables chosen must have the broader relevance to ensure that the budget becomes the culmination of the narrowing down of strategic options, i.e., is consistent with the broader contextual limits given through the objectives and strategic programs.

accountability for budgets

Let us now change our discussion to a third implementation issue associated with the budgeting stage, which might be analyzed together with the integration of the so-called management by objectives (MBO) approach in the corporate planning process. One important aspect of the budgeting process is that each manager should be in a position to identify clearly the tasks that will fall to him as a consequence of carrying out the budget. A related requirement is that each manager internalize and associate himself with the relevant part of the budget; next year's operation should make sense to him to the extent that he is indeed motivated to move toward its fulfillment. There are several ways to reinforce this. The major factor is of course the participation of managers in the corporate planning process itself, which has involved several levels of management in the development of a consistent set of corporate objectives as well as strategic programs, i.e., has provided a basis throughout the organization for understanding the broader strategic implications of the budget through participation in the previous stages. The budgeting stage with its culmination of the narrowing down should therefore result in a clear task and rationale identification for each manager with his part of a coordinated corporate-wide action plan. A desirable effect of the process, therefore, is the likely development of broad-based managerial commitment to a particular strategic direction, through inviting the managers to participate in the process in a manner which will make sense to them.

To reinforce this sense of commitment even further, it might be useful to tie this added sense of direction in with an MBO scheme. A first step in this direction is to have meetings between each manager and his superior to review what the budget implies in terms of an action program for him during the coming year. Each manager relevant to the implementation of the budget in the organizational hierarchy should go through this. This might provide a basis for evaluation of each manager's short-term job performance after the year is over to underscore the longer-range strategic significance of near-term performance. Management incentives might be tied to such an evaluation; we shall discuss this later.

One implementation problem with respect to the above is that the budgeting process may not emphasize enough the action-oriented task implications for each manager. It is not only necessary that the budget has been developed with enough detail to facilitate this but also that near-term action responsibility on the part of a manager can be reconciled with longer-term program responsibility. Failure to develop this degree of specificity in the budgets is often an indication that the entire corporate planning process is not functioning as expected. To ameliorate this, attention should be focused on cycles one and two of the process to determine whether the outputs of these cycles are specific enough to be useful as well as whether preliminary patterns of management accountability have been established. Addressing the above question is a critical check of whether the corporate planning process has been functioning so far, i.e., that the stages of the process which are concerned with identification and narrowing down of strategic opportunities are operational.

An implementation problem that is smaller and much easier to handle stems from the fact that the MBO approach in many companies often tends to be detached from the strategic planning effort. This might actually result in dysfunction unless modified to be consistent with the rest of the strategic management process. MBO might have been introduced well before planning to create more of an action-oriented task emphasis to the traditional budgeting. As such, MBO would have a highly bottom-up-dominated nature, with lower-level managers playing major, roles and with heavy emphasis on behavioral/job evaluation aspects. Of course, it could not be expected that the MBO process would bring out an adequate general management strategic context for such task identification. With the advent of a corporate planning approach what is needed is the modification of the MBO approach so that it can be executed within the necessary strategic context and thereby become a useful reinforcement of the strategic management process.

We have discussed a total of ten implementation issues that relate to the three first stages of the strategic planning process. All these issues are concerned with aspects of how to establish strategic direction for the company and/or its parts. Thus, they deal with how a company might prepare itself to improve the pattern of strategic resource allocation before it has to act. Any of the issues discussed might constitute stumbling blocks against the development of strategic direction. We shall now change focus and discuss four additional implementation issues, fundamentally different in nature from the former in that they deal with aspects of cycles four and five of the planning process, i.e., post facto concerns for modifying and improving one's strategic direction.

Implementation Pitfalls and Problems
During the Monitoring Stage

We shall discuss two implementation problems that seem to be common when it comes to an effective monitoring of progress toward the fulfillment of the strategies decided upon during the previous three cycles of the corporate planning process. These issues relate to taking a mechanistic approach toward monitoring actual results relative to plans without proper reflection on the specific nature of the phenomenon being monitored, its predictability, the strategic response potential at hand, and the relative importance of the phenomenon in a risk/return sense. A second implementation concern is that the monitoring often tends to overemphasize short-term progress, with little or no regard for the monitoring of progress toward long-term objectives. We shall discuss each of these issues in turn.[9]

tailor-made monitoring to the phenomenon at hand

We recall from our discussion of the concept of risk/return as part of the corporate portfolio analysis in Chapter Three that it is meaningful to consider the degree to which we are able to predict a particular phenomenon as well as the extent to which we are able to respond in a discretionary fashion to the phenomenon. We isolated four environmental factor archetypes according to differences along the above two dimensions, each factor having a different degree of risk associated with it. However, the diminished risk associated with a strategy which is heavily dominated by an environmental factor that can be reasonably well predicted and which also can be responded to will not automatically be enjoyed; we have to carry out an adequate monitoring in order to be able to predict the factor, and we also have to prepare the form of ameliorating response we might want to take. Thus, the approach that is taken to monitor performance is critical in containing strategic risks to the levels we assumed when we developed and approved the strategy. Given the different environmental archetypes, we shall benefit from employing a situational monitoring/control systems approach, contingent on the degree of predictability and the degree of discretionary response potential. It will thus be a major requirement to the successful implementation of the monitoring stage that a too general overly standardized monitoring approach be avoided.

For the monitoring of a phenomenon which has a relatively high degree of predictability potential and also a relatively high degree of discretionary response potential, an approach that we shall label *steering control* is the one most appropriate. This implies that forecasting of environmental phenomena will be done with enough frequency and detail to predict changes, if any, with a reasonable degree of accuracy. This in turn allows for a relatively immediate response as soon as the predicted deviation emerges and permits carrying out the corrective action before the strategic program actually has been completed; this reduces the potential for adverse effects by making corrections in time or increasing the potential for favorable effects by taking action in time to go after a particular opportunity. Because the nature of the corrective action typically will be rather incremental, it is analogous to a self-correcting positive feedback phenomenon; it is being *steered* toward the target through the monitoring process.

Our capability to carry out this highly advantageous before-the-fact steering control depends above all on the potential for reasonably accurate forecasting. However, in many situations forecasting an environmental phenomenon will be virtually impossible, even though we might have been able to respond if we had some reliable forecasting information. In such a situation we shall propose a *contingency control* approach. This implies that for each of several alternative outcomes of such an unpredictable environmental phenomenon a particular managerial response is developed. The monitoring function then consists of observing when a change actually takes place and as rapidly as possible executing the appropriate predetermined response pattern. A strategy which relies on this type of environmental phenomenon is more risky than one that relies on a more predictable phenomenon; however, a contingency control monitoring approach which lays out prepared response patterns beforehand can at least significantly reduce the risk.

We may also be in a position where there is little we can do to respond to development of a particular environmental phenomenon; even though we might be able to predict the development of an environmental factor, we are unable to take corrective actions after we have committed ourselves to the particular strategy. We shall apply an *anticipative go–no go control* approach in monitoring this class of environmental phenomena. This implies that we might be able to scale the strategic program activity up or down or abandon the program altogether; however, we might be able to reduce the consequences of an adverse development (or increase the potential for benefiting from a positive development) if we take advantage of the early warning that the relatively high degree of predictability can give us. Thus, this monitoring approach implies that ample attention should be put on forecasting and that the necessary reactive managerial consequences for the strategic program in question should be faced up to at once.

The final situational setting implies that the key environmental phenomenon influencing a strategy can neither be well predicted nor easily responded to. In such an instance we might adopt a *post facto go–no go control* approach. Given that there is little we can do through monitoring in terms of taking corrective actions to contain the risk associated with a strategy, there is not the same compelling reason for allocating time and money to the monitoring function in this case. We might therefore conclude that monitoring should be kept to a minimum or abandoned, except for the following two secondary benefits. First, to register through monitoring that an environmental event has taken place which is different from that assumed in the plans will allow for reassessment of the corporation's portfolio strategy in case the effects are serious enough. Second, through careful monitoring we might be able to learn and improve our judgment so that we can make sounder strategic choices the next time around.

A related benefit from the fact that we have been able to designate different modes of monitoring for phenomena with different risks is that we also may make use of this to set guidelines for when to pass on information and decision responsibility upwards in the organization versus when to carry out corrective actions at the decentralized level. A strategy which might be monitored primarily through a properly developed steering control approach can to a much larger extent than a more risky strategy be left in the hands of subordinate management in terms of discretionary responsibility for execution. Thus, the bottom-up flow of monitoring signals in cycle four should also be tailored to the nature of the monitoring task.

The contingency approach toward monitoring just discussed seems unfortunately to be far from the state of the art of implementation of the monitoring function. Instead, much of the monitoring tends to be standardized according to principles that do not substantially allow for differentiation between the monitoring tasks at hand or for tailoring centralized versus decentralized responses to monitoring data. This emphasis reflects a tradition of making use of the budgets as simplified tools of measuring by the end of a given period whether an organizational subunit has actually achieved its results or not. This stick-and-carrot approach clearly puts too little emphasis on developing innovative strategy-based monitoring tailor-made to various subunits of the organization. An effective monitoring approach represents an essential element in the implementation of strategies, providing an opportunity to modify strategic programs in time and thereby reemphasizing an element of responsiveness and alertness to critical factors outside the firm in order to reduce and contain risk. It is a serious implementation problem that the monitoring function tends to be so deficient as an element in our strategic decision-making context, particularly in that opportunistic responsiveness is quashed and unnecessarily high risk taking will be the result.

near-term monitoring only

Let us now turn to a second and highly related implementation issue which has particular relevance to the monitoring stage, namely, the need to monitor not only short-term performance but also longer-term performance. We recall that the budget should represent the iceberg in terms of next year's action plan toward the fulfillment of agreed-upon longer-term objectives, goals, and strategic programs, the tip of the iceberg. However, as we also discussed, budgets are not complete mappings of strategic programs or objectives, not the least because they represent only near-term aspects of the longer-term strategic direction. Thus, monitoring of budget fulfillment does not necessarily imply that we are progressing as intended toward the fulfillment of strategies; hence, it is necessary to monitor separately progress toward the fulfillment of particular objectives and strategic programs.

When it comes to strategic programs, milestones should be established for the progress review and reevaluation of each, as already discussed. Separate monitoring should be done for the longer-term progress of each of these programs. Similarly, when it comes to business objectives, the progress along a transition path toward achieving a particular new long-term position for one's own competitive strength, say, by increasing market share, should be monitored. Changes in business attractiveness and consolidation attractiveness should also be monitored. We have already discussed the choice of appropriate variables— monetary as well as nonmonetary—for facilitating the monitoring of long-term performance in addition to short-term performance. We have also discussed the need to monitor key environmental factors, particularly in connection with the monitoring of progress toward the fulfillment of business as well as corporate objectives. The implementation issue of providing for both longer-term and shorter-term monitoring is related to these issues already discussed and will not be elaborated further here.

The nature of the so-called time span for control needs to be raised at this point. The typical control approach consists of four interrelated steps: (1) the establishing of a prior performance target or output standard; (2) the measurement of actual position output performance relative to this standard; (3) analysis of eventual deviations between actual, particular output and the previously set output standard; (4) execution of modifying actions, if deemed necessary and/or feasible. For the control approach to be useful, however, it must be a requirement that the time span between when a prior standard is being set and the posterior output performance is being measured not be too long. If too long a time goes by, it will no longer be meaningful to analyze deviations and carry out timely corrective actions.

For instance, if we establish as a prior standard a goal to reach a particular competitive strength position ten years into the future, it will not become possible to see whether we actually achieved the goal until ten years later. By that time, however, it may typically be too late to carry out eventual modifying actions that might have been at our option. To observe the actual output this long time later may have little more than curiosity value.

For instances with long time spans of control, which typically will be the case when we are dealing with objectives and strategic programs, it will therefore be necessary to modify the control approach. Two useful modes of modification have implicitly been eluded to during the control-related discussions in this and other sections. We shall restate these modifications more formally here.

One useful and obvious approach in dealing with this will be to monitor progress toward the target in terms of intermediate, incremental steps, such as whether we are achieving milestones or interim goals. This implies that we must make the following two modifications of the basic control approach: (1) The prior performance target must be broken down into intermediate performance targets; (2) the measurement of actual posterior output performance will be relative to the intermediate performance targets, so that the time span of control thereby can be reduced.

Unfortunately this modified control approach still frequently has serious shortcomings when it comes to dealing with control within the context of objectives and strategic programs. Take, for instance, our previous example, where we have established a ten-year market share goal and translated this into interim goals as well. Even though we may be progressing as planned by meeting the interim goals on target, we are frequently still not able to determine whether the final goal itself is valid. Thus, even though we are able to control our progress in a certain direction, this control approach does not put sufficient light on whether the basic direction itself is an appropriate one. Again, there is a need to modify our control approach.

The critical environmental factors that we have identified as the basis for our risk assessment approach and which establish the basis for different control modes in fact contribute a set of environmental premises that the various objectives or strategic programs will be resting on. If one or more of these environmental factors changes in a different direction than assumed, then there will be a need to reexamine whether the objective or strategic program in question is still valid. Thus, to reexamine the continued relevance of basic strategic direction, we need to control how the underlying assumptions are holding up.

The steps of the basic control approach thus need to be modified as follows: (1) The critical environmental assumptions behind a specific objective or strategic program must be delineated—these serve as prior standards; (2) the monitoring will emphasize whether there are extraordinary changes in the prior standards set for each environmental factor—thus, we are *no longer* monitoring an output measure, a dramatic departure from the basic control mode model; (3) analysis of extraordinary deviations with respect to any of the critical environmental assumptions must be performed; and (4) modification, if possible, of the objective or strategic program in question must be carried out, so as to reflect the new, emerging environmental premises.

We need to make use of the basic control mode as well as both the modification approaches outlined when it comes to carrying out any balanced control function. The one aspect of this most often overlooked seems to be the lack of emphasis on controlling critical environmental assumptions.

One final aspect of the implementation of monitoring long-term progress relates to the attention that senior management puts on the interpretation of these monitoring signals relative to the attention being paid to the interpretation of short-term results. There is a tendency among some senior managers to pay inordinate attention to short-term performance deviation problems, going from one fire-fighting situation to another. For lack of time (or mental energy) relatively little or no attention will be paid to monitoring signals that indicate more fundamental weaknesses with the general strategic path. Also, pressures toward showing consistent short-term performance, a feature which tends to be highly appreciated by the stock market, might diminish senior management's attention to long-term corrective actions. We are of course not claiming here that short-term performance should be ignored. Rather, our position is that monitoring of both long-term and short-term results should be attempted. The issue of how much relative emphasis should be put on short-term versus long-term performance fulfillment attention is a question that will depend on a company's particular situation, and we shall discuss this further in Chapter Five, which deals with tailor-making the corporate planning system's design.

Implementation Pitfalls and Problems
During the Management Incentivating Stage

Let us now discuss two implementation problems that relate to the fifth and final stage of the corporate planning process, the determination of management incentives. The first implementation issue here is that the granting of management incentives should reflect the nature of the strategic tasks at hand. If a particular strategic success is due largely to environmental effects outside the control of a manager, then he should not receive additional compensation for this; if, on the other hand, the success was largely attributable to the manager's strategic insight, then this should be reflected in the way he is compensated. The second implementation issue in connection with the final cycle is to pay attention not only to incentives that honor short-term performance excellence but to strike a balance between these and those that honor long-term performance excellence. Let us discuss each of these two issues in turn.

strategic focus of managerial incentives

The nature of the strategic task at hand should be reflected in the incentive system, so that managers can be motivated in a way which facilitates congruence between the strategies to be pursued by the organizational unit and the manager's personal goals. Let us illustrate this issue by considering how to motivate the manager of a strategy center as an example.

The nature of the strategic task facing the manager might, for instance, vary significantly with the type of life cycle that the strategy center's business is in. For instance, the major determinants to success for a strategy center which is in its early growth stage are probably adaptive entrepreneurial moves to develop an effective niche in the marketplace, breadth and type of products, channels of distribution, pricing and financing policies, and so on. To a large extent success is likely to depend on the manager in charge of the strategy center. He might be further motivated by receiving a relatively large share of his compensation as a variable function of his organization's performance. The emphasis on the key role of this manager may further be underscored by giving the major part of the incentive to him as an individual and not to the broader group of managers in the strategy center.

If, on the other hand, we have a strategy center which is positioned within a business which is considerably more mature, the keys to strategic success will probably be different from those in our growth-business strategy center example. Now the success is more likely to hinge on outperforming one's competitors in terms of cost efficiency, a smooth production and distribution process, lean policies for purchasing and inventories, maintenance of stable levels of product quality, and so on. In this case the managers working as a team rather than individualistic performance is likely to be more critical. Thus, incentives should be focused more on the performance of the management team as a group. However, a relatively larger number of factors outside the team's control will probably also dictate performance in this case—above all, the strategy center's built-up position of business strength over past years. Thus, a larger fraction of the executives' compensation should probably be considered as fixed; the incentives should probably only apply to a relatively small proportion of the overall compensation. In line with this, a strategic emphasis on managerial incentives might involve a tailor-making to the given situation; individual versus group incentives, as well as relatively high emphasis on fixed compensation versus compensation variable with performance.

However, we see that incentives should reflect the nature of the strategic task of a particular business, depending on the life-cycle stage that the business is in. There will typically be an additional consideration that might further modify the nature of the strategic task, namely, the extent to which the management of a business is in a position to predict and respond to the development of key environmental factors. If a manager has little or no opportunity to predict significant developments in the environment that might dramatically influence his strategic performance, then his incentives should reflect this: A relatively smaller share of the incentives should be variable, so that effects from unpredictable fluctuations can be eliminated. Similarly, if there is little the manager can do in terms of discretionary reaction to environmental factors, then, too, the variable fraction of the incentives should be relatively smaller; it would be meaningless to develop incentives that are not the function of discretionary managerial action. Thus, incentive systems should be applied only in situations where opportunities exist for forecasting events external to the business and/or for discretionary managerial responses.

Unfortunately, in practice there seems to be relatively little reflection regarding the nature of the strategic tasks in the design and implementation of managerial incentive schemes. The incentive systems often seem to be designed as a general set of rules that apply across the company, with no regard to whether strategic success will be heavily dependent on variable factors outside the control of the managers or not. Whether a manager has a relatively large or limited potential for influencing his strategy does not seem to be reflected in most incentive schemes. Worse than this, in several instances there is no apparent tie between the incentive scheme and the strategy fulfillment performance of managers; rather, informally set incentives, often with a strong element of nepotism, tend to be common. This lack of emphasis on the reinforcement of strategic direction setting when developing management incentives may not only be an important barrier to the implementation of strategic planning as such. Worse, it is even conceivable that the implicit thrust of managerial motivation might be counterstrategic, thus providing even more serious countermomentum against the implementation of planned strategic direction.

balance between incentives for long-term and short-term performance

This brings us to another implementation problem, namely, that incentive schemes do not tend to reach a reasonable balance between motivating toward short-term versus long-term performance. Unfortunately, in most cases the emphasis seems to be heavily skewed toward appreciation of short-term performance in the incentives schemes. For instance, year-end profit performance, particularly when it exceeds the budget, tends to count heavily. This is likely to introduce a short-term performance maximizing bias into a company, with possibilities of dangerous nonstrategic suboptimizations that might erode the potential for long-term success. One of the more common objections to including long-term performance fulfillment criteria in management's incentive schemes is that these schemes must be based on reasonably objective measures; thus, it is often deemed to be too subjective to assess a manager's contribution toward long-term performance. However, with the advent of the set of variables and measures that has been devised during the previous four cycles of the strategic planning scheme, there is a much better basis for carrying out assessments of longer-term performance; hence, this concern should no longer be seen as a major objection.

We remember that when it came to controlling the soundness of basic strategic direction we needed to partly abandon our reliance on monitoring output performance solely. Instead, we also had to monitor the continued relevance of critical environmental assumptions. This will have implications for management incentives. Normally, incentives will be based on the attainment of a particular output performance, such as meeting this year's interim goal toward a particular long-term objective. However, we would typically also want to include in the incentives scheme for those managers who are responsible for a strategy an inducement to examine whether the strategic direction in question is still valid. As we have seen, we can no longer rely on output measures to facilitate this but rather must focus on the continued relevance of the critical assumptions underlying the objective.

A part of a manager's incentives package should thus be modified to incorporate such a close concern for the strategic direction. We might do this as follows. Partly, this fraction of a manager's incentives should be a function of the extent to which he has been able to come up with a robust set of critical environmental factors; if it subsequently turns out that he had failed to identify several critical changes, the manager may simply not have been thinking hard enough about developing a viable strategy. However, whether a set of key environmental factors will continue to be valid will of course to at least some extent be outside the control of the manager, given impacts from environmental changes. Thus, this part of the manager's incentives should partly also be based on how well the manager is able to cope with a change in a critical environmental factor, so as to motivate him to face an environmental change in a timely way, carry out proper analysis of ameliorating options, and propose an eventual plan of action for modifying the strategy.

Another factor which traditionally has detracted from emphasizing long-term performance as a criterion in the incentive schemes is based on the observation that the frequency of job rotations among managers is so high that it will be virtually impossible to hold a manager accountable for longer-term performance. This is a valid objection, indeed a fundamental potential obstacle to the implementation of a strategic mode of managing the firm. One approach to reducing this problem would be to cut down on the frequency of managerial job rotations. Excessive job rotations may in many companies indicate a lack of thorough planning of key management resources and may also be seen as a symptom of underestimation of this obstacle's role as a barrier to the implementation of strategic planning. The epitome of this may be a rapid assignment of a succession of managers to try to turn around a troubled business, instead of attempting to come to grips directly with the basic strategic problems facing the business. In any case, rapid job rotation seems to have become a part of the management style of some companies, probably with more negative than positive benefits. However, a conscious attempt to reduce the frequency of job rotation of course does not mean that one should have to go to the other extreme.

Some companies systematically reassess managers' key strategic decisions even after the responsibility for a manager's business domain has been transferred to his successor. Such a dossier of a manager's back history of substantive input on strategic decisions and plans might be a useful tool in ameliorating some of the dysfunctional effects of job rotation by reserving a sense of long-term accountability for strategy fulfillment. The administration of such a file would of course have to be done carefully, both in terms of who should have access to it and the right of each manager concerned to include his point of view in the file. Probably the most useful purpose of such a file system is to have on record the backgrounds for the business successes; credit is very easily given to the manager who happened to be at the helm at the time when a business experienced a successful break and not to the managers who laid the foundation through long-term strategic insights.

Lack of proper balance between longer-term and shorter-term criteria for performance as the basis for managerial incentive schemes provides an important implementation barrier to strategic planning, above all because of the decline of the important opportunity to bolster planned strategic direction that this represents. While this implementation problem as well as the other one discussed in the context of the final cycle of the planning system may be seen as relatively indirect barriers to the implementation of corporate planning, they are still important. Proper integration of management incentives with the rest of the planning system can provide a significant reinforcement of the intended strategic thrust.

Summary

In this chapter we have laid out the initial issues in our discussion of how to implement corporate planning systems. Rather than embarking on a contingency-based discussion at this point, we found it useful to discuss 14 different types of implementation pitfalls and problems that tend to be common when adopting the three-by-five conceptual approach to corporate planning. The issues raised here should serve as a first checklist for the implementation of corporate planning; without at least being aware of, or even better, having attempted to resolve these issues, it is more or less futile to expect planning to be effective. Having tackled the problems outlined in this chapter does not, however, guarantee success in the corporate planning function; additional tailor-making of the system to the particular situational setting at hand will have to be done—the topic of Chapter Five.

Let us briefly review the 14 areas of immediate concern when implementing a planning system. During the objectives-setting stage there *I* were five issues that seemed particularly common: the active and open involvement of the chief executive and senior management during the first step of the planning process; the penetrating assessment of business opportunities by each of the divisions through open-ended assessment of key environmental factors rather than through a mode of extrapolation; the mode of review of planning inputs by the corporate management, emphasizing a portfolio approach whereby each business is assessed in relation to the others; the limited and informal involvement by the functional departments during the objectives-setting cycle—instead, this aspect of planning is predominantly a general management key concern; and the need to make decisions to narrow down options in order to close planning gaps.

It should be noted that two of the issues discussed in connection with the implementation problems of the objectives-setting cycle have general applicability in all five cycles of the planning process. Thus, we should always be concerned with stressing the need for a corporate-level portfolio review of bottom-up planning inputs as well as the issue of closing the planning gaps during the various stages of the planning process by executing the necessary decisions. For practical reasons, we have found it useful to discuss these implementation issues when they first occurred, namely, during the objectives-setting stage.

During the strategic programming stage we discussed two common *II* implementation concerns, namely, that the development of strategic program alternatives is typically cross-functional and that when aggregating and choosing between strategic program alternatives there should be consistency with the objectives set during the previous stage. *III* During the budgeting stage we raised three areas of implementation concern: that strategic resources should be allocated to the strategic programs and not to the proposals of the capital budgeting process or to the departments' discretionary expenditure budgets; that the budget should be seen as an action plan reflecting next year's intended progress toward the fulfillment of strategic programs, objectives, and goals and hence should be built up around key variables; and that the budget should assign clear responsibility for execution to the relevant managers, consistent with the underlying objectives, goals, and strategic programs. During the monitoring stage there were two issues of particular concern: that the monitoring task should be strategic in outlook, i.e., have a focus on the forecasting of a given environmental phenomenon as well as the strategic response potential; also, that the monitoring task should reach a balance between a long-term primary external focus and a shorter-term primary internal focus. Finally, during the management incentive-setting stage we raised the issues that the specific nature of the strategic task should be reflected in the management incentive system's execution and that the incentives should reach a balance between emphasizing shorter-term and longer-term performance fulfillment.

Having by now completed our task of identifying and discussing a set of general planning implementation and pitfall issues, which seem to be more or less relevant to all corporate planning settings, our next step will be to discuss how to approach the tailor-making of a planning system so that it possesses an appropriate set of capabilities to meet the particular needs for planning that a given company might face. We shall discuss this in Chapter Five.

NOTES

1. This chapter follows a structure which in most instances is similar to that reported in Peter Lorange, "Implementation of Strategic Planning Systems," in *Advances in Operations Management*, ed. Arnoldo C. Hax (Amsterdam: North-Holland, 1978), pp. 99-116. For other discussions of pitfalls and problems, see E. Kirby Warren, *Long-Range Planning: The Executive Viewpoint* (Englewood Cliffs, N.J.: Prentice-Hall, 1966); Xavier Gilbert and Peter Lorange, "Five Pillars for Your Planning," *European Business* no. 33 (Fall 1974), 82-90; Gunnar Eliasson, *Business Economic Planning* [New York: Wiley (also Swedish Industrial Publications), 1976]; and George A. Steiner, *Strategic Managerial Planning* (Oxford: Planning Research Institute, 1977).

2. See H. Koontz, "Making Strategic Planning Work," *Business Horizons*, 19, no. 2 (April 1976), 34-47; and James Brian Quinn, "Strategic Goals: Process and Politics," *Sloan Management Review*, 19, no. 1 (Fall 1977), 21-38.

3. For good discussions of aspects of opportunistic, adaptive planning, see William W. Simmons, *Exploratory Planning: Briefs and Practices* (Oxford: Planning Executives Institute, 1977); James B. Whittaker, *Strategic Planning in a Rapidly Changing Environment* (Lexington, Mass.: Heath, 1978); and Ian H. Wilson, "Corporate Environments of the Future: Planning for Major Change," *Special Study No. 61* (New York: Presidents Association, 1976).

4. A fundamental aspect of closing the loop will be to review the consistency of the tentative objectives with the critical strategic assumptions that should be underlying the objectives; for an approach to this, see James R. Emshoff, and Ian I. Mitrof "On Strategic Assumption-Making: A Dialectical Approach to Policy and Planning," *Academy of Management Review*, 4, no. 1 (Jan. 1979).

5. See H. Igor Ansoff and John M. Steward, "Strategies for a Technology-Based Business," *Harvard Business Review*, 45 (Nov.–Dec. 1967), 71-83; Richard F. Vancil, "Better Management of Corporate Development," *Harvard Business Review*, 50 (Sept.–Oct. 1972), 53-62; and Alan R. Fusfeld, "How To Put Technology into Corporate Planning," *Technology Review* (May 1978).

6. See E. E. Carter, "The Behavioral Theory of the Firm and Top-Level Corporate Decisions," *Administrative Science Quarterly*, 16 (1971), 413-428; Peter A. Phyrr, *Zero-Base Budgeting: A Practical Management Tool for Evaluating Expenses* (New York: Wiley, 1973); Paul J. Stonich, *Zero-Base Planning and Budgeting* (Homewood, Ill.: Dow Jones-Irwin, 1977); and Sudeep Anand, "Resource Allocation at the Corporate Level of the Firm: A Methodological and Empirical Investigation of the Dimensions Used by Managers for Evaluation of Investments" (unpublished Ph.D. thesis, M.I.T., 1977).

7. See Norman A. Berg, "The Allocation of Strategic Funds in a Large Diversified Company" (unpublished D.B.A. thesis, Harvard Business School, 1963); R. W. Ackerman, "Organization and the Investment Process: A Comparative Study" (unpublished D.B.A. thesis, Harvard University, 1968); Joseph L. Bower, *Managing the Resource Allocation Process: A Study of Corporate Planning and Investment* (Boston: Division of Research, Harvard Business School, 1970); E. Eugene Carter, *Portfolio Aspects of Corporate Capital Budgeting* (Lexington, Mass.: Heath, 1974); and Sudeep Anand, "Resource Allocation at the Corporate Level of the Firm: A Methodological and Empirical Investigation of the Dimensions Used by Managers for Evaluation of Investments" (unpublished Ph.D. thesis, M.I.T., 1977).

8. See M. Schiff and A. Y. Lewin, "Where Traditional Budgeting Fails," in *Behavior Aspects of Accounting,* eds. M. Schiff and A. Y. Lewin (Englewood Cliffs, N.J.: Prentice-Hall, 1974), pp. 132-140; and E. E. Carter, "Designing the Capital Budgeting Process," in *Prescriptive Models of Organizations,* eds. Paul C. Nystrom and William H. Starbuck (Amsterdam: North-Holland, 1977), pp. 25-42.

9. See Note 6. Also, see W. H. Newman, *Constructive Control* (Englewood Cliffs, N.J.: Prentice-Hall, 1975); Peter Lorange, "Strategic Control: A Framework for Effective Response to Environmental Change," *Sloan School Working Paper* (Cambridge, Mass.: Sloan School of Management, M.I.T., 1977); C. F. Bales, "Strategic Control: The President's Paradox," *Business Horizons* (Aug. 1977); and Rochelle O'Connor, "Planning Under Uncertainty: Multiple Scenarios and Contingency Planning," *Report No. 741* (New York: The Conference Board, 1978).

chapter five

Tailor-Making the Corporate Planning System's Design

Introduction

We have developed a conceptual scheme for corporate planning (Chapter Two) but have seen that the successful implementation of such a scheme depends on the avoidance of a number of pitfalls of implementation (Chapter Four). Equally important, however, we must be able to tailor-make the planning system's capabilities to reflect the needs of the situational setting of the firm. The strategic position of the firm (Chapter Three) was the most important source of determination for planning needs. In this chapter we shall develop an approach toward tailor-making the design of a firm's planning system in order to meet the needs requirements at hand.[1] We shall do this by identifying a set of variables relating to the design of a planning system. These variables will be under our discretionary control and can be manipulated in such a way that the corporate planning system will achieve desired capabilities for matching the planning needs. It is clear that this will be an important step of sharpened focus beyond the more general implementation issues discussed in Chapter Four. However, we saw that these issues have relevance for all corporate planning systems and therefore represented a necessary step of clarification of the conceptual scheme.

We shall start our discussion of situational design of the planning

system by approaching how to tailor-make those aspects of the planning
system that apply to a product/market element or a division in particular.
We shall see how the planning system might facilitate the setting of an
appropriate strategic direction of a product/market element or division
by reflecting its needs for adaptation and integration.

When it comes to designing the part of the planning system intended to facilitate the development of business element and family
strategies, our approach will thus be one of suggesting a format for the
business plans design which reflects the specific strategic setting at hand.
Thus, by focusing on setting appropriate strategic direction for this kind
of business element or family, as well as choosing an appropriate strategic
program thrust for this particular setting, the planning format will add
focus to the particular business planning task, not distract, as would have
been the case if all business planning were carried out according to an
essentially standardized format. Seen in isolation, such a static set of
suggestions for tailor-made business planning systems design would not
appear to be all that useful in that it might seem too mechanistic and
uninspiring. However, we shall suggest that it is critical to provide
improved tailor-made business planning strategic focus. Too often the
individual strategic needs of different business units might be overlooked
as a consequence of the common tendency to require standardized business plans from all parts of a company.

The corporate-level portfolio planning needs will of course dictate
the design of the overall planning process. The individual business's
differing planning needs will thus be put into the context of the particular
corporation; while still adhering to each business's unique needs, these
will to a greater or lesser extent have to be tempered to reflect the needs of
the particular portfolio of which they are part. We shall discuss a set of
six tailor-making systems design devices which at least to some degree
might be controlled or manipulated in a discretionary sense by the systems designer to achieve the desired adaptation and integration
capabilities of the overall planning process. These factors will be the
following: the design of a planning system format to meet a strategy
center's planning needs; the choice of relative emphasis on *top-down*
versus *bottom-up* focus of the strategy opportunity identification and
review activities; the relative amount of executives' penetrating involvement and time spent on each of the five cycles of the planning process—
the layout of the planning calendar; the nature of the linkage among each
of the five cycles in the planning process—*tight* versus *loose*; the relative
emphasis in the control system on monitoring front-end versus near-
term phenomena; and, finally, relative emphasis in the managerial
incentives system on assessing front-end versus near-term performance
fulfillment. As a way of summarizing our approach to tailor-made design

of the planning system we shall finally illustrate by means of an extensive example how this battery of planning systems design factors can be changed when needed in order to reinforce a strategic shift either for the company as a whole or in some of its parts.

Revising a Planning System's Format to Meet a Strategy Center's Planning Needs

We recall from our discussion of a strategy center's planning needs in Chapter Three that the absolute and relative need for adaptation and integration will be a function of the location of its strategic position within the business attractiveness/competitive strength matrix. Thus, a so-called question mark position would imply a relatively high need for adaptation but a relatively low need for integration; a star position implies a relatively high need for both adaptation and integration; a cash-cow position implies a relatively higher need for integration than for adaptation; and a dog position implies a relatively low need for both adaptation and integration. We also recall that to evolve a product/market element from a question mark to a star position will require an inordinate emphasis on adaptation as well as integration but that the integration dimension typically will have to be strengthened the most. When a product/market element is evolving from a star to a cash cow, the adaptive needs actually will tend to diminish somewhat relative to integration. The challenge for a strategy center's planning system is thus to facilitate the choice of a strategic direction that actually provides the adaptive/integrative thrust to meet these identified needs.[2]

We shall propose three sets of checklist factors which should facilitate the proper focus on the execution of strategic direction. These checklists relate to the choice of basic strategic direction, the choice of strategic program thrust, and the choice of competitive mode reinforcing policies. The contingency-based design approach of business planning systems for strategy centers implies that the actual span of each of these choices will indeed be relatively narrow, given that there will be a few natural strategies that will provide the desired adaptive and integrative thrust for a particular strategy center. Thus, a major purpose of the design of the strategy center's planning system is to ensure that the relevant checklist factors are chosen which allow such a natural strategy to be followed, consistent with the strategy center's needs. The system should be a tool for the business element or family manager for his own planning of his strategic direction. Let us, in turn, discuss the three classes of checklist systems design choice factors for a strategy center's strategic planning systems module.

When it comes to the first set of factors, namely, to check where to go, or, in other words, to focus on what should be the basic direction coming out of a strategy center's objectives, there seem to be five broad directional alternatives:

H.A. 1. To *enter* into a business, creating a new product/market element within the question mark area.

H.A. 2. To *build* a strategic position. This will imply the development of competitive strength, say by increasing one's market share.

A 3. To *hold* one's strategic position. This implies embarking on a strategy that attempts to maintain one's competitive strength posture without major shifts in, say, market share.

L A 4. To *harvest*, which will imply that one's strategic position will gradually be allowed to be weakened. There will probably be more resources extracted from a product/market element than what is reinvested to maintain its competitive strength.

NO A 5. To *exit*. This implies withdrawing from the business by divesting of the strategy center or closing down its activities.

We recall from Chapter Two that the objectives-setting stage of the strategy formulation process is particularly important for influencing the adaptive thrust of a strategic direction. Considering the above directional alternatives in this light, we might say that the entry and build direction choices will imply a rather highly adaptive thrust. A hold direction will probably imply a less intensive adaptation thrust. This is likely to be even more so for a harvest setting, where the basic directional posture has long since been established. Finally, to exit no active adaptation thrust is implied. It is thus important that the format requirements for a business plan be such that they reinforce the articulation of a relevant direction for this strategy center.

Let us now move to a second class of factors to add proper focus to the execution of a useful strategic direction for a strategy center, namely, the type of strategic program that most appropriately should be chosen. We shall identify seven broad classes of strategic program directions all signifying alternative ways of how to get there but each being the natural choice in a different product/market element's direction need situation:

L.I. 1. *Initial entry* into a business by means of initial new market and new product development.

L.I. 2. *Market penetration*. This implies the execution of strategic programs, either for penetrating new markets with existing products, for penetrating existing markets with new products, or for penetrating new markets with new products.

L.I. 3. *Market maintenance*. A strategic programming effort of this type implies that the present markets and products are being maintained.

I 4. *Vertical integration*. Such strategic programs will attempt to facilitate either backward integration or/and forward integration.

I 5. *Rationalization*. Strategic programs of this kind might include making moves to trim excess capacity, attempting to carry out market rationalizations, distribution rationalizations, product line rationalizations, and/or production process rationalizations.

6. *Increased efficiency*. Such a strategic programming thrust would include attempts to gain increased technological efficiency, elaboration of methods for further pursuance of functional efficiency improvements, as well as traditional cost-cutting efforts.

7. *Terminal exit* would imply strategic programs for gradual abandonment and/or divestiture.

We recall from our discussion in Chapter Two that the strategic programming activities imply a relatively much higher emphasis on integration, given that this activity is taking place "later" in the planning process than the initial, highly adaptation-oriented objectives-setting stage. If we consider the seven types of strategic programs that have been identified above, however, we see that they are not all equally integration-oriented. For instance, a programming thrust that emphasizes initial market development, market penetration, or market maintenance seems to have a relatively low orientation toward integration. Strategic programming activities which are based on rationalization or improved efficiency, on the other hand, will be relatively more integration-dominated. Thus, if we exclude for now the terminal exit strategic program thrust, we see that the integrative dominance of the strategic programming activities seems to increase as we go from the first type of programming to the sixth.

Before introducing the third list of factors for providing appropriate formats to business plans, policies for the fine tuning of a product/market element's competitive niche, let us see how the two format checklists already discussed provide the management of a strategy center with quite accurate guidelines for developing a natural strategy to correspond to its identified needs for planning. In Exhibit 5-1 we have plotted each of the five basic strategic direction alternatives along the horizontal axis according to its degree of adaptation-orientation. Along the vertical axis we have ranked the six strategic program alternatives according to their integrative orientation. We have indicated with check marks relevant natural strategy combinations of these objectives and strategic program thrusts. For instance, if the basic direction of the objective is entry, then one type of strategic program will fit logically with this, namely, initial entry. If we take any of the other strategic program thrusts, such as vertical integration or rationalization, none of these will blend with the entry objective into a natural strategy. If we take the build objective, on the other hand, we see that there are three alternative strategic program types that fit with this, namely, market penetration, market maintenance, and/or vertical integration. One or a combination of these strategic programs will form another natural strategy when connected with the build objective. Similarly, from Exhibit 5-1 we can see in an analogous manner what the other natural strategy alternatives might be.

From the vertical and horizontal axes of Exhibit 5-1 we can determine the nature of the adaptation and integration capabilities of the various natural strategies. For instance, a natural strategy of build by means of market penetration will imply a relatively high adaptive but low integrative thrust. A harvest by means of efficiency improvement strategy, on the other hand, will imply a low adaptive but high integrative emphasis. Given that we therefore can classify all the natural strategies in terms of adaptation/integration capabilities, it follows that specific sets of these strategies will provide the most adequate response to different business element planning needs. Specifically for a product/market element which is in a question mark strategic position and thus is facing relatively high adaptive needs but relatively low integrative needs, we have indicated that only the following alternative natural strategies might be relevant. These are located inside the area marked I and are either entry or build by means of initial market development or market penetra-

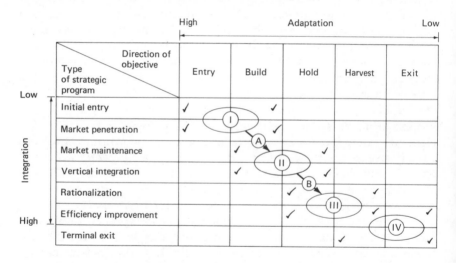

EXHIBIT 5-1 Checklist of Business Plan Formats for Natural Strategies in Terms of Basic Strategic Direction and Type of Strategic Program

√ = *feasible objective direction/strategic program strategy combination*
○ = *borderline for strategy combination alternatives for different strategic positions*
I = *question mark (high A/low I need)*
II = *star (high A/high I need)*
III = *cash cow (low A/high I need)*
IV = *dog (low A/low I need)*
A = *from question mark to star*
B = *from star to cash cow*

tion. Let us similarly consider what the natural strategies would be that would fulfill the needs of a strategy center in a star position. These have been encircled within the area marked II in Exhibit 5-1. We see that there are four potential strategies that would have the appropriate capabilities in this instance, namely, to build or hold by means of market position maintenance or by means of vertical integration. In a similar fashion we can see from Exhibit 5-1 what the natural strategies will be for strategy centers in the cash-cow or dog positions.

We can also see from Exhibit 5-1 the natural strategies of primary relevance to consider for a management which intends to evolve a product/market element from a question mark to a star position. This is indicated by arrow A in Exhibit 5-1. Clearly the basic direction of the strategies to follow in this case would be to build. In line with this, the arrow falls within the build column in its entirety. We see, however, that there are three natural strategies that are applicable in this case, namely, to build by means of market penetration, build by means of market maintenance, and/or build by means of vertical integration. In a similar fashion, we can see the relevant strategies for a product/market element which is to be evolved from star to cash cow, as indicated by arrow B in Exhibit 5-1.

From the discussion of the preceding paragraphs we see that the approach to the design of a business planning system for the product/ market element level helps its managers to maintain a relevant strategic focus, given that the particular needs for planning are identified. The potential distraction that might have been caused from a standardized business planning format is avoided.

We shall now introduce a third class of planning format checklist factors that are intended to be helpful devices in sharpening the strategic capabilities even further. As indicated, these factors relate to reinforcing an appropriate competitive niche for a product/market element. We shall indicate four different competitive mode factors for reinforcing a competitive niche:

1. *Image.* A product's image might be developed to reinforce the strategic direction, probably with particular effect in the build and to some extent in the hold strategic direction cases.
2. *Quality.* The quality of the product that the strategy center is offering might be developed to reinforce a strategy. This is probably particularly relevant for reinforcing a build or a hold strategic momentum.
3. *Service.* This factor, which also includes reliability of delivery, might be particularly useful to employ for a strategy center which is following a hold general strategic direction and is attempting to further strengthen its competitive niche.
4. *Price.* While the price of a product has to be competitive for the strategy center to stay in business at all, it will probably be for strategy centers which follow a

general hold or harvest direction that price might be a particularly useful tool to
strengthen one's competitive niche position. Still it should be noted, however,
that price might be one of the best ways to build market share; i.e., you buy it.

We have attempted to order these factors in terms of how they might
reinforce an adaptive or an integrative thrust. The first factor, image, for
instance, is appropriate for strengthening a highly adaptive strategic
thrust, particularly for a product/market element in an entry position. On
the other extreme the price factor seems to be particularly appropriate to
reap competitive benefits for product/market elements that are following
a highly integrative strategic direction, such as harvest. The quality and
service factors would seem to have strengthening effects above all on
general strategic thrusts that fall between the two examples cited, applying in particular to build and hold strategic directions, respectively. Thus,
we see that the competitive niche reinforcement factors 1 and 4 seem to
apply along the upper-left to bottom-right continuum indicated as the
evolutionary stages of a product/market element in Exhibit 5-1. Consequently, this third set of checklist factors contributes to an even further
sharpening of the strategic capabilities in response to a strategy center's
particular planning needs.

Before concluding our discussion of how to tailor-make the set of
checklist factors to different situational settings in order to come up with
useful planning system components at the product/market element level,
let us briefly touch on the particular problems associated with exit decisions. We have seen that while it has been relatively easy to come up with
a concept for matching the planning system's capabilities with the particular needs for planning when we are dealing with strategy centers
which find themselves in various ongoing operations settings, it is difficult to extend this analysis to an exit decision setting, given that this
implies the discontinuance of this operation. In such cases the intended
mode of exit will determine the needs for planning and the corresponding
planning system support. If, for instance, management's decision is to
phase out a dog product/market element slowly as its net funds-
generating capabilities dwindle, then the future business potential of the
product/market element will indeed be so low that it will not be well
justified to spend extensive management resources on revitalized adaptation and/or integration directions. As such, we might state that the relevant, opportunity-weighted needs for planning would be low, both with
respect to adaptation and integration. The planning system should reflect
this. If, on the other hand, management is attempting to divest itself of
the business, then different planning needs will be created. There might
be a need to dress up the product/market element itself, calling for the

pursuance of various adaptive and/or integrative moves at the business element planning level. In addition, the need to search for buyers to divestiture candidates will typically create added adaptation planning needs at the corporate level. We shall not, however, pursue the issue of modifying further the approach proposed in this book for matching needs and capabilities when it comes to product/market element exit situations, given the highly atypical nature of these situations.

We have now concluded the first part of our analysis of how to approach the task of tailor-making the design of a planning system so as to reflect a particular situational setting's needs. Specifically, we have seen how at the business element level a strategy center with a particular set of planning needs might be equipped with a planning system which facilitates the development of a focused business strategy relevant to the setting of the product/market at hand. The design of the guidelines for the format of such a business-level planning system took place by choosing format factors for facilitating the establishment of the relevant basic direction as reflected by proper choice of objectives, by devising factors to guide the development of an appropriate strategic programming thrust, as well as by pointing toward factors for developing an appropriate competitive mode to strengthen the strategy center's competitive niche. Thus, the planning guidelines for the strategy center level should be tailor-made along three sets of dimensions, for each of which we have suggested a relatively narrow set of values to reflect a given situational setting.

It should be clear, however, that while this approach has the potential of providing useful guidance for the development of more focused plans at the strategy center level, this formulating approach might easily lead to mechanistic and static business element plans if used as the only planning system tool. When integrated as part of a larger, overall corporate-wide strategic planning system, however, the business planning format approach becomes highly useful. We recall from Chapter Two that our conceptual framework is heavily based on interaction, iterations, and information exchange. It is as a vehicle to sharpen this group decision-making process that the business planning format approach becomes particularly useful, so as to underscore the necessity to tailor-make planning to the various business settings within the company and avoid treating all businesses in the same way.

Let us therefore turn to a discussion of how the overall corporate planning system in a broader sense might be tailor-made to reflect a particular corporate setting. The task at hand will be to develop guidelines for tailor-making the conceptual framework for corporate planning that we developed in Chapter Two to the particular needs for planning that a company faces, as seen for the corporation as a whole. Thus, the corporate planning system's design should reflect the corporate portfolio needs for planning, as determined in Chapter Three.

Top-Down Versus Bottom-Up Emphasis During Planning Reviews

Before discussing any of the corporate planning systems design tailor-making issues, it is useful to recall the nature of the situational design task that we are faced with.[3] We recall from our discussion of the needs for planning at the corporate level in Chapter Three that three basic types of need imbalances might be created as a result of shorter-term financial as well as longer-term structural pressures on corporate management. One situation would indicate a high need for facing integrative types of issues. This might dictate a corporate planning system design approach which modifies the conceptual scheme in such a way that its integrative capabilities will be strengthened. To do this, added emphasis should probably be given to the elaboration of the strategic programming and budgeting cycles as well as to the tie-ins between these two cycles and the monitoring and incentives-scheme cycles. A second corporate planning need situation, we recall, might indicate that the pressures would be of an adaptive nature. In such a case the design of the objectives-setting cycle of the corporate planning system should be elaborated, together with the aspects of the monitoring and incentives-scheme cycles that relate to this. The third major type of corporate-level planning need indicates that there might be both adaptive and integrative pressures. This would call for a strengthening of the planning system's capabilities when it comes to both adaptation and integration.

It should be stressed that the task of tailor-making the design of the corporate planning system is one of starting out with the conceptual scheme that has been outlined in Chapter Two, i.e., viewing this as a base case. The particular need pressures which apply to the corporate level should then dictate how to modify the basic scheme so that relevant planning capabilities might be put in place to contribute toward the lessening of the pressures that apply to the corporate level over the longer run. Each of the five classes of design factors that will be discussed in this and the next sections are thus primarily intended for tailor-making the overall capabilities of the corporate planning system in accordance with what we just have discussed. The five corporate-wide tailor-making design considerations to be discussed are:

- The degree of top-down versus bottom-up emphasis in the planning process, particularly when plans are being reviewed.

- The degree of concentration on the front end versus the later stages of the planning process
- The nature of linkage of each of the stages of the planning process to the monitoring and management incentive cycles
- The emphasis of the performance monitoring process on objectives fulfillment versus fulfillment of more near-term performance
- The emphasis of the management incentives process on rewarding objectives fulfillment versus rewarding more near-term performance fulfillment

Let us now turn to a discussion of the planning systems design issue which relates to the nature of the top-down/bottom-up balance which should be attempted for various situational settings. The terms *top-down* and *bottom-up* are examples of the unfortunate tendency toward jargon which so often tends to creep into the field of planning; a digression for a clarification of their meaning is consequently in order. Top-down is used as a label for the initiative and direction that top management gives to the planning process. This will of course typically be associated with portfolio planning; a top-down emphasis might be seen as almost a prerequisite in order to achieve a deliberate shift in strategic direction through influencing the resource allocation pattern. Such top-down emphasis will thus be manifested through the resource allocation decisions by the deliberate transfer of funds from one business to another as well as deliberate curtailing of some business involvements through divestiture and/or expansion into other areas through acquisition. A key to achieving such strategic shifts is a strong corporate-level integrative focus on the funds-flow patterns within the company, so that it will be quite explicit which will be the sources of strategic resources and which will be the users. Through imposing an integrative focus on the ongoing, funds-generating businesses the corporate management diminishes the likelihood of surprises and unexpected changes in these planned shifts of its strategic resources.

Another aspect of the top-down/bottom-up balance emphasis, however, relates to the relative impact that senior management might have on planning within the divisions through its guidance or involvement in the setting of assumptions and premises for divisional plans as well as through reviews, discussions, and approval of these plans. Let us see, for instance, what effect a highly bottom-up orientation might have with respect to the planning activities of the businesses, particularly in terms of planning for the ongoing success of each of the businesses. Such a heavy bottom-up emphasis will put strong pressure on the management of each of the businesses to show initiative in coming up with internal growth opportunities and in attempting to tackle potential threats facing its business as well. Thus, a bottom-up orientation will also be necessary to achieve effective adaptation of the business level to pursue internal growth. In this way it will be possible for the corporate level to receive more relevant inputs about the potentials of each business. It seems that a bottom-up emphasis is likely to yield strong business-level adaptation planning dominance. On the other hand, as we have seen, a heavy top-down emphasis is likely to yield strong integration planning dominance at the business level in that the businesses will have received much more specific inputs from the top with respect to where they are expected to go and how to utilize their internal strengths.

In summary, we see that a relatively heavy bottom-up emphasis might tend to strengthen the organization's capabilities for internal growth through adaptive moves of its existing businesses. A relatively heavy top-down emphasis, on the other hand, will have as an effect the strengthening of the integrative planning capabilities with respect to the firm's ongoing businesses. The significance of the latter will be that strategic resources might be freed more easily for redeployment by the corporate level, either by means of significant shifts in emphasis among the company's internal businesses or by means of acquisitions. This implies that the corporate level must have an adaptive planning capability to orchestrate these portfolio strategy shifts. It is important, however, to recognize that this is a different adaptive planning capability from that which will be created through a bottom-up design choice, because the latter refers to the ongoing operations. Thus, a separate corporate-level adaptive capability is needed when one wants to change the basic balance of the mix of the ongoing operations. One might prefer to develop such a strong portfolio change adaptive capability in combination with a strong top-down corporate integration capability with respect to the ongoing businesses.

It may well be that neither an extreme top-down nor an extreme bottom-up approach will be appropriate in most situations. A reasonable balance between the two is often more in line with what is needed, allowing for some internally generated growth through business-level growth as well as for facilitating some corporate-level portfolio adaptation.

The top-down/bottom-up balance has implications for the nature of the planning review process. In the case of a more top-down-oriented approach senior management will tend to be relatively more directive. When a predominantly bottom-up approach exists, however, senior management's role will be more one of listening, stimulating debate around the bottom-up inputs, and attempting to "bring out the best" from the lower organizational echelons. As discussed, what will be an appropriate top-down/bottom-up balance should be determined as a function of the particular strategic planning needs at hand. It follows that the style of review that senior management adopts should differ as it applies to divisions in diverse strategic settings. Top management's review style is thus an important tailor-making element in the design and implementation of effective strategic planning systems. Unfortunately, this factor is often overlooked.

In the argument outlined in the previous paragraph we have of course assumed that top management is willing and able to adopt such a flexible review style. Any problem in this respect, however, is probably just as much due to lack of specific recognition of review style as a design factor as to lack of flexibility on the part of the CEO.

Front-End Versus Back-End Emphasis: The Planning Calendar

Another systems design issue related to the top-down/bottom-up design consideration just discussed is the degree of emphasis on the front end of the planning process versus the back end, i.e., the relative amount of management time and intellectual effort invested in planning activities that relate to the first planning cycle versus the second cycle versus the third. This will typically be manifested by the layout of the planning calendar, i.e., the time-spending pattern allotted to the various planning activities. A relatively heavy emphasis on the front end of the planning process will imply a relative strengthening of the adaptive planning capabilities, with added emphasis on an assessment of the attempt to improve the objectives and goals of the organization and added emphasis on reexamining the relevance of strategic programs. A relatively heavy emphasis on the back end of the process implies that the integration capabilities of the system will be strengthened because of the closer emphasis on strategic program efficiency through budget emphasis.

The choice of front-end emphasis relative to back-end emphasis or vice versa will have to take place at the corporate management level as well as at the division management level. The key is how much real intellectual effort and commitment is being put into the development of plan proposals and plan reviews and discussions by the various management groups. One achieves neither proper adaptation nor proper integration just by committing a lot of time unless the quality of the time spent is high.

It should be noted that the balance between front-end versus back-end management emphasis does not need to be even when it comes to each of the organizational subunits within the firm. Some product/market elements or divisions, for instance, may be primarily into the cash-cow strategic mode, with heavy need for integration. The management of these units should spend their efforts more heavily on the back end of the process. When a strategy center is heavily into a growth mode, on the other hand, such as a star or a question mark, its management should spend relatively more efforts on the front-end process issues. The corporate management may have to spend relatively more effort interacting with the internal growth business units by merely stating relatively clear top-down guidelines for these. Later in the process, however, relatively more top management effort might be spent with the detailed strategic programs and budgets of the mature businesses. The growth businesses, on the other hand, would need relatively less corporate attention at this point, given that the objectives already chosen will more or less dictate what types of programs and budgets to follow.

A relatively simple but straightforward device to influence the adaptation/integration capabilities, as we have seen, is to manipulate the effort-spending pattern that managers follow when it comes to their involvement in planning. With relatively more effort being spent on the front-end planning activities than the back-end activities, the more relative emphasis will be given to adaptation and vice versa. One design aspect of the formal planning system which therefore is important is the layout of the so-called planning calendar. This spells out the deadlines for the various inputs, presentations, and reviews that have to take place according to some time sequence. A critical constraint on the layout design of the planning calendar must be that it sequences the various planning activities in a way which is consistent with the conceptual planning framework that we have outlined. Beyond this, however, there is ample flexibility to design the planning calendar to give relatively clear suggestion as to the time limits that various line executives should spend on the different aspects of planning. Thus, the planning calendar is a simple and important device for influencing the time-spending pattern. Too often, unfortunately, the design of the planning calendar is done without keeping in mind that we have here a useful source for influencing the planning capabilities. At worst, a carelessly designed calendar can actually influence the planning capabilities in unintended directions.

There will of course be considerable flexibility in determining the actual time-spending pattern within the relatively broad limits set by the planning calendar. However, given the need to have the entire set of the businesses' planning inputs available at the corporate level in order to make portfolio considerations and facilitate the closing of each particular planning cycle, it is also important that the planning calendar be strictly adhered to. Failure of one strategy center to deliver its planning input on time will delay the progress of the entire corporate planning effort.

Exhibit 5-2 illustrates the design choices which apply when determining a useful and flexible planning calendar.

There are two major classes of concerns in determining a usefully tailor-made planning calendar. First, the needs for adaptation and integration of the corporation as a whole should play a major role in the overall time allocation to each of the three direction-setting cycles. For instance, if the corporation as a whole is facing major structural portfolio pressures, thus having an overall need for adaptation, then relatively more time should be allotted to the objectives-setting stage. If, on the other hand, the corporation is facing major integrative pressures, then relatively more time should be allotted to integration. The drawing of the date lines marked I and II in Exhibit 5-2 should thus reflect the over all corporate planning needs.

The second major class of concerns relates to establishing a planning calendar which is reflecting the planning needs of each individual business. The task in this respect is to tailor-make a calendar for each business, within the room for flexibility left by the establishing of the corporate-wide deadlines for the completion of the objectives-setting phase (I) and the strategic programming phase (II). In Exhibit 5-2 we have given three examples of this. Business A is facing highly adaptive planning needs; hence, relatively much time will be allotted to its objectives-setting activity. Business B, on the other hand, is having a relatively even need for adaptation and integration. Its planning schedule reflects this, with relatively even amounts of time allotted to each cycle. In an absolute sense we also see a difference in the overall time spent on planning between businesses A and B, however. This reflects that business A is in a turnaround situation, requiring a heavy time commitment to determining a new direction. Business B, on the other hand, has its basic direction already determined, thus calling for relatively less time spent on planning in an overall sense. Finally, business C is an example of a planning schedule tailor-made to reflect a heavy integrative need.

As in the top-down versus bottom-up design issue discussed in the

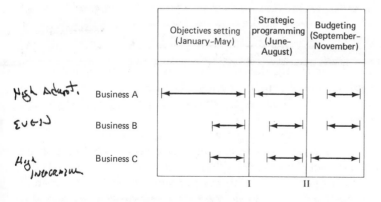

EXHIBIT 5-2   Planning Calendar for Company X.

previous section, senior management will have a considerable impact on the final determination of planning time spending. If the CEO through his own example shows his determination to influence the planning effort in the way needed, then the rest of the organization will pick up the signal. Unfortunately, however, planning takes time, and it might be tempting for the CEO not to spend the time needed, particularly on more far-reaching adaptation planning issues; the rest of the organization will be quick to cut down on its own time spending too. Thus, what might at first have looked like fairly insignificant concessions to short-term pressures by the CEO in terms of postponing planning might in the end have serious adverse effects for planning as a strategic decision-making tool. The planning calendar is therefore an important and flexible tool for the CEO in signaling to the various parts of the organization how he expects them to spend their time in planning.

Linkages Between the Five Cycles of the Planning System

Another useful planning systems tailor-making device is the nature of the linkage between the five-stage elements of the planning system.[4] To consider what we mean by the linkage concept, we may recall that there will be a set of outputs from each of the three planning cycles relating to the identification and narrowing down of strategic options. One cycle's output will thus constrain the execution of the planning function that has to be undertaken by the next stage in the planning process. If the output from one planning stage heavily constrains the span of the next cycle's planning activities, then we shall say that there is tight linkage between the cycles. If, on the other hand, the output of a prior planning cycle to a considerably lesser extent constrains the planning activities of the next planning cycle, then we are dealing with a looser linkage. A tight linkage implies a rapid narrowing down of strategic options; a loose linkage implies a slow narrowing down. Exhibit 5-3 indicates the difference between a rapid narrowing down of the alternative strategic options, i.e., a tight linkage between the cycles (dashed line), versus a slow narrowing down of the strategic alternatives, i.e., a loose linkage between the cycles (solid line).[5]

We might also consider extending the linkage concept to address how the monitoring and managerial incentives cycles relate to the three strategic direction-setting cycles. When it comes to looking at the monitoring cycle's relationship with the previous three cycles we shall want to apply the concept as follows: If progress toward fulfillment of the output of a given cycle is monitored in much detail and with quite

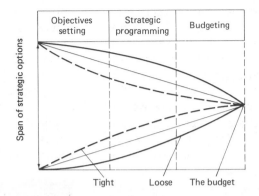

EXHIBIT 5-3 Loose vs. Tight Linkage; Slow vs. Rapid Narrowing Down of Strategic Options

accurate measurements attempted, then we have tight linkage; if, on the other hand, the monitoring efforts are done in less detail and one is attempting to measure progress in a broader manner, then we have loose linkage. In an analogous way we shall apply the linkage term with respect to the incentives system: If managerial incentives and compensation are closely tied to the fulfillment of the output of a particular cycle, then we have tight linkage; if, on the other hand, the compensation is more informally and loosely tied to the performance fulfillment of a given cycle, then we have loose linkage.

We shall distinguish among three types of linkage. The most obvious one, *substance linkage*, relates to the relationship between the substantive output of one planning cycle and the substantive inputs to the next planning cycle. For instance, at the corporate level it may be decided that the discretionary funds-flow resources of a certain magnitude might be channeled into a new business area, primarily through internal developments within a new direction. These issues have been identified and resolved in principle during the objectives-setting cycle. Thus, important limitations will thereby have been set for what the substantive context of the subsequent strategic programs will be like.

Another type of linkage will be labeled *organizational linkage*. This refers to the extent to which the same managers are centrally involved in the execution of and with the responsibility for planning, all the way through, the five planning cycles (tight linkage) or to which different managers have basic responsibility for the different cycles of the planning process (loose linkage). We might, for instance, have the corporate and divisional planning departments heavily involved in the execution of the objectives-setting and strategic programming cycles, while the controller's department might be centrally involved with the execution of the budgeting and monitoring cycles. Further, a human resources department might be responsible for administering the management incentives cycle. Thus, in this case we have a situation where three different corporate management staff groups are involved in various aspects of the planning process—what we would consider a loose organizational linkage. If, on the other hand, we are assuming that the three groups report to a common senior vice president for administration, then we would have a tighter organizational linkage. If, at the extreme, one manager is directly in charge of the staff activities relating to all five cycles, then we have a tight organizational linkage.

The third type of linkage might be labeled *timing linkage*, relating to whether or not the activities on the planning calendar follow each other in such a rapid sequence that there are few or no vacant periods between the activities to complete the various cycles (tight linkage) or that there is considerable unused time between two cycles that thus is not being spent on planning activities (loose linkage). We have already discussed the role of the planning calendar; whether we have tight or loose timing linkage between two cycles can be seen from this. From Exhibit 5-2 we can see that business A is faced with a relatively tight timing linkage in that there is little unused time between the various planning activities. Businesses B and C, on the other hand, face relatively loose timing linkage in that there are significant time periods left on the calendar where no planning activities go on.

Exhibit 5-4 shows the various linkage possibilities among the five elements of the planning system. As we see, we have a total of eight different linkage types. First, we have two linkage types which are directly associated with the interrelationship of the three elements that represent the narrowing down procedure of the planning process. These are labeled types 1 and 2 in Exhibit 5-4. Then we have three linkage types associated with the relationship between the monitoring cycle and each of the three cycles that perform the narrowing down part of planning, marked as types 3, 4, and 5 in the exhibit. Finally, we have three linkage types between the management compensation cycle and the three narrowing down cycles, indicated as types 6, 7, and 8 in Exhibit 5-4.

Let us now consider how the linkage concept can be utilized as a design tool to influence the adaptation and integration capabilities of planning. Let us first assume that we intend to strengthen the adaptation capabilities. Hence, we want to emphasize the front-end objectives-setting-related aspect of the overall planning effort. This means that we would attempt to make linkage types 1, 5, and 8 tight. In a tight linkage of type 1, the objectives and goals would be fairly explicitly developed, so that they provide a relatively narrow set of constraints for the strategic

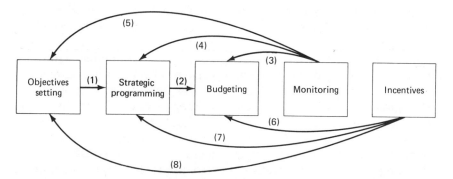

EXHIBIT 5-4   Linkage Types in the Planning Process

Linkage type 1: Between the objectives-setting and strategic programming cycles
Linkage type 2: Between strategic programming and budgeting
Linkage type 3: Between performance measurement and budgeting
Linkage type 4: Between performance measurement and strategic programming
Linkage type 5: Between performance measurement and objectives setting
Linkage type 6: Between the management incentive scheme and budgeting
Linkage type 7: Between the management incentive scheme and strategic programming
Linkage type 8: Between the management incentive scheme and objectives setting

programming activity; i.e., the objectives and goals would be followed up by the development of a set of strategic programs that correspond to the intended adaptive direction. Assuming, of course, that the objectives and goals cycle has produced an appropriate adaptive strategy, then the tight linkage of type 1 will facilitate the follow-through with the implementation of this. Linkage type 5 ensures that progress toward objectives and goals is closely monitored. A tight linkage implies that we shall have a careful and relatively detailed monitoring of progress toward the intended strategic direction. Linkage type 8, which connects the objectives and goals cycle with the managerial incentives cycle, should also be tight in order to emphasize the importance of encouraging managerial performance toward the longer-term strategic direction necessary to achieve adaptation.

Let us turn now to a situation in which we want to strengthen the integration capabilities of the planning system. Tight linkage should be attempted for types 2, 3, and 6 for the following reasons: Linkage type 2 ensures that strategic programming and budgeting fit together as one efficient activity so that the budgets merely represent more detailed developments of the strategic programs, thereby strengthening the integrative thrust. Linkage type 3 facilities a close monitoring of the budget fulfillment performance, again essential for efficient integration so that corrective action can be taken in time. Linkage type 6 ties executive compensation to managerial performance's fulfillment toward budgets, underscoring the importance of integration. We have not discussed linkage types 4 and 7 because they seem to possess a middle-ground position between adaptation and integration in terms of their emphasis. However, while they might have no extreme effect in reinforcing either adaptation or integration, they may still have important effects in strengthening a particular adaptive or integrative capability thrust. For instance, tight linkages of types 4 and 7 should facilitate monitoring and motivating progress of the strategic programs directly as part of an attempt to strengthen integration. An examination of the specific nature of the strategic programs, whether they are primarily adaptation-oriented or integration-oriented, would, however, be necessary in each such case.

Let us now consider the interplay between the linkage types that primarily facilitate adaptation and those that primarily facilitate integration. To some extent we might be able to strengthen adaptation further by loosening up somewhat on the linkage types associated with integration, types 2, 3, and 6, in addition to the tightening of the adaptive linkage types 1, 5, and 8. Conversely, if strengthened integration was the intention, then we might have implemented exactly opposite linkage tightening and loosening procedures. It is necessary in this context to remind ourselves that both adaptation and integration capabilities are needed in any planning system; what we want to do when redesigning a system is to change the relative emphasis on the one versus the other aspect of planning, but within limits. We must, therefore, be particularly careful not to dichotomize adaptation and integration by overemphasizing one aspect of planning to such an extreme that the necessary absolute minimum capability level of the other dimension is violated.

When it comes to treating linkages as a tool in the design of a strategic planning system, then, we should again raise two classes of concerns. First, the overall portfolio-level planning needs should dictate an overall pattern of linkage choices. Within the broad pattern established this way, however, we should tailor-make the linkage pattern further for each business, reflecting its particular planning need.

The Monitoring System

As already implied in the previous section, the monitoring system might play a significant role in affecting the adaptation/integration balance of the planning capabilities of a planning system, depending on how the monitoring stage is linked to the other cycles of the planning system. We do not need to discuss this further. There are, however, additional aspects of the monitoring cycle's interplay with the rest of the system that need to be pursued.[6]

A major concern is the almost generic tendency of the monitoring cycle to reinforce stronger integration than actually intended and thereby often to weaken the adaptation emphasis indirectly. This is probably due in part to the nature of the traditional role of the control system as a key tool for managing companies that do not have a planning system. The emphasis in such cases tends to be focused on more near-term, often somewhat crisis-laden issues rather than on systematically pursuing a long-term strategic direction. Thus, even though a firm's senior management may have participated wholeheartedly all the way through the implementation of a planning process, there is always the danger that when an adverse quarterly performance report hits the desk of the CEO he may overract. His old working habits may call for his involvement in the details of sorting out a problem, including putting heavy immediate pressure on the subordinate managers in question to ameliorate the problem, but often with little or no regard for the underlying strategies previously decided upon. This is, however, exactly the kind of situation in which the homework done during the planning process should pay off to avoid hastily perceived and executed reactions which might violate the strategic thrust agreed upon for the business. The involvement of senior management in near-term fire fighting has a somewhat overpowering effect on the subordinate managers, who should be primarily accountable for the strategic success. Erosion of discipline in connection with reacting to monitoring outputs might thus represent a serious problem.

The nature of superior management's involvement in interpreting and reacting to monitoring feedback is a function of the degree of autonomy that subordinate organizational units may be enjoying. What constitutes an appropriate level of delegation is a complex issue which we shall be able to touch upon only in part, and briefly, in the next paragraphs. Our position is that the pattern of delegation, i.e., the degree of decentralization, is an issue that should not be decided as an overall general policy but that should reflect the strategic issues of the corporation at hand and its parts.

We can illustrate one aspect of this by extending our analysis for assessing the riskiness of a business strategy when strategic risk is seen as a function of the nature of the strategy's exposure to the environment. We recall that we might be able to position each environmental factor critical for the success of a particular strategy in terms of its degree of predictability as well as in terms of the organization's own options for making a discretionary response to such a development in the environment. We argued that the riskiness of a strategy was high if its links to the environment were more heavily dominated by factors that might neither be easily predictable nor offer much response flexibility. Conversely, if the strategy were dominated by more easily predictable factors that also offer much response flexibility, the risk would be lower. Assuming for now that the environmental factors which we have identified to be of potentially major significance in terms of their impact on a strategy fall within the low-predictability and low-response potential category, we might presume that management would be less inclined to delegate extensive autonomy to subordinates, given the high risk of such a strategy. When, on the other hand, the riskiness is less, say when key environmental factors fall within the high predictability and high response potential category, we expect senior management to be more willing to delegate responsibility for evaluation of and response to monitoring feedback. In Exhibit 5-5 we have indicated how the pattern of delegation, autonomy in monitoring and responding, might be seen as a function of the riskiness of a strategy. Let us stress again, however, that environmental risk posture typically will be only one of several factors determining patterns of delegation. Let us therefore raise two related additional issues with respect to this.

First, while one factor to influence the general degree of a strategy center's autonomy with respect to monitoring and discretionary authority to carry out corrective action will be the overall pattern of environmental exposure, there might be one or a few environmental factors in a particular situation that cause a risk exposure substantially different from the general pattern. Consequently, there might be a need for a different mode of top management monitoring and control involvement when it comes to such exceptional factors. For instance, a strategy center which is facing generally low risk might, however, also be exposed to one critical environmental factor that implies high risk exposure. Therefore, while the management of this strategy center might enjoy a high degree of

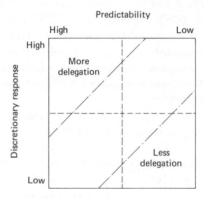

EXHIBIT 5-5   Influence on the Pattern of Delegation in the Monitoring and Control System Stemming from Environmental Risk Exposure

autonomy in monitoring, reporting on deviations, and carrying out ameliorating decisions in general, the monitoring of this exceptional environmental factor might involve a higher degree of senior management involvement in analyzing deviations and deciding on what corrective steps potentially to take.

Second, in general one might expect that the frequency of decisions tends to be higher and the magnitude of each single decision tends to be less when it comes to corrective response to phenomena that fall within the lower risk segment in Exhibit 5-5. The normal mode of corrective action here will be relatively small incremental steps, often in sharp contrast to more fundamental changes that may have to be taken as one moves toward the bottom-right side of the exhibit. Thus, while such major decisions might be reserved for senior management, the more incremental decisions can more easily be delegated. Again, we see the need for a tailor-made monitoring and control approach.

Let us conclude this section with a caveat: It should be obvious from the discussion of the planning approach advocated here that a strategic mode, as opposed to an ad hoc mode, of interpreting performance evidence from the monitoring cycle does not imply that management would have to be insensitive to significant changes and fail to make decisions. It will in fact be an indication that the corporate planning system is not effective as a strategic decision-making tool if the planning exercise contributes to indecisiveness. All that is required is to make use of the homework already done through the planning process when interpreting monitoring feedback for making a corrective strategic decision. Environmental alertness is essential. Needless to say, the planning process will not give us the right answer about what the future will look like, and it will not reduce the uncertainty in our business environment. Meaningful monitoring of progress toward plans fulfillment can improve a firm's ability to cope with this uncertainty, so that the risks in business policy decision making can be contained at an acceptable level.

The Management Incentive System

As was apparent earlier, the management incentive cycle also offers a unique opportunity to influence the adaptation and/or integration capabilities of the planning system. Specifically, when we put relatively more emphasis on motivating managerial performance which contributes toward the fulfillment of objectives and goals as well as strategic programs, as opposed to more near-term budget-fulfilling behavior, then we strengthen the adaptive capabilities of the system. To create more goal congruence between long-term performance fulfillment and managers' individual goals, there will thus have to be tight linkages between the objectives-setting cycle and both the monitoring and the management incentives cycles (linkage types 5 and 8 in Exhibit 5-4). In the event we want to strengthen the integration capability, an analogous argument can be made for this by strengthening linkage types 3 and 6. It follows that the incentives cycle also must be linked to the three first cycles.

As we have discussed, the major leverage points for facilitating adaptation typically lay within the front end of the planning process, particularly during the objectives-setting stage. We recall that the number of executives participating during this stage typically is relatively low, general managers down to the level of division heads only. As progress is made in identifying the strategic options and in narrowing them down, however, a gradual shift takes place toward involving more and more executives. Thus, by the time organizational consensus has been reached for next year's budget, a large number of executives will have been involved. They must have a delineation of their roles in the fulfillment of the near-term, primarily integrative tasks by this point. The implication of this for the tailor-making of incentives schemes would be that incentives for the individual executives might be relatively more applicable when it comes to inducing adaptive behavior, while group or team incentives, on the other hand, may be relatively better suited for inducing integrative behavior. Thus, we would find relatively more individual incentives tied in with the fulfillment of objectives and relatively more group incentives when it comes to near-term performance fulfillment. In many companies this is manifested by the distinction between an MBO system's role versus the budget's role in the management incentives process—while the MBO system tends to focus on individual managers' contributions toward the attainment of more long-term, strategic goals, fulfillment of a budget for an organizational unit tends to result in a group incentive for the managers of the part of the unit in question.

It has been postulated that when it comes to the management of strategy centers in different strategic positions, different executive styles might be appropriate. For instance, a strategy center in a start-up position would benefit from more of an entrepreneurial-type manager, while a strategy center in a cash-cow position might better be managed by a manager with a strong aptitude toward cost efficiency and performance detail. The implication of this for the design of incentive schemes would be that managers of the former types of strategy centers, with their relatively high adaptive challenges, would receive predominantly individual incentives, while the managers of the latter type of strategy centers would receive relatively more group incentives, given their integrative tasks.

There is, however, another incentives tailor-making dimension in addition to the individual versus group incentive trade-off. This stems from the fact that the actual degree of success in the fulfillment of adaptive targets tends to be lower than the success rate for the fulfillment of integrative targets. The reasons for this might be several: longer-term versus shorter-term time horizon, less versus more highly structured managerial tasks, the inherent degree of risk involved, and so on. Thus, if a manager is given a certain fraction of his salary as fixed, i.e., independent of his success in target fulfillment, and another fraction of his salary as a potential bonus, dependent on his success in achieving the targets, then it follows that the degree of variability of compensation for the managers who face more integrative tasks will tend to be less than for the managers who face more adaptive tasks. The implication is that bonuses can have a relatively higher effect when it comes to motivating adaptive behavior. Thus, the function of variable to fixed compensation might be higher for strategy center managers who are managing question marks than for cash-cow strategy center managers.

It also follows that since the nature of each manager's strategic tasks typically will be distinctively different it will be necessary to individually tailor-make incentives for each. It will thus be difficult to capture the incentives in a simple formula. Instead, each manager should receive an individually negotiated incentives *package* which summarizes his incentives along the following three dimensions:

1. Relative emphasis on objectives setting versus strategic programming versus budgeting. This will provide the weights for the importance of the following five performance components in a manager's incentives package:
   a. Output performance relative to intermediate goals, pursuing an established strategic direction
   b. Performance in reassessing strategic performance, by means of critical assumption analysis
   c. As in (a) for strategic programs
   d. As in (b) for strategic programs
   e. Output performance relative to the budget
2. Types of incentives to be distributed for different types of performance:
   a. Salary, bonus
   b. Promotion
   c. Discretionary freedom
   d. Fringe benefits
   e. Stock options
3. Split between individual and group incentives for different types of performance:
   a. Individual
   b. Subgroup
   c. Organization-wide

The number of factors playing a role in inducing different types of managerial behavior is large. It is beyond the scope of this book to discuss the many incentive schemes that have been proposed. In summary, however, we shall stress the need to see the decisions on choice of management incentives as part of the overall strategic management system design task. Too often incentives are developed in a less than adequately focused strategic decision-making context, the result invariably being that the incentives are at odds with the strategic decision-making thrust of the firm.

Tailor-Making the Planning System to Reinforce Shifts in Strategic Direction: An Example

Let us consider a company with annual sales of approximately 500 million dollars. The company is active in business domestically and internationally in food products, children's toys, and industrial chemicals. Diversification internationally and into toys and chemicals has involved relatively recent strategic moves, primarily through acquisitions. The company has recently reorganized from what was predominantly a functional to a divisional structure. Presently there are 4 groups, more than 20 divisions, and close to 70 strategy centers. The recent reorganization called for a relatively higher emphasis on integration during the years just after the reorganization, so that transitional inefficiencies associated with the institutionalization of the new management tasks might more rapidly be sorted out.

The CEO has adopted a philosophy of high-performance aspirations, including, as noted, heavy emphasis on growth through acquisitions. The diversity of the company is therefore rapidly increasing. One consequence is that senior management can less and less comfortably know all the businesses in detail. Senior management thus increasingly realizes that it will have to rely on the more specialized business knowledge of the various division managements. The portfolio/business division of labor with respect to the strategic planning tasks of the firm has thus only recently been delineated.

In terms of the planning needs facing the company, the continued acquisition drive might call for strengthening of the adaptive planning capabilities at the corporate level in order to identify, analyze, and consummate acquisitions. Also, however, a strengthening of the integrative planning capabilities when it comes to the ongoing operations of the company seems in order, so that dysfunctional efficiency problems due to the recent reorganization might be overcome. This would apply to the existing operations at the division/business level but would also be reflected in the corporate management's mode of interaction with the divisions. We thus seem to have a different adaptation/integration balance need for planning at the corporate level and at the divisional level; at the former level it seems appropriate to have relatively more emphasis on adaptation, while at the latter level, relatively more emphasis on integration should probably be the case. Of course, if at some later stage the emphasis on internal growth through the existing businesses is to be stressed, then the adaptation capabilities at the division/business level need to be strengthened relatively more at the time.

The key implication in terms of designing the linkages of the planning system, however, is that the needs for linkage might be different at various organizational levels—relatively tight linkages of types 1, 5, and 8 (see Exhibit 5-4) at the corporate level and relatively tight linkages of types 2, 3, and 6 at divisional levels. Also, we see that changes in linkage patterns might be appropriate at a particular level when the adaptive/integrative balance of a subset of organizational subunits changes. In instances of this kind, linkage changes across the entire organization would be inappropriate; a potential loosening of linkage types 2, 3, and 6 and a tightening of linkage types 1, 5, and 8 would be appropriate for those divisions at the business level where more internal growth gradually would be pursued.

The increased diversity of the company provides the company's senior management with the opportunity to develop a corporate portfolio strategy that emphasizes the balance between net funds-generating business divisions and funds-consuming growth divisions, as we have seen. This added diversity calls for increased realism with respect to adaptation needs and capabilities among the high-growth divisions, so that the corporate level can be fully aware of each business's growth potential. Also, there is a need for increased integration needs and capability realism, particularly among the net funds-generating divisions, to facilitate the gauging of the discretionary funds-flow generation. This is necessary to estimate reallocation capacity for going into other business segments. Thus, added diversity calls for increased adaptation emphasis at the corporate level so that appropriate rebalancing of the portfolio can be carried out. Given their different roles in the portfolio strategy, the nature of the linkage might be different among different divisions, as we have seen with relatively tight linkage of types 1, 5, and 8 among the growth divisions and relatively tight linkage of types 2, 3, and 6 among the net funds-generating divisions. This again underscores the need to tailor-make planning among divisions within a company—the application to all divisions of formalized planning rules that are too inflexible for the company as a whole may be dysfunctional. Thus, we see an added dimension to the richness of the linkage problem in that the nature of linkage probably should be expected to differ depending on the life-cycle/competitive strength posture of the division.[7] In general, we see that the maturity of the system, the nature of the company's growth strategy, and the characteristics of its portfolio pattern of diversity are factors that will be relevant in dictating the needs for tailor-making the linkage aspects of the planning system.

As we have seen, the emphasis on pursuing a corporate or business strategy is likely to change over time in most real-life settings, so that the relative need for adaptation versus integration changes. It will therefore be a normal procedure that the relative emphasis on the different linkage types should change. This management of the shifts in linkage emphasis is probably one of the most important "plan for planning" tasks. We shall pursue this further in Chapter Six. At this point, however, let us give another example which describes how such shifts actually might come about.

A 1.5 billion-dollar sales company was pursuing two major groups of businesses, one rapidly growing and high-technology-based and one more mature and within the consumer products area. It went through an evolutionary pattern for planning, which in many ways gives a quite typical illustration of the linkage problems associated with changing the relative balance between adaptation to more long-term environmental opportunities and/or threats and integration in order to cope with the more near-term internal issues of utilizing strengths and diminishing effects from weaknesses.

The company got started in an emerging high-technology business area three decades ago and grew rapidly, thanks to the entrepreneurial insight of its founder and CEO. The company's performance was outstanding, as measured by means of its growth in sales as well as in return on stockholders' equity (ROE) over the first two decades. However, from year to year the performance was quite erratic, a phenomenon which the CEO felt was natural, reflecting his strong desire to continue to take innovative risks, some of which would result in success, some in failure. Through a major acquisition about a decade ago, the company took over a well-established stable consumer products company, the strategic rationale being that it would provide a stabilizing effect on the corporation's cash-flow pattern. The high-technology business end of the company soon experienced a series of serious setbacks; even with the stable cash flows from the other end of the company, the overall corporate performance became so poor that both stockholder pressure and pressure from the firm's bankers eventually caused a dramatic shift to near-term actions to get costs under control and to clean up obvious inefficiencies. This manifested itself within the high-technology business by the adoption of a rigid budgeting system; cost cutting across the activity areas, particularly in personnel; and a dramatic reduction of discretionary expenditures. Within the consumer business end, a more conservative, heavily contingency-oriented plan was adopted. The result of this reorientation toward more integration was a stabilization of the company's performance, as indicated by a more stable ROE.

The level of the more stabilized ROE trend was, however, far below the performance levels of comparable competing corporations. Thus, to improve on long-term performance prospects beyond the gains from stabilization achieved through the integration-dominated efforts, increased emphasis was being put on allocation of resources, discretionary development expenditures, and channeling of capital to new profit lines judged to have higher longer-term strategic potentials. Soon it was felt that the more or less even approach toward cost cutting across the company also needed to be adjusted, so that costs were not cut as hard in instances where this would clearly frustrate the attempts at new strategy development. For the senior managers of the high-technology group to see better where to allocate discretionary resources and where to cut free resources, they more and more felt a need for concern with longer-term priority setting. In fact, what was taking place was a relative increase in the adaptation emphasis. Thus, the pendulum was swinging back again for the high-technology part of the company, away from a one-sided integration emphasis and toward a more balanced adaptation/integration planning thrust. For the mature consumer products part of the company, however, the predominantly integrative emphasis largely remained.

The major lesson from this example is that it took the top management of the company a long time and a lot of frustration and agony to realize that shifts in the company's direction might more fruitfully be pursued on a less grand scale. It was neither necessary nor beneficial to encourage cross-company changes of such magnitude. Belatedly, the senior management came to the conclusion that tailor-making of the planning system was necessary within the company itself. Not only should the linkage design be more front-end-oriented for the part of the planning system that applied to the high-technology part of the company versus more back-end-oriented for the consumer products part. Also, the other tailor-making design features should be applied differently. Thus, in handling the task of management of the evolution of a planning system, one must recognize the need to allow different parts of the organization to receive the types of planning support that they need, while of course also keeping an overall corporate focus in mind.

As a way of summarizing the major systems design options available for influencing the capabilities of the corporate planning system, let us consider Table 5-1. We recall from Chapter Three that the overall corporate planning needs generally were focused on bringing the corporate planning system back to an equilibrium position in terms of its adaptation and integration capabilities by redesigning the corporate planning system so as to improve either its adaptive or integrative capabilities or both. We have identified a total of five systems design variables that fall into these classes, combinations of which might be employed to facilitate such tailor-made design. The choice of values for these design variables will thus depend on the direction toward which we wish to change the planning system, as indicated in Table 5-1.

TABLE 5-1 Corporate Planning System's Tailor-Making Design Options

Corporate Planning System's Tailor-Making Design Factors	Strengthened Integration	Strengthened Adaptation
1. Focus of planning: top-down vs. bottom-up	Top-down	Bottom-up
2. Time-spending pattern: front-end vs. back-end	Back-end	Front-end
3. Nature of delegation in planning:		
a. Linkages	To back end of budgets fulfillment	To front end of objectives fulfillment
b. Performance monitoring	Tied to budgets	Tied to objectives
c. Management incentives	Tied to budgets	Tied to budgets

Summary

In this chapter we have attempted to discuss approaches toward tailor-making the strategic planning system so that the capabilities of the system can be developed to meet the particular needs for planning that different companies have in accordance with the adaptive and integrative planning needs patterns identified in Chapter Three. We approached this task at different organizational levels.

For the business planning level we saw how adaptive versus integrative tasks would call for different sets of strategic guidelines for the development of the desired strategic thrusts. We identified several aspects of such guidelines.

We then examined several corporate systems design factors that the planner to a greater or lesser degree might control in order to achieve the needed adaptation/integration focus of the planning system. These tailor-making factors were the following: relative emphasis on top-down versus bottom-up inputs in the planning process, relative emphasis on the front end versus the back end of the strategy opportunity identification and narrowing down stages, the nature of the linkage among each of the five cycles in the planning process—tight versus loose, the pattern of executive involvement, time-spending patterns, the focus of the control systems for monitoring the front-end versus back-end parts of the planning process, and, finally, the relative importance of the front end versus the back end in the management incentives formula.

Finally we gave examples of how the tailor-making emphasis might differ in relation to different organizational subunits within the same company. We also saw an example of how changes in tailor-making emphasis might reinforce successful shifts in firms' strategic directions.

NOTES

1. The contingency approach or situational design approach to the design of management systems underlines this chapter. Among the more influential articles and books that have relevance within the context of corporate planning are Alfred D. Chandler, Jr., *Strategy and Structure* (Cambridge, Mass.: M.I.T. Press, 1963); James D. Thompson, *Organizations in Action* (New York: McGraw-Hill, 1967); William H. Newman, "Strategy and Management Structure," *Journal of Business Policy* (Winter 1971–72); Jay W. Lorsch and Stephen A. Allen, III, *Managing Diversity and Interdependence: An Organizational Study of Multidivisional Firms* (Boston: 1973); Division of Research, Harvard Business School, John W. Newstrom, William E. Reif, and Robert M. Monczka, *A Contingency Approach to Management: Readings* (New York: McGraw-Hill, 1975); Peter Lorange and Richard F. Vancil, *Strategic Planning Systems* (Englewood Cliffs, N.J.: Prentice-Hall, 1977), Part Two; and Rochelle O'Connor, "Corporate Guides to Long-Range Planning," *Report No. 687* (New York: The Conference Board, 1976).

2. The following articles or books address important aspects of how to develop situationally tailor-made product/market strategies: Donald G. Marquis, "The Anatomy of Successful Innovations," *Innovation* (Nov. 1969); Charles W. Hofer, "Some Preliminary Research on Patterns of Strategic Behavior," *Academy of Management Proceedings* (Aug. 1973); *A System for Managing Diversity* (Cambridge, Mass.: Arthur D. Little, Inc., 1974); Dan E. Schendel, Richard Patton, and James Riggs, "Corporate Turnaround Strategies" (unpublished working paper, Purdue University, 1974); C. R. Wasson, *Dynamic Competitive Strategy and Products Life Cycles* (St. Charles, Mo.: Challenge Books, 1974); and Charles W. Hofer, "Towards a Contingency Theory of Business Strategy," *Academy of Management Journal*, 18 (1975), 784-810.

3. See Peter Lorange and Richard F. Vancil, "How To Design a Strategic Planning System," *Harvard Business Review*, 54 (Sept.–Oct. 1976).

4. See John K. Shank, Edward G. Niblock, and William T. Sandalls, Jr., "Balance Creativity and Practicality in Formal Planning," *Harvard Business Review*, 51 (Jan.–Feb. 1973), and J. M. Hobbs and D. F. Heany, "Coupling Strategy to Operating Plans," *Harvard Business Review* (May–June 1977).

5. See Peter Lorange and Richard F. Vancil, "How To Design a Strategic Planning System," *Harvard Business Review*, 54 (Sept.–Oct. 1976), Exhibit 2.

6. See H. Igor Ansoff, "Managing Surprise and Discontinuity—Strategic Response to Weak Signals," *Working Paper No. 75-21* (Brussels: European Institute for Advanced Studies in Management, 1975); William H. Newman, *Constructive Control* (Englewood Cliffs, N.J.: Prentice-Hall, 1975); S. I. Ansari, "An Integrated Approach to Control System Design," *Accounting, Organizations and Society* , 2 (1977), 101-112; Les Metcalfe and Will McQuillan, "Managing Turbulence," in *Prescriptive Models of Organizations*, eds. Paul C. Nystrom and William H. Starbuck (Amsterdam: North-Holland, 1977), 7-25; William G. Ouchi, "The Relationship Between Organizational Structure and Organizational Control," *Administrative Science Quarterly*, 22 (March 1977), 95-113; Richard F. Vancil, *Decentralization: Managerial Ambiguity by Design* (New York: Financial Executives Research Foundation, 1979); and Ben C. Ball and Peter Lorange, "Managing Your Strategic Responsiveness to the Environment," *Sloan School Working Paper* (Cambridge, Mass.: Sloan School of Management, M.I.T., 1978).

7. See Donald K. Clifford, Jr., "Managing the Product Life Cycle," in *The Art of Top Management: A McKinsey Anthology*, ed. Roland Mann (New York: McGraw-Hill, 1971).

chapter six

Managing the Evolution of the Corporate Planning System

Introduction

In Chapter Five we discussed the needs for, and approaches to, tailor-making a corporate planning system to the particular needs of a given corporation, so that the capabilities of the planning system might be developed in a useful direction. The particular planning needs will, however, seldom be constant; rather they keep changing. Partly this will be due to changes in the firm's environment, thereby creating new strategic pressures on the corporation. Also, however, revised planning needs might stem from changes in the strategic position within the firm itself.

In this chapter we shall first discuss how one might approach this issue of how to modify the planning system so that it stays current over a longer period of time. Our approach will be that the task of managing the evolution of the planning system should be based on an anticipation of the nature of upcoming planning needs and should not be a reactive process. We shall take an overall management systems point of view to carry out such an evolution, since we want consistency among the five systems elements of the management system.

Having established a general framework for how to manage the evolution of the strategic planning system, we are in a much better position to approach a number of specific evolutionary issues that also need to be tackled. We shall be focusing on seven issues relating to managing of the planning system approach: how to cope with overloading of the planning system, how to minimize potential dysfunctions of the firm's hierarchical structure so that an added group level does not become a filter in the strategic process, how to assess whether a particular product/market element pattern remains reasonable or whether further delineation of organizational boundaries between product/market elements should be undertaken, how to modify the planning system so that it is workable within a so-called matrix organization structure, how to facilitate a relatively consistent pattern of risk taking over time while coping with differences in executives' attitudes toward risk, how to attempt to maintain vitality as a central ingredient of planning as the process becomes older, and, finally, how to incorporate considerations for particular strategic problems of planning within the multinational corporate scene, not only as a company grows abroad but also as the multinational scene becomes more complex. Finally we shall discuss an important procedural question when it comes to managing the evolution of strategic planning systems, namely, when to carry out a more complete audit of planning needs.

The Task of Managing the Corporate Planning System over Time

Exhibit 6-1 gives our view of the dynamic nature of the task of managing the evolution of the corporate planning system. Let us first give a brief general description of the nature of this task by explaining the rationale of the process implied by the exhibit. Subsequently we shall elaborate as needed on several aspects of the process.[1] Starting with the top box of the diagram in Exhibit 6-1, we state that the particular need for planning is a function of a specific organization's strategic position. This is in accordance with what we discussed in Chapter Three. The planning system, then, should be designed in such a way that the capabilities built into the system will meet the particular needs identified. This is exemplified by the middle box in Exhibit 6-1. The actual approach to tailor-making the planning system's design was outlined in Chapter Five. Strategic plans will be shaped through the planning system, leading in turn to strategic decisions which will be functions of the strategic plans. We have illustrated these outcomes of strategic planning as a tool in decision making in the bottom box in Exhibit 6-1.

At a first glance we might conclude that our task of designing a useful corporate planning system will have been successfully concluded at this point, particularly if the capabilities of the system seem to reflect the company's needs. On second thought, we shall, however, probably

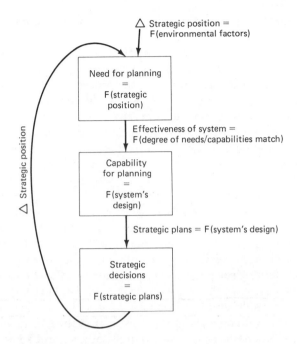

EXHIBIT 6-1   Dynamic (Closed-Loop) Task of Managing
the Planning System

realize that the emerging strategic decisions in turn will inflict changes on
the previous strategic situational position of the firm and thereby cause
changes in its planning needs. Environmental factors are also likely to
inflict changes on the firm's strategic position. We have indicated this in
Exhibit 6-1 by means of the two arrows which, respectively, identify
internally and externally generated changes in the firm's strategic position, both impacting the needs for planning. Thus, the company's planning needs will be expected to change over time, partly because of
environmental factors outside the control of the firm but also as a result of
the firm's own discretionary decisions. Revisions will have to be incorporated in the design of the planning system in order to provide for the
modified capabilities that will be called for by the new needs. Recognizing
that we have a closed-loop system at hand, a more or less continuous
updating of the planning system will be required for the system to
maintain its effectiveness. If not, the planning system will contribute to its
own obsolescence by self-destructing.

As indicated in Exhibit 6-1 we can in fact develop a concept of
planning's effectiveness as a function of the degree of match between the
planning needs and the system's capabilities to meet these needs. The
preceding paragraph should make us realize that effective planning is a

fragile phenomenon and might easily deteriorate unless one works at it almost continuously.

Having now completed the discussion of the basic dynamic issues applying to the evolution of planning systems, let us attempt to get a better perception of how this evolutionary process might work in actual life. We shall start by giving some examples of strategic decisions and seeing how they might affect the company's strategic position.

For a product/market element, for instance, these strategic decisions might relate to changing its strategic direction—to build a stronger competitive strength position or to harvest by allowing the competitive strength position to become weakened. For a division we might have decisions that relate to developing new product/market elements as well as phasing out older ones. For the corporate level we might have strategic decisions that cause a relative shift in emphasis on certain businesses at the expense of others in that some will be allocated a relatively larger share of discretionary resources than others. Other examples of portfolio-level strategic decisions are acquisitions and/or divestitures. In all these instances we see that the internal situational setting of the firm will change as a result: emphasis on new product lines—deemphasis on others, expansion into new geographic areas, investments in new plants, entry into new businesses—divestiture from others, and so on. Clearly, the planning needs of the firm will change as a consequence of this. Therefore, unless the planning system is modified to reflect the evolving planning needs, the system will less and less reflect the needs dictated by the situational setting. As already stated, the planning system itself will influence the strategic directions taken. By thereby contributing to changes in the firm's situational setting, the system will cause the situational setting that its own design is based on to no longer be up-to-date. Thus, we might say that the planning system contributes to its own destruction.

The other major element to influence the situational setting will of course be changes in the firm's relevant environment. Some companies are such dominating factors in their business settings that they can significantly affect their environments through their own actions. Typically, however, such companies are relatively few. Most companies will not be in a position to affect the major factors of their environments, at least not for an extended period of time. Thus, most firms' environments will change largely due to factors outside the control of the firm.

It is important to make a distinction between changes in the planning needs that stem from internally generated decisions versus those that stem from external environmental pressures. The latter factors are particularly significant not only because they too might affect the need for planning but because they are largely outside the control of the firm's management and cannot easily be anticipated in most cases. This is in contrast to the effects on the firm's internal situational setting which will be derived from its strategic decisions and which thus at least in theory should be anticipated reasonably well, facilitating modification of the planning system in time. The environmental factors are often much harder to anticipate, and it should be a major task in the effort to manage the planning system's evolution to pay attention to this, so that the reactive element of the mode of evolution of the planning system can be kept to a minimum.

When analyzing the history of many planning systems in the light of the dynamic evolutionary model for a planning system's design that has just been developed, we find that many commonly found growth-pain problems can be better understood. First, it makes us realize that the planning system is in a sense similar to a temporary management system in that it will only be applicable in a particular design configuration for a relatively short period of time. Thus, it will be important that the system be brought up to speed relatively early to contribute usefully to at least certain aspects of strategic decision making. Many corporations, unfortunately, take such a long-term approach to the installation of a planning system that it might be partly obsolete by the time it is put into operation. There is in fact some danger in allowing the consideration for learning during the planning start-up to be played up too much because of this. Although there is a legitimate need for learning, little time should be wasted in emphasizing decision-making considerations. It might be deduced from this that a modular approach to planning would be useful, allowing the process to come up to speed within certain areas of planning at a time. In these instances there is, however, the danger that overall consistency among the various elements of the planning system might get lost. We shall discuss this in the next section.

A second evolutionary planning issue relates to finding a proper degree of rigidity and formality for the planning system. In general, rigid formalization will be less desirable in the case of temporary systems than in the case of more permanent systems. Unfortunately, many companies tend to formalize aspects of the planning system more than necessary for the purpose at hand. As one indication of this we find that some companies go through great efforts in having their planning manual printed, with fancy artwork and all. Although admittedly not necessarily a major stumbling block for proper evolution of planning, this might nevertheless easily lend a notion of permanence to the planning system that could be unfortunate. Formalization and institutionalization might easily lead to the development of plans for the sake of planning. In fact, the planning approach to strategic decision making discussed in this book would typically not be characterized by overly formalized systems routines, such as highly extrapolative, numbers-oriented plans à la long-term budgets found in some companies.

Third, as for all temporary management systems, the corporate planning system needs to be associated with and managed by a specific group of managers, who should be easily identifiable. The manager who is the prime customer of this temporary system will be the CEO. As such he is also the one ultimately responsible for seeing that the planning system in being managed. He will of course have to draw on staff assistance in having this task carried out. However, he should not delegate the management of the system to a staff planner to the extent that he loses familiarity with the system and is unable to judge whether it is effective. Such familiarity is a requirement for building confidence in the planning system. Also, it will open the possibility for the CEO to control the evolution of the planning system in order to reinforce the strategic changes he is pursuing.

Let us stress as a preliminary conclusion then that it should be clear that there will be a strong need for managing the evolution of a planning system, since the situational setting, and thereby the planning needs, will be almost constantly changing. It is useful to consider a planning system as being analogous to a temporary management system, stressing flexibility over formality, requiring a relatively immediate payoff in terms of results from the system, and requiring the CEO's involvement in the system's design in his capacity as its key user. Beyond establishing the need for managing the corporate planning system in general, as we have done in this section, there will be several critical issues that relate to carrying out specific aspects of this task. The rest of this chapter will in fact be devoted to pursuing this. One critical issue in this respect is to provide for a continued sense of consistency among the various elements of a planning system as the system evolves over time. This topic will be discussed in the next section.

A Strategic Management System Point of View: Consistency

The key issue when discussing how to achieve an overall strategic management point of view for the design and implementation of the corporate planning system is the need to remind ourselves, in accordance with our conceptual scheme for planning discussed in Chapter Two, that there are five cycles or subsystems in our strategic management system, namely, the objectives-setting system, the strategic programming system, the budgeting system, the monitoring system, and the management incentives system. There will be the same need to tailor-make each of these subsystems to the situational setting at hand. Needless to say, the same general situational setting applies to all of these subsystems as the tailor-making base. Therefore, this imposes a requirement for consistency among the subsystems in terms of their design and capabilities.[2] Exhibit 6-2 illustrates the need for a tailor-made design for each of the elements of the strategic system to underscore that the elements will have to be consistent with each other. The effectiveness of the strategic system, then, is a function of the matching of each system element's design to the particular needs of the situational setting. Assuming that an appropriate matching of needs and capabilities has taken place, we see that this automatically implies that internal consistency in design is ensured among the elements of the strategic system.

Unfortunately, there seem to be major problems in real life when it comes to achieving overall internal consistency within the strategic sys-

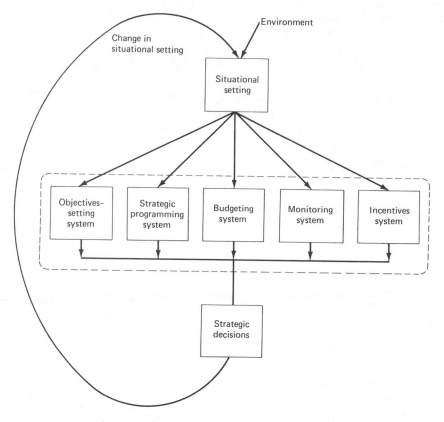

EXHIBIT 6-2   Tailor-Making Each Element of the Strategic System to the Situational Setting and with Consistency Among Elements

tem. Typically, management's attention will be on redesigning and/or modifying one of the subsystems in particular at a given time, leaving the other systems as they are. For instance, the objectives-setting or strategic programming systems may receive major attention, i.e. be strengthened to reflect the given setting as of today. The budgeting system, however, may not receive the same critical scrutinizing to assess whether modifications are needed here too. This system may have remained essentially the same over quite some time, having been tailor-made to a situational setting long since changed. In such a case the budgeting system will not provide capabilities in accordance with the emerging needs and in line with what would be necessary to follow through with the benefits from the strengthening of the prior cycles. Hence, we might have a potentially serious element of inconsistency. For exactly analogous reasons to those above, we might also have a monitoring system or incentive system which does not reflect the present situational setting.

A typical reason for the serious inconsistencies among the various systems elements might be that the subsystems were not installed at the same time, as already mentioned. The age distribution of the subsystems might even be so wide that the systems might reflect entirely different prevailing management settings. Another potential source of inconsistency might be that different management groups may have been responsible for the management of the different subsystems, thereby not necessarily perceiving the same needs from the situational setting. For instance, a corporate planning group might be responsible for objectives setting and strategic programming, a corporate controller's department may have major responsibility for the budgeting and monitoring stages, and a human development function might be primarily involved in the managerial incentives stage. These executives will approach the needs for system support from their own frame of reference. Thus, unless coordinated, management responsibility segmentation, and potentially also an element of parochialism, might be likely to hamper the attempt to achieve overall consistency. Finally, it might be that the management of a corporation is simply not sufficiently aware of the issue of potential inconsistency in subsystems, not being used to seeing the five elements as part of one overall strategic system.

What might be the consequences of lack of consistency among the elements within the strategic system? We have seen in our discussion of how an integrated overall strategic management system is supposed to work that each element of this system is dependent on the others. Thus, the strategic decision-making tool will not function unless there is a tight logical interrelationship among all the elements. There will be several specific consequences when such lack of overall consistency is the case, and we shall discuss each of them.

First, let us consider the consistency requirements among the objectives-setting, strategic programming, and budgeting stages. If, for instance, the strategic programming activity is not done within the context of the focus set by the objectives-setting stage, the effect will probably be that a much larger number of strategic program alternatives will have to be prepared and analyzed in order to come up with enough viable choices to be able to select a reasonably good package of strategic programs. Little or no prior focus will have been provided to limit the areas of search for strategic programs, the most likely consequence being that much additional effort will have to be spent on the strategic programming aspects. This of course is normally not desirable at all, given the heavy work load involved in preparing and analyzing a typical strategic program. A weakening of the quality of the strategic programs to be followed is likely to result, given that management attention almost inevitably will have to be more thinly spread over a larger set of less focused strategic programs. Thus, inconsistency between the stages is less likely to lead to both a heavier work load and an inflated quality of the managerial inputs into the process. Similarly, with inconsistencies between the strategic programming and the budgeting stages there will be an analogous set of problems in that the strategic options will not have been substantially narrowed down beforehand. We recall that the lack of narrowing down was also discussed in Chapter Two and illustrated in Exhibit 2-3.

It should be noted that the necessary narrowing down prior to the budgeting process might be hampered even if we have a reasonable consistency between the stages of the process, because of management's lack of willingness to execute the necessary decision-making discipline during the earlier stages. Unless management is willing to resolve which strategic choice to make among several potential directions to go, i.e., to commit to a particular set of objectives, it will be next to impossible to carry out a more focused strategic programming. Similarly, unless decisions are made concerning which of the many potential programs to follow the budgeting process will be out of focus.

Returning to another issue that was touched upon during our discussion relating to Exhibit 2-3 we see that the distribution of time spent on planning through the year is also critical in terms of regulating the work load for reaching the best possible strategic direction. With the gradual narrowing down of strategic options the work load can be spread out reasonably well over the year. However, without the prior narrowing down management will be faced with the same broad set of strategic options during the much shorter budgeting period. This probably means an extraordinary peak work load for the management team, again likely to result in reduced quality of the strategic decision-making efforts. Given that such a work-load peak exists, one would typically expect this to lead to a natural and probably necessary tendency toward more ad hoc elimination of certain options. Thus, there will be a real danger that the truncated narrowing down that takes place will be out of line with what would seem to be optimal had the full range of relevant options been considered. A less than ideal final action program package might be the result.

We have argued that poor time utilization among the first three stages of the strategic process might lead to serious distortions in the strategic decision making due to dysfunctional effects on the narrowing down process. Beyond the arguments discussed in the previous paragraphs a more fundamental underlying problem will be that the adaptation/integration balance in the strategic decision-making process might get distorted. This, however, can more easily be discussed in connection with inconsistencies relating to the interrelationships with the remaining two factors, the monitoring and the management incentives components. We shall pursue this in the next paragraphs.

Considering problems that might arise due to inconsistencies between the monitoring function and the other stages, a basic requirement will be that the monitoring system be structured in such a way that it is able to monitor progress toward the fulfillment of the outputs for each of the three previous cycles. When the monitoring system is out of focus, a serious consequence might be that neither adaptive nor integrative corrective action will be taken. Beyond this fairly obvious requirement that the monitoring system adequately reflect the variables it is supposed to monitor, there often exists a more subtle inconsistency: The balance in the monitoring efforts, i.e., the relative emphasis on the monitoring of objectives versus monitoring of strategic programs versus monitoring of budgets, might not fully reflect the intended adaptation/integration balance for the first three cycles. Specifically, most monitoring systems tend to put almost exclusive emphasis on near-term budget fulfillment monitoring. Some also put emphasis on monitoring progress toward the fulfillment of longer-term strategic programs, while relatively few monitoring attempts tend to be focused on the long-term objectives-setting fulfillment. Thus, there might easily develop a bias toward the near-term and toward integration. At least two factors tend to reinforce this bias. First, the fulfillment of the budget might receive so much attention that management might become geared too much toward integration problems. Second, the lack of monitoring of the predominantly environmental issues associated with the relevance of one's longer-term objectives might cause a further lessening of the sensitivity toward adaptation-related issues. In Chapter Four we discussed how to operationalize the monitoring of key environmental variables and how to cope with the problem of excessively long time spans of control.

We shall turn now to the management incentives phase; this is the element which is most often substantially inconsistent with the other parts of the strategic management system. For instance, a management incentives system might consist of monetary elements, such as executive bonus and stock option plans. Most often, however, these are not specifically tied to each executive's performance in contributing to the fulfillment of the output targets in the first two cycles. In cases where explicit rules exist for the distribution of bonuses and options, these tend to reinforce short-term budget fulfillment performance. For nonmonetary incentives, too, there often seems to be a lack of explicit tie-in with strategic performance. For instance, the promotion and reassignment of key executives is often not systematically tied to explicit performance assessments.

The management incentives system often is not explicitly coordinated with the other elements of the strategic system because the task of administering the system falls to staff executives who are not directly involved in the planning and control functions. Even more critically, these executives may not be very familiar with the major strategic decision-making shifts that line management may be attempting. Thus, by segmenting staff tasks without being explicitly concerned about the system consistency issue, a company might be denying itself this source of reinforcement of the strategic direction. Even worse, however, this might create pressures that would actually counteract the implementation of the strategic plans.

It should be pointed out that to bring the incentives system in line with the other elements of the strategic system will depend critically on the availability of relevant information about strategic performance fulfillment. Thus, the intention to emphasize both long-term and short-term strategic behavior with management incentives presupposes that the monitoring system has been developed sufficiently to allow for a useful assessment of managers' longer-term performance. Unless this is realistic the basis for credibility would be gone.

Given the importance of consistency among the elements of the strategic system, let us discuss a few approaches that management might take in facilitating this. A first step might be to carry out a consistency audit at certain regular intervals, say every third or fourth year. The task here simply should be to determine whether the elements of the strategic system seem to reflect the same common situational setting. This consistency audit approach is useful because it explicitly creates an opportunity to focus on the overall consistency issue in large, complex organizations where the lack of an overall common viewpoint seems to be the norm.

A second approach for ameliorating inconsistency is to recognize the management task consequence of the overall integrated strategic approach, namely, that it will be one task to manage the design and evolution of this system. Consequently, there should be one staff executive who has responsibility for this task; this leadership will facilitate cooperation among, say, a corporate planner's department, a controller's department, and a human resources department. Given the critical importance of the strategic system as a vehicle for achieving strategic direction in a large, complex organization, it is necessary that the executive responsible for the overall system be sufficiently close to senior management to internalize a realistic sense of direction that relates to the company's strategic direction. Thus, a remote staff executive will not suffice in this position, for such a person would not have the insight to be able to line up the strategic system behind the desired strategic thrust.

Third, and probably equally important, by recognizing the complexity of the task of managing the strategic system so that it stays relevant and remains internally consistent, a company should develop a *plan for planning*. This should consist of an explicitly spelled out conceptual framework for the system, identifying its components, how they are intended to function, and their interrelationships. One example of a useful conceptual scheme is the one proposed in Chapter Two and summarized in Exhibit 2-5. Having put down, communicated, and internalized such a conceptual framework for planning, this should serve as a benchmark for any development and improvement of aspects of the system, ensuring that improvements and modifications will contribute in a common direction. Otherwise energy is wasted in developing aspects of a planning system that will not fit into a common scheme. Thus, an integral part of the plan for planning will be to specify when to change and what to change in the planning system and how as well as why such changes might be deemed desirable. Without such an explicit plan for planning it is very common that the planning system is subjected to shifts in direction, modifications and additions that do not consolidate into a common strategic decision-making thrust. Little by little the system might become so diffuse, illogical, and complicated that its effectiveness as a management tool is diminished. A common feeling among the users in such situations is that the strategic planning system has been *overloaded*, an issue we shall discuss in more detail in the next section.

Overloading of the Strategic System

A common problem in the design, implementation, and evolution of a corporate planning system is that there might be a tendency for such a system to mushroom, i.e., gradually become so complex, time-consuming, and difficult to use that we might talk about a work-overload phenomenon on the part of the systems users. In such instances it will be exceedingly hard and time-consuming for the various line managers to prepare the necessary inputs to the various aspects of the planning documents, to participate in planning meetings, to report progress on strategic programs that they manage, and so on. That this additional heavy work load and pressure may lead to a feeling of frustration is quite natural, especially when the perception develops among line managers that they seem to be preparing plans that are more useful to their superiors than to themselves. Further, they feel that the planning activities take time and energy away from the day-to-day business activities. Given the formidable work load for a line manager, it should therefore be an essential requirement that the planning system be both conceptually sound and carefully implemented, so that there should be no wasteful activities. Whatever requests on line managers' time, in the forms of additional meetings, new data input reports, extra follow-up studies, etc., that are not absolutely essential for the fulfillment of the strategic planning task should thus be eliminated.

Unfortunately, there seems to be a tendency for all management systems to keep growing as a function of time. In the previous section we discussed an aspect of this, namely, that the system might thereby become less internally consistent and less logically focused over the years. Another real problem, however, is that management tends to add new routines to the planning system, usually in response to a particular pressure: For example, energy shortage leads to a need for the planning of energy sources, conversion, and conservation; soaring labor wages, social costs, and legislative labor restrictions trigger off a corporate response in the form of a manpower plan; and so on. While such ad hoc additions might be necessary and legitimate given the circumstances, there is not a similar tendency to delete those parts of the system that might have become less relevant; hence, the system tends to grow.

We shall offer three suggestions for dealing with this problem of keeping the line's time commitment within reasonable limits. The first will be to adopt a zero-base audit approach to the planning system. At certain time intervals, typically not too frequently, an audit might attempt to raise the question of why each particular element of the planning system is justified in terms of the benefits it yields relative to the costs of expending management time on executing this aspect of the system. Essentially, the planning system will be examined as if it were redesigned from scratch. It would be natural to perform this type of audit in conjunction with the consistency audit discussed in the previous section.

A second approach would be to rely on ad hoc one-shot studies of various kinds to a larger extent in the planning process. For instance, a special-purpose task force might be created to come up with strategies for how to approach each of the particular issues, such as energy or labor, referred to before. In line with this, it should be explicitly stated that certain planning procedures that are being introduced are intended to have a very specific lifetime.

There is another ad hoc aspect of planning which involves senior management primarily and has proven to be very useful in several companies. Through this, senior management will get involved in an in-depth strategic audit review of a few of the operating units each year, outside of the recurrent reviews and interactions that are part of the annual strategic planning cycle. This might give senior management an opportunity to learn more intimately about the subtleties of the particular business and give the managers of the particular business an opportunity to understand better senior management's point of view. In-depth strategic interchanges of this kind might strengthen senior management's insight and feel for the business, which is essential for giving the recurring annual planning process corporate reviews a sense of realism rather than aloofness. Also it might open up a more free-flowing communication within the organizational hierarchy. Incidents such as a corporate management visit to an operating unit, for example, in connection with an in-depth strategic review, might have dramatic effects on creating a sense of shared commitment to the company's strategic direction.

This more in-depth business understanding on behalf of senior management seems essential not only for efficient planning, in that it will pave the way for a more focused, quicker, corporate-divisional pattern of interaction for narrowing down strategic options, but, more importantly, it may provide an impetus for better strategic decisions. As already stated, the corporate-divisional planning review process might too often deteriorate into an overly formalistic, intellectually unchallenging exercise, overly financially dominated. Instead of pursuing planning with such an unreal touch, a sound senior management business understanding and judgment will better enable the corporate and business strategic levels to work together to improve the strategic decisions. The recognition of the need for appropriately chosen and insightful top management contribution to the business plans is essential; no top-down contribution should create a feeling of animosity at the business level; artificial or shallow top-down contribution might, more than most factors, lead to the deterioration of the effectiveness of the planning process.

A final suggestion for keeping the overloading pressure of planning under control has to do with the relationship between the corporate planning staff and the line. It is not entirely uncommon to see corporate planning staffs that cannot resist the temptation to project themselves as whiz kids relative to the line or that even develop an image of slight disrespect for the line. They may underestimate the time implications for the line of various suggestions the planning staff may come up with for planning systems improvements. An effective corporate planning staff, on the other hand, will put much emphasis on working closely with the line to establish a line-staff consensus about the need to add to or to modify the planning system. It might be advisable, for instance, to try out the format of any systems additions or modifications on a pilot subset of the divisions. It should be a requirement that a particular planning procedure has been thoroughly debugged. If the line is involved in the implementation of modifications of the planning process, the likelihood of the line's acceptance of the modifications will be increased. Equally important, the quality of the changes themselves will probably improve.

Despite the arguments in the preceding paragraphs to keep the time involvement required by both top management and the line within reasonable proportions, it should be emphasized that good plans do not materialize without hard work. The considerable time and commitment needed in order to make planning work are real requirements. Given that it is so time-consuming, it follows that planning will probably not survive unless it provides sufficient useful input to the strategic decision-making process. It is through demonstrating a positive contribution that the planning tool can convince management (senior management in particular) that this is a worthwhile way of spending time and energy.

Despite the requirement for extensive taxing of management's time and involvement, it turns out that strategic planning, when properly functioning, actually might lead to savings in time spent by management on other management tasks within the firm. For instance, senior management's time spent on budget deviation analysis and short-term fire fighting might actually be freed. As a result of the planning efforts, a much more solid basis for the strategic direction of the firm now will exist. Thus, a larger degree of delegation can typically take place when it comes to making decisions with regard to corrective actions for the implementation of strategies and programs. We recall from our discussion in Chapter Five, however, that extreme care must be exercised so that delegation is not carried out in such a way that senior management might miss critical signals when significant changes are taking place, thereby hampering senior management's involvement in executing a change in strategy. Despite this, having made the investment of involving a larger group of management in internalizing the strategic direction through planning should provide senior management with a real opportunity to free time from ad hoc fire fighting. Another potential area for senior management time saving can be found when it comes to involvement in the review and approval of capital budgeting proposals and expenditure proposals. With prior planning and thereby an established strategic direction as stated in a set of objectives and goals as well as a focused set of strategic programs, the investment proposal and expenditure review and approval process should be significantly changed. Given that investments and expenditures of course are parts of particular strategic programs, the major review and approval effort from a resource allocation viewpoint should take place when scrutinizing the strategic program. Any investment or expenditure proposal should therefore be evaluated in this context, i.e., as a way for fine-tuning particular strategic programs and for checking their continued validity. Capital budgeting and expenditure budgeting should consequently not be seen as a primary decision-making tool for strategic resource allocations as such. Given the considerable senior management time involvement that the traditional capital budgeting and expenditure review and approval procedures require, planning might provide an opportunity to free considerable time. Even more important than the actual time saved, however, is probably senior management's increased influence on the firm's direction through the resource allocation process, as opposed to the rubber stamping of investment and expenditure proposals.

Let us finally discuss an approach for keeping a potentially very time-consuming aspect of planning within more reasonable proportions, namely, carrying out the analysis and evaluation of new product leads as well as potential acquisition leads. It seems clear that a firm should strive to receive a substantially larger number of such leads than what they actually decide to go ahead with. Such an intentional overflowing of alternatives will probably be a significant factor in increasing the batting average of the acquisitions and/or new product leads that turn out to be successful. In terms of reducing potential overloading of the planning system, then, it seems beneficial to develop a sequential approach for screening new product or acquisition proposals, with each proposal having to pass increasingly more elaborate analyses. A minimum of time might thereby be expended on proposals that are quite likely to be less attractive. Instead, efforts might be concentrated on analyzing the more serious contenders.

Previously we discussed approaches for evaluating R&D projects as part of a business strategy. As we recall, these approaches developed overall measures of attractiveness based on a number of relevant underlying factors. A similar approach might be developed as the basis for a screening procedure for acquisitions. When developing such an index-based sequential screening procedure it is important to find the right level of discrimination. If the prescreening is too heavy, then one runs the risk of turning down proposals that in retrospect prove advantageous. If, on the other hand, the prescreening is too light, then the problem of overloading the planning system will remain.

There are two additional sets of issues that should be considered when instituting prescreening procedures for the handling of new product and/or acquisition proposals in planning. First, the specialized know-how relevant for the evaluation of a new product and/or acquisition will have to be collected from a relatively wide number of executives within the firm—staff specialists, various functional representatives, line managers providing a business strategy perspective, and senior management providing a portfolio strategy viewpoint. It is therefore essential that a formalized and standard information/interaction flow be established among the relevant executives, so that it becomes clear who should evaluate particular aspects of a new product and/or acquisition proposal as well as when this should be done. Such unambiguous assignment of tasks provides accountability in the time saving that this is likely to lead to on the analysis—another critical factor, for in many instances the ability to make a quick decision will be paramount in order not to lose an opportunity.

Problems of overloading the planning system which stem from the time and efforts that planning requires have potentially serious dysfunctional effects on strategic decision making. Other factors in addition to overloading might lead to a diminishing of the decision-making focus. With the large number of executives involved in aspects of strategic analysis, the pressure to decide might easily become diffused. Planning might easily lead to a situation where nobody has clear responsibility to make a decision. In the next section we shall discuss how the decision-making focus of planning might become blurred due to elements of inappropriateness in the ways the organizational subunits interact through the planning process. What we shall identify as strategic filters hamper the development and implementation of strategic direction.

Strategic Filters

Let us first elaborate on what we mean by strategic filters as another aspect of managing the evolution of the planning system. A strategic filter is a feature of the organizational structure, formal or informal, that will potentially jeopardize the development and implementation of appropriate strategic direction in a corporate portfolio strategy, divisional business strategies, and (inter-) functional strategic programs. As we shall see in this section, the organization's structure is of major importance as a facilitator of or, alternatively, as a barrier to the achievement of a strategic direction. We have stressed earlier that it might be useful to distinguish between a strategic structure mode and an operating structure mode. At the center of the problem of strategic filters often lies the issue of lack of explicit reconciliation betwen these two structures, particularly the difficulty of seeing how a set of product/market elements, our strategic building blocks, fits with the existing operating organizational structure. Such strategic filters might of course arise even when the strategic structure exists only in a less articulated sense or maybe exists only implicitly. It may even be easier to assess whether strategic filters might exist in settings where the strategic structure is explicitly manifested, such as in Texas Instruments, Inc. or in General Electric Company (see the appendix to Chapter Two).

It will of course normally be outside the scope of the corporate planning system to be responsible for overseeing an organization's structure. Thus, in a narrow sense, it will not be an available planning systems design factor to suggest organizational changes in order to improve the climate for strategic management. However, we have made two arguments throughout this book that strongly suggest that the organizational structure issues must be seen together with corporate planning, both being integral elements of setting and implementing strategic direction: (1) The strategic systems fundamentally belong to the CEO and should thus strongly reflect his management style and strategic vision—both the organization structure and the corporate planning system are part of his strategic system; (2) we have stressed the need to strive for consistency among the various elements of the strategic system—thus, the planning system and the organization structure must be seen in the same scope. It follows that the corporate planners should not only be aware of potential dysfunctions associated with the organizational structure so that the planning system may be modified to ameliorate such effects on the strategic focus. The planner should also be prepared to point out organizational dysfunctionalities explicitly and to provide his inputs for having them ameliorated. This, of course, must be done with a sense of perspective. As we shall see, it is often possible to modify the planning system as an alternative to undertaking large, expensive, and disruptive organizational changes to improve a company's strategic focus. We feel that this opens up a potentially very important benefit in managing the evolution of the planning system. By allowing an updated planning system to remain a reasonably current strategic tool for coping with the firm's challenges and threats at given points in time, the organization will already have a tool in place to respond to these emerging challenges without having to reorganize the firm's structure. To respond by means of reorganization is of course very expensive, given disruptions in communication and learning patterns. If the use of an evolving planning system can cut down somewhat on the need for and frequency of major reorganizations, the benefits might in fact put the costs of planning into a new perspective.[3]

Let us now turn to a discussion of three specific types of strategic filters which are suprisingly common. We shall discuss approaches both for identifying and for modifying the planning system so as to be able to cope with them. We shall in fact see that emerging from our discussion will be a further operationalization of the concept of a dual organizational structure, a strategic structure as well as an operating structure, the latter then being synonymous with what we have called the organization structure.

The first type of strategic filter can occasionally be identified in connection with the so-called group organization structure commonly found in larger and more complex organizations. The group structure typically might emerge in one of two ways. One scenario takes place when a company grows in size and/or diversity and as a result the work load from day-to-day operation pressures might gradually become so great for the CEO that he feels unable to interact adequately with all of the businesses. A response to this is to create groups of businesses, so that each of the businesses may report to one of several group vice presidents. The group management will in turn report to the chief executive. This type of group structure formation is created primarily to reduce pressures on the CEO. The roles of the group vice presidents should therefore be seen as extensions of the corporate office of the chief executive, i.e., sharing in the responsibility to develop a portfolio strategy. As an alternative scenario, groups might also be created when a company expands within the same business through several channels, such as acquiring and/or developing several organizational entities that will operate essentially within the same business. One example of this was a highly diversified corporation which acquired several companies that were in the pleasure boat business. Instead of integrating them into one division, a pleasure boat group was formed to avoid disruptions in the operations of each of the organizations by breaking up the well-established patterns of functional interaction. In this case a group structure might be seen as a way to coordinate the related organizations' efforts within essentially the same business area. The group structure here becomes the vehicle for developing a coordinated business family strategy. For both types of group structures, however, this might create problems for maintaining a proper strategic direction of the planning process. In the next paragraphs we shall discuss these issues in turn.

When a number of business divisions report to a group executive who in turn reports to the corporate chief executive, it seems at the outset as if we might have created a four-level strategic hierarchy, adding the task of developing strategic direction for the groups. In many companies this is in fact exactly what happens; the group vice president attempts to develop a miniportfolio strategy for his subgroup of businesses. The group plan which is in turn presented to the corporate management will, together with the inputs from the other groups, serve as the basis for the development of a corporate portfolio strategy. The corporate strategy, then, will have as a primary focus balance among the groups. By dividing the portfolio strategizing task into two stages, which is implied by the scenario just described, serious dysfunctions may occur. First, each of the group executives will see only a subset of strategic business opportunities and threats, namely, those that occur within his own business sphere. There may consequently be better strategic opportunities in other parts of the firm that conceivably may not receive sufficient resources. For instance, suppose that one of the groups is fairly heavily dominated by relatively funds-rich, slow-growth, cash-cow businesses. Instead of planning to make these funds available for a high-growth business with proven potential within another group, there will be a natural tendency within the group plan to develop its own growth opportunities, which of course will be largely unproven. On the other hand, a group which faces the prospects of ample growth opportunities may have to scale down its plans due to lack of funds. Thus, the tendency toward at least some internal balancing of the groups' subportfolios of businesses will imply that the corporate level no longer can see the entire pattern of business opportunities and/or threats when determining where to allocate its resources. The company does of course still consist of the same portfolio of businesses. However, senior managers may no longer see this, but rather a set of filtered group aggregates. This obstruction of the corporate level's opportunity to deal with the relevant portfolio pattern is a serious obstacle to meaningful corporate portfolio strategy development and to the top-down strategic resource allocation task.

A related potential dysfunction from this source will be that the risk taking of the firm might become unintentionally biased, leading to overly conservative strategic choices. This might come about as follows: In developing his group subportfolio plan, a group vice president might evaluate his risk-taking capacity for going after a particular business opportunity as being contingent upon the safety levels that he feels he can count on from the other businesses in his portfolio. If he already has involved his group in a few risky but potentially high-payoff ventures, he may therefore be reluctant to take on another project. Another group within the corporation may, however, have been looking for opportunities of this kind given a relatively low overall risk exposure of that group. The development of group plans might easily lead each of the group managements to consider a risk in the context of its own smaller base and not in the larger context of the risk-taking capability of the company as a whole. Thus, overly strong conservatism might creep into the strategizing picture. This is indeed a serious problem in that it might prevent a large firm from going after and capitalizing on one of its major advantages over smaller firms, namely, that it is in a better position to take on a few selected projects with high risks and correspondingly high return potentials. A clear corporate portfolio strategy focus is essential for achieving this. The group structure thus might add to the difficult problem of how to address the issue of risk handling in planning.

A common notion in the planning efforts of many companies is that risky alternatives are bad and that a major purpose of planning should be to contribute toward the reduction of risks. A more relevant approach would probably be that selected high-risk/high-return opportunities should be sought out to take advantage of the overall risk-taking potential of the firm. To pursue this, however, it is important to establish an explicit view of the actual as well as desired overall risk exposure of the firm. If not, it might easily be led into an overly conservative path, such as just described. Alternatively, the firm might be unaware of major environmental changes which may actually lead to increased risk exposure. Sociopolitical developments, for instance, may have such effects. We shall, however, not pursue here the issue of how to conduct such a risk assessment for a corporation but shall return to this later in this chapter when we discuss managers' personal risk preference patterns as strategic filters. Instead, let us turn to approaches for modifying the planning system to cope with the other planning dysfunction issues raised in connection with the group structure.

As a starting point, let us ask ourselves two questions: Which aspects of the planning capabilities might potentially be weakened the most by separating the portfolio strategizing task into two levels? Further, we need to question for each given situation which of the two major rationales for the introduction of the group level will be the closest to actuality. The answers to these two questions might provide us with a useful way of delineating the role of the groups in the planning process in such ways that several of the filter problems can be minimized. In terms of the first question it seems to be a particularly serious consequence that corporate management might be obstructed in its view of the overall, relevant portfolio picture, particularly when it comes to the adaptation planning task. Successful portfolio adaptation depends, above all, as we know, on a realistic overall corporate portfolio outlook. As such, it will be essential to take into account the complete picture of opportunities, threats, risks, and environmental exposures stemming jointly from all the businesses.

Turning now to the second question of what was the nature of the groups' roles, we recall that in one instance the groups were instituted in order to relieve corporate management of some of the day-to-day burden of coping with an exceedingly wide spectrum of businesses. Thus, the planning task transferred to the groups in connection with this decentralization move would fall primarily within the integration area. What emerges is the following: The chief executive and his close corporate-level aides should elect to deal directly with the businesses when it comes to the objectives-setting stage, where the major impact of adaptation planning on the portfolio should be centered. Each respective group executive should of course also take part in this interaction but primarily as advisors to the CEO. Thus, when it comes to objectives setting they should act as teammates of the CEO, being extensions of the corporate office. Corporate management should make every effort to stress that there exists no group structure when it comes to establishing a corporate portfolio objective consisting of a set of business objectives as the building blocks. There is no shortcut around the need for the CEO to be directly involved in the development of the adaptive adjustments of the overall corporate portfolio, despite the fact that this might require a significant portion of his time.

We see that it is thus not necessary to require consistency between the hierarchical levels of the strategic structure and the operating structure. The groups are parts of the corporate level in the strategic structure but constitute a separate, additional level in the operating structure.

In certain instances one might of course expect that some group vice presidents might resist this redefinition of their roles and view it as if their importance is being downplayed. However, when it comes to planning for the implementation of this strategic picture, the group managements should play a much more active role. The development of strategic programs as well as the subsequent development of budgets should be coordinated by the group executives. This predominantly integrative planning task can usefully be carried out within the group structure. The corporate-level CEO will of course be involved in these planning stages, too, in reviewing the groups' strategic program suggestions as well as their budgets. Considerable time will be freed for the CEO by relying on the group management structure in the strategic planning process in this way. At the same time the potential dysfunction of weakening the portfolio adaptation capability associated with a two-level portfolio planning approach can be controlled. We thus see that the role of the groups will be different within a corporation's strategic structure than within its operating structure. Within the former the groups do not have a central function; otherwise, they become strategic filters. Within the latter, however, the groups play an important role in easing the predominantly operations-oriented and integrative management burdens from senior management.

Let us now turn to a discussion of the planning implications associated with the second type of group structure creation, namely, when several divisions which are in more or less the same business form one group. In this case the group level is analogous to what we have been calling a division throughout this book from a strategic decision-making viewpoint. Consequently, the group management should take a major responsibility for the development of one coordinated business family strategy involving all the related business elements. If, on the other hand, each of these pseudodivisions were left with the task of developing its independent business strategies on its own, we might expect to come up with plans that in all likelihood will be suboptimal, particularly when it comes to the execution of consolidation attractiveness-related integration planning needs. In cases like this, the planning system might be an excellent vehicle for initiating coordination and consolidation moves among the various organizational entities so that one consistent strategic business family direction can be followed, giving the units an impression that they are losing their semiautonomous entity. Too often in instances like this, however, a group (i.e., business family) strategy is not pushed heavily enough, the result being that consolidation synergy benefits from one overall business family strategy are lost.

Let us now turn to another potential strategic filter source frequently associated with the evolution of planning. Effective planning might be hampered when the product/market element pattern of the firm is illogical. A logical product/market element pattern from a corporate planning viewpoint should facilitate the identification of logical strategies. Thus, a strategy center should ideally be independent of other strategy centers to the extent that this might facilitate the development and implementation of a business strategy in a reasonably straightforward manner. Often, however, a product/market element's strategy is exposed to major effects from actions taken within the strategic domain of other product/market elements. We shall discuss how to modify the planning system to ameliorate some of the problems stemming from this in the next section.

Evolutionary Pressures: Reconciling the Strategic and the Operating Structures

A major problem with the structure of a corporation's product/market element pattern, seen from a planning systems design and evolution point of view, is that the formal operating organization structure might not reinforce the strategic structure delineated through the product/market elements. Thus, the implementation of the strategies for which the businesses are planning might be hampered. As an example, we might have a situation with a rapid evolution of a firm's product mix, implying that some businesses that were added within a particular strategy center might become increasingly important, while some of the traditional businesses might have become relatively insignificant. A particular strategy center might even start to resemble a smaller-scale portfolio of businesses on its own, merely through an evolutionary process of mushrooming. However, while the natural tendency for most companies to emphasize different businesses over time might be quite profound, modification of the formal operating organization structure might be lagging, and hence the structure would not adequately reflect where the business strategizing pressures are. The problem is to reconcile the operating structure with the more rapidly evolving strategic structure.

The structural fit might be further diffused when extensive acquisition activities are going on. It usually will be impossible then from a practical point of view to dismantle acquired firms structurally and to parcel out businesses in terms of fit with already existing strategy centers, new strategy centers being established only in cases where the parent company is not already actively involved. Needless to say, reasons such as concern for employee morale, hesitancy to downgrade certain strong managers, desire to reach for know-how reserves, and reluctance to cause immediate changes in the funds-flow patterns associated with an acquired company all might call for advancing carefully when integrating newly acquired strategy centers into an existing formal operating organization structure. The consequence again, however, would be an increased discrepancy between where the business strategizing pressures and challenges are and the formal operating pattern.

Why is it that from a planning systems point of view the formal operating structure should reflect the actual business strategizing activities in a relatively accurate or explicit manner? Several studies have shown that strategy and formal structure seem to be highly interrelated. Not only is the formal organizational structure itself an essential management tool for facilitating the development and implementation of strategic direction. Even more, it seems as if companies with an explicit match between intended strategies and formal organizational structure tend to perform better than companies with less of a match. This problem probably comes about because of an inability to take advantage of the information-handling capabilities associated with a formal organizational structure. The pattern of communication is normally influenced through the formal organizational structure; thus, if this pattern reflects the strategic communication needs, it might be a definite advantage in implementing strategic planning. If not, the planning system itself will have to open up the relevant channels of communication.

Another planning implementation problem might arise when the organization structure is illogical in terms of managerial practicality. This might happen when the sizes of the various strategy centers in a corporate portfolio are dramatically different. For instance, when a company is faced with a portfolio strategizing setting with one or a few large strategy centers contributing the bulk of the firm's sales and revenues and, in addition, a relatively large number of smaller strategy centers, we still are faced with the requirement that large and small strategy centers should be reporting to the CEO in a proper portfolio mode. In practice, however, the firm's critical businesses might receive relatively too little and inadequate top-down input in the strategizing process, given that the CEO easily might be distracted by the strategic problems of the smaller businesses. This might be a dilemma, given that in a narrow business strategizing sense a smaller business, too, might need much top-down interface. Managerial time and effort spent on a business's strategy formulation and implementation will only to a small extent be a proportionate function of business size. A small business in a strategic turnaround situation might require as much or even more of top management's time than a larger business. However, the cognitive capability of the CEO and his closest associates might be a bottleneck when it comes to dealing with these small strategy centers while still giving the larger business the required attention, given the overall importance of the latter for overall corporate success.

We shall discuss two approaches for modifying the design of the formal planning system so as to deal with the often serious problems stemming from strategic overlaps or excessive size differentials among businesses, as reflected in the formal organizational structure. First, it should be underscored that any acquisition program should be carried out with this issue in mind. For instance, it might make sense to establish a minimum size for potential acquisition candidates. In line with this, some of the smaller businesses presently in a firm's portfolio might be divested, largely as a result of lack of corporate management capacity. This is in fact not an uncommon reason for larger companies' divestiture of small and peripheral businesses that do not fit closely with the other business activities of the firm. Another approach would be to put several of the smaller businesses together into one miscellaneous ventures group. This relieves the CEO from the pressure of dealing directly with all the small businesses in the planning process. However, as discussed in the previous section, this introduces another potential strategic filter, namely, that the overall corporate-wide business portfolio pattern might get blurred. There may, however, be instances in which senior management decides that the benefits from ameliorating the first type of strategic bottleneck outweigh the disadvantages of creating the second type of strategic filter. Some companies do not fully recognize, however, that they are creating a new strategic filter through a miscellaneous ventures group approach. One major oil company, for instance, recognized that the sheer size of its major business lines—the integrated oil operations as well as coal and chemicals businesses—would make it difficult to create the momentum for developing new businesses beyond mere extensions of the company's traditional businesses. Lack of capacity to provide enough senior management attention would be one inevitable problem in case of diversification. The strong business style or culture within the traditional business areas of operation as well as the existence of ample attractive investment opportunities within the traditional businesses might further complicate a viable diversification drive. To deal with this, the oil company established a separate new venture organization as a very autonomous group. This miscellaneous ventures group soon resembled a small conglomerate in many respects. This new venture group approach proved to be quite successful in that it gave the company a vehicle for acquiring new venture companies as well as pursuing new internal developments. Given the small size of the group's activities relative to the major business activities of the firm, it would have represented an almost unacceptable toll on senior management's attention to treat the new units in the planning process on a similar basis to the larger elements of the company's portfolio. The potential problem of overall portfolio pattern distortion has not been serious thus far, because of the relatively small size of the new activities. However, as the new venture group grows, the issue of portfolio strategy distortion should be of increasing concern, and the autonomous mode of planning within the miniconglomerate may have to be modified.

The approach for addressing the potential strategic filter problem associated with strategically illogical formal organization structure patterns, stemming from evolution of the business mix shift, mergers, and/or strategy center size distribution imbalances, should in part be to create an alertness to the need for undertaking reorganization changes focused specifically on containing this problem. The other part of the approach, then, will be to focus the design and/or evolutionary improvement on meeting these problem areas, so that communication channels may be opened to develop relevant strategies to units recently being merged into the mainstream strategic planning system of the firm and to reach a reasonable balance when it comes to expending management resources on the planning of larger, highly critical business elements versus smaller, less important businesses. Thus, to restate our position, a continuing amount of reorganization of the strategic organizational structure might be necessary as a part of the evolution of a tailor-made corporate planning activity. However, it will be a delicate judgment to decide how extensive a reorganization would be appropriate. On the one hand, as previously explained, the scope of the organizational changes must be kept under control. On the other hand, if the formalized organizational structure is not modified to reflect the actual strategic tasks, there might not be enough of a formal framework to build on in order to implement a meaningful planning system.

We thus need to reconcile the lines of argument given with respect to reorganizing to deal with an illogical product/market element structure as a potential strategic filter with our basic premise that a strategic planning system which is managed in an evolutionary sense should facilitate a reduction in the frequency and degree of operating structure reorganizations. In this respect we shall find it useful to introduce a distinction between two types of reorganization steps. On the one hand, initial steps may have to be taken in order to bring the formal operating organization structure into shape to allow for a minimum degree of communality with the strategic tasks. This should be done before strategic planning is pursued and should be seen as a one-shot reorganization undertaking. On the other hand, a firm's management is faced with the strategic responses that the company has to make toward its environmental opportunities and/or threats on a more or less ongoing basis. The corporate planning system should play an important role in facilitating the responses to these pressures. Planning should be a major vehicle for allowing adjustments or shifts in the organization's capability to meet changing needs. For instance, when the environment seems to open up for a more aggressive pursuit of new opportunities, the need for adaptation will increase relatively. The planning system should be modified accordingly in order to respond to these needs. Similarly, in cases where the economic climate seems to become harder, a relative shift toward more integration needs is taking place. Again, the planning system's capabilities should be modified in this direction.

Traditionally, a major element of organizational response to major environmental pressures like the ones just indicated in the previous paragraph has been through reorganization of the operating structure. For instance, to strengthen adaptation a company might break off from traditional divisions several lines of business that it considers particularly promising in terms of growth opportunities and create new divisions out of them. Alternatively, to strengthen integration it might combine divisions to eliminate duplication of, say, sales forces and/or distribution channels. Typically, however, given the relatively static nature of a formal organizational structure, to adjust this way would mean a pattern of stop and go in terms of impacts on the organization. Thus, this mode of response offers relatively little capability to carry out incremental responses on a more continuous basis. An evolving planning system will represent a complementary tool to the more far-sweeping formal organization response route. Thus, we have a vehicle for changing the strategic structure without changing the operating organization structure. Therefore, we should have much less need for and be much more careful about initiating large and usually disruptive formal reorganizations. However, although the frequency of using reorganization as a response to environmental changes thereby should go down, this should of course not eliminate entirely the need for ad hoc organizational structure overhauls, but at less frequent intervals.

To reiterate, our approach to reorganization emphasizes its role of assisting managers in carrying out their changing strategic tasks. We do not advocate reorganization as a tool for enhancing a more logical organizational structure. On the contrary, we have emphasized that a longer time commitment to a particular strategy is difficult in an atmosphere of frequent organizational changes and rapid job rotations. Also, an attempt to strive for an overly pure and narrow business strategy focus, arrived at, for instance, by reorganizing so that all the business activities of each strategy center fall into one segment of the business life cycle, does not necessarily produce the intended improved strategic performance. By not being forced to manage the strategy center as a somewhat broader composite of growing and maturing elements, managers might develop unrealistic attitudes. Managers in complex strategic settings need the assistance of the strategic planning system in order to see clearly this strategic position and how to facilitate implementation of strategic progress in this setting. Thus, the organizational units should be able to maintain a reasonable strategic focus through planning, reducing the need for major reorganizations by not overemphasizing narrowly logical business units. Unfortunately there seems to have been a tendency in many organizations to equate formal reorganization with improved strategic performance capability; exactly the opposite is probably true. An improvement of each manager's understanding of how to operationalize strategic management is essential, and the pressure should be on management to facilitate this through the strategic planning process, not through formal reorganizations *per se*.

Modifying the Planning System
to the Matrix Organizational Structure

Let us briefly touch upon a third area of potential organization structure-related strategic filters in connection with the evolution of effective strategic planning systems.[4] This might occur with the emergence of a so-called matrix structure found in some organizations. This type of structure has come about primarily as a response to the need to recognize interdependence among business elements within the company. Often a matrix form is chosen to deal with operational interdependency. In other instances, although probably less often, the matrix attempts to capture strategic interdependence. Given the way we have defined product/ market elements or strategy centers, there may well be strategic interdependence among business element strategies. However, given our definition of a division, there would rarely be interdependence among business family strategies. Analogously with the latter, the way the General Electric Company has defined its SBUs, for instance, would preclude that there ever would be strategic interdependence among its SBUs. In the following paragraphs we shall discuss examples of the implications on planning from both strategically interdependent as well as operationally interdependent matrixes, starting with the more common latter situation.

For instance, when it comes to businesses which share a common (typically process-oriented) intermediary production facility but which might be sold through distinctive marketing channels, a matrix structure might be very useful so that duplication of production efforts can be avoided. Certain specialty chemical corporations might fall into this category. Similarly, when it comes to high-technology companies that are active in several businesses but based on predominantly the same technological base, a matrix structure might be applicable. The implication of such a structure is that an explicit set of operating interdependencies will be created between, say, a functional activity and several business-related activities. Thus, a pattern of two bosses is created. A manufacturing manager, for instance, will not only be responsible to the vice president of manufacturing but also to the manager of the particular business for whom he attempts to provide his manufacturing output.

We can identify three classes of dimensions that might be operationally or strategically interrelated in a matrix mode: the business dimension, the geographical area dimension, and the functional dimension. We shall not discuss how to design and implement such a matrix structure here or assess its appropriateness. This is amply analyzed elsewhere and is outside the scope of this book. Our concerns relate to the potential strategic filter problems stemming from a matrix structure as part of the planning process.

While a matrix structure certainly will have important benefits in selected applications, there are also several problems that might arise when it comes to planning in such a structure. For instance, it may become increasingly time-consuming and burdensome to carry out the interactions among management which typically are so essential to the development of good plans. Given the dual lines of responsibility patterns that predominate, both the frequency and size of planning meetings might increase.

A more fundamental problem might easily arise when it comes to carrying out major adaptation-related strategic moves within an operations-interdependent matrix structure. It should be kept in mind that an underlying rationale for developing an operations-interdependent matrix structure is the sharing of selected functions and facilities, thereby diminishing duplication of efforts; thus, an integration-oriented concern is prominent. It is often difficult for matrix structures to adapt effectively, partly because of the tilting of the balance toward integration but also due to the fact that extensive compromising between a relatively larger number of executives when it comes to setting strategic direction, as we shall have in a matrix structure, might make it difficult to come up with major deviations from the present direction. Thus, the operating structure, based on a matrix approach, might add to the problem of meaningfully striking a delineation with the strategic structure; the rigidity of the matrix structure might drive out the strategic dimension.

One way of at least partially ameliorating this problem is to develop a somewhat clearer division of labor among the matrix dimensions in the planning process. If, for instance, we consider a manufacturer of specialty chemicals, the matrix organization might consist of a set of two dimensions, the functional activities, such as manufacturing, marketing, distribution, and R&D, as well as the business activities, which will consist of several distinct product/markets. When it comes to carrying out the planning tasks within this particular matrix structure, we might ask which of the two dimensions should be given the integrative planning tasks and which dimension would have to focus primarily on adaptation. We see that in this example the functions can be characterized as the integrative dimension, while the business can be seen as the adaptive dimension. While the efficiency of this matrix organization's strategy depends on how well the functions are performing their tasks, the strategic effectiveness will above all depend on how successful the organization will be in developing and maintaining a good business product mix. Thus we see that there is a natural division of labor between the two matrix dimensions, one being focused primarily on the adaptation planning tasks and the other on integration planning tasks.

Often we can identify such a duality in the planning tasks among the dimensions in a matrix organization. It is, however, necessary to determine which will be the adaptive and which will be the integrative dimension in each case; we do not necessarily have a division of labor similar to the example in the previous paragraph in other settings. A facilitating factor in the task of isolating the adaptive and integrative dimensions stems from the fact that matrix structures with more than two dimensions tend to be rare. In most cases a combination of only two of the functional, business, or area dimensions is at work. Thus, we can normally work with one adaptive and one integrative dimension.

We recall that the objectives-setting stage would play a major role in facilitating the development of an adaptive strategy. Conversely, the budgeting stage tends to be central in the development of the integrative aspects of a strategy. This, however, implies that the adaptive dimension and the managers associated with this should be centrally involved during the objectives-setting stage. The integrative dimension's involvement at this stage should be more limited, merely focusing on providing awareness of potential internal constraints that might make a particular adaptive move difficult. The managers associated with the integrative dimensions would, however, be centrally involved in the budgeting stage, while the adaptive dimension managers would not. In Exhibit 6-3, we have indicated the shift in involvement in the planning process between the two matrix dimensions.

We see that the division of labor among an adaptive and an integrative dimension might provide a useful vehicle for the simplification of the task of carrying out planning within a matrix structure. The pattern of interaction among managers can be simplified, and the frequency and size of planning meetings might be reduced. Only when it comes to the development of strategic programs during cycle two will there be a full-fledged simultaneous involvement from both matrix dimensions. While in all likelihood this will continue to be a difficult step in the planning process, the degree of ambiguity and complexity will at least have been reduced when it comes to the objectives-setting and budgeting stages. Not only will this be important in trimming the managerial burden of planning down to reasonable proportions. Even more importantly, the adaptive as well as integrative points of focus will have been strengthened. A potentially serious barrier to strategic planning within matrix organizations will thereby have been reduced.

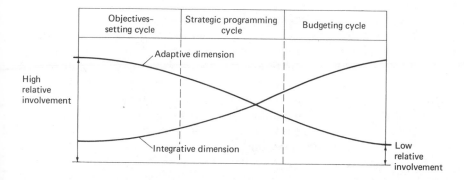

EXHIBIT 6-3   Shifts in Matrix Dimensions' Involvement in the Planning Process

Planning Considerations in Multinational Corporations

Needless to say, the field of multinational management is exceptionally broad and complicated. It would not only require an inordinately extensive discussion to cover all substantive aspects of this field that might potentially be relevant for strategic decision making in the multinational firm, but this would clearly also be outside the scope of this book, given that our concern centers around the design of the planning process, not the development of a multinational strategy. What does fall within the scope of this book, however, is to identify a few critical aspects of the multinational planning setting that need to be considered in order to avoid barriers to the implementation of a planning process in such companies. The basic conceptual scheme for planning applies to the multinational firm as well. A few planning process capability issues need to be considered in addition.[5]

Specifically, we shall deal with four critical planning issues unique to the multinational firm. Two of these apply most directly to the portfolio-level planning task. These are the increasing lack of flexibility in making significant changes in a company's portfolio due to sociopolitical pressures outside the control of the firm as well as the added complexities in developing the funds transfer aspect of a portfolio plan due to currency valuation changes. At the business planning level a third factor to take into account involves potential patterns of differences when it comes to the attractiveness and competitive strength of a business from one country to another. A final factor relates to strategic management in different countries, where several of the five stages of the planning process play an often different and more limited role than presumed in the discussion thus far in this book, particularly when it comes to the roles of incentives, monitoring, and budgeting. We shall discuss the four classes of factors in turn.

There seems to be an increasing lack of flexibility among many multinational corporations when it comes to being able to modify their portfolios. The problem is not only that investment to increase the activity level in a particular country may become increasingly difficult in that there will typically be a growing number of strings attached to such investments. Potentially much more serious is the lack of flexibility to scale down or change the nature of a particular operation. In most of the European countries as well as in such developing countries as Venezuela, for instance, tough labor laws make it next to impossible to fire part of the work force, making it very difficult to scale down unprofitable operations. Political and union pressures also tend to stifle such relatively near-term portfolio adjustments. Leaving aside the substantive strategic choice question as to whether it in fact will be attractive to have a presence in a particular country at all, the presence of these key environmental factors calls for several modifications of the planning process. First, even more elaborate prior analyses would probably have to be carried out before resources are committed to a particular project. This is a self-evident consequence of the lack of flexibility of subsequent corrective response possibilities and does not need to be elaborated on further. Second, senior management must pay particularly careful attention to signs of potential deterioration of any of its businesses located in such restrictive national settings. If a weakening of the position of a particular business is detected, a long-term strategic program of internal development for repositioning this business should be initiated. By vigorously pursuing structural change challenges before they become a crisis there will be a much better likelihood that a problem situation can be avoided. Given that internally generated development projects for restructuring typically take a long time before reaching fruition, it is important to start as early as possible. One European company has extended this philosophy in its planning efforts by having developed alternative usage pattern plans for each of its physical facilities and also pursuing an extensive central development program intended to come up with new activity options that might be transferred to existing plants in need of restructuring. A third area of modification in the corporate planning approach will be the increased emphasis of direct corporate-government contact to resolve major structural portfolio issues. The government typically plays a more active role in many countries in influencing corporations' portfolio choices. It is important to provide accurate government inputs for the portfolio plans of companies in such settings.

A second major area of modification of the planning system of a multinational corporation will be with respect to the planning of the portfolio level's transfer of strategic resources. Central in this respect is the focus on funds-flow patterns to deal with potential disturbances due to currency fluctuations. Again, it will be beyond the scope of this book to discuss issues of international finance. What seems important, however, is that a company explicitly address the riskiness of its planned international funds-flow transfers. Other important dimensions will be the transfer of key management resources as well as the transfer of technological resources, both often causing considerable problems in developing and implementing plans in an international setting. Given that an added element of uncertainty thereby has been added to the portfolio strategizing task, one would expect that planning routines should be developed for providing the appropriate information for the stability of the strategic resources aspect of the strategy as well as for monitoring these factors. Too often, for instance, there is too much of a split between strategic planning and multinational financial planning. The latter is clearly an important element of the former, and the planning system should be designed to recognize this. Failure to achieve such a coordinated view might lead to several dysfunctions. The potentially most serious one is probably a danger to become too risk-prone in both portfolio strategy decision making and international finance strategizing. The reason for this is that by seeing each of the strategic tasks in isolation there might be a tendency to overlook the constraints imposed on one strategy by the other, thereby perceiving more flexibility to ameliorate a problem than actually will be the case.

Turning now to the business-level planning task within the multinational corporation, we note that there are several important issues that should be addressed. One issue relates to how to measure business attractiveness in situations where several countries are involved. We recall from our discussion in Chapter Three that a product's position in its life cycle is a major determinant of the growth rate that it will enjoy at a given point in time, thereby determining the attractiveness of the business. It has, however, been demonstrated that a product's life-cycle position might differ from country to country, depending on the level of economic development that each country enjoys, on the country of a product's origin, as well as on other factors. For instance, a product which has reached a highly mature stage in the United States may still enjoy limited growth in Europe and Japan, while enjoying strong growth in various developing countries. Thus, the attractiveness of the product will differ from country to country and so will the adaptive planning needs— from relatively low adaptive planning needs in the mature U.S. market to highly adaptive needs in the developing economies.

There might also be important differences from country to country when it comes to a company's competitive strength. We recall again from our discussion in Chapter Three that market share typically will be a major determinant of competitive strength and that experience curve advantages are likely to benefit companies the most which enjoy the highest market shares. We also recall, however, that experience curve advantages do not tend to come automatically but only when actively being pursued through an interactive planning effort. An important issue which follows is to determine the extent to which and why the experience curve benefits might differ from country to country, recognizing that there will probably be aspects of the experience curve effect that will apply worldwide, other aspects that will apply on a country-to-country basis, and even aspects of the experience curve phenomenon that will apply on a plant-by-plant basis. One determinant will be the absolute size of the market. With large production runs the experience curve effect is expected to be greater. Another determinant which will be less obvious but potentially more important is the slope of the experience curve, as found with respect to the same product in different countries. A country which has a highly competent, learning-oriented work force is likely to have the steepest experience curve and enjoy the biggest benefit. Factors that determine this are probably not only the general educational level of the work force but also such factors as the relevance of the work force's training and experience, degree of absenteeism, attitudes toward innovations, flexibility of labor laws and union attitudes, and so on. Such cross-country experience curve comparisons would probably have to be done on an industry-specific basis, given that the basic skill requirements needed will depend largely on the specific nature of the production and management processes of a particular industry. Thus, some countries may have the skill advantages when it comes to some industries, while for other industries other countries might lead. For these reasons, a country's comparative experience curve advantage might often also change over time relative to other countries.

We see that a complex and challenging worldwide business strategizing picture emerges from the global business attractiveness/competitive strength analysis. This will probably have significant consequences with regard to where to invest in new production capacity, where to attempt to develop new star positions, where one's cash cows ideally should be located, as well as from which areas to withdraw. Only through a careful planning need/capability analysis, carried out on a sufficiently broad-focused basis, might we expect that planning can be carried out in a relevant manner to facilitate a worldwide business strategy across a large number of countries.

Let us finally turn to a fourth major consideration with regard to modifying a company's planning system to fit a multinational setting. This has to do with planning's acceptance as a management tool in different business cultures. As several multinational corporations might testify, there can be strong resistance to planning within their subsidiaries in certain countries. While the reasons for this may be numerous and in fact not necessarily much different from resistance to planning in general, we shall point out three implementation factors that may be more or less unique to the multinationals.

A first reason for resisting planning might be due to the fact that some of an organization's parts, in some countries, might have been familiar with a relatively limited number of formal management systems beforehand. Thus, exposure to a relatively full-blown planning system easily becomes a culture shock, not a meaningful evolutionary step. When, say, an organizational unit has just started its struggle to implement budgeting, it becomes a serious problem to be able to implement a planning system on top of this. There is no definite solution to this problem. The major issue will be to stress the overall logic of the planning approach, which in its simplicity should be both appealing to and reconcilable with intuitive ways of managing. Paradoxically enough it may actually turn out to be an advantage not to have been too imbedded with an integration-biased budgeting culture.

The second reason for resistance to planning is more fundamental. The notion of holding an executive accountable for strategic performance, and thereby not only explicitly associating him with measures of strategic progress but also providing him with incentives based on his individual performance, might to a larger or lesser degree be resisted in many national cultures. This is largely due to the emphasis on group cultures and group success rather than on the individual in these business settings. For instance, loyalty to the firm may make it relatively rare that executives change from one employer to another in such settings. To some extent too the personal income taxation system as well as other value norms may be such that financial incentives mean little to an executive, at least beyond a certain point. There is little one can do to get around value norms like these. The best approach is probably to accept them and to attempt to honor them. To be explicitly aware of them will at least save a company from problems arising from attempting to transplant their original planning system.

It will probably above all be within the area of management incentives that sensitivity will have to be called upon to modify a multinational's planning system. In this respect it seems important to take a sufficiently broad view of incentives in order to be able to answer the following basic question: What factors establish a manager's status and prestige in the particular setting at hand? While bonus payments may play a relatively low role, such factors as promotion, discretionary freedom, praise from superiors during reviews, and fringe benefits may be exceedingly important. Also it may be appropriate to carefully reassess the degree to which incentives should be given to the individual versus to larger teams, recognizing the importance of group loyalty in many international settings. Sensitivity to the incentives issues on behalf of the planning systems designer thus is critical.

The final reason that we shall discuss is an increasing resistance to aspects of decision making which will add an element of centralization in larger companies attempting to pursue a portfolio strategy. At first this may sound like a paradox, given that decentralization seems to be less common outside the United States. However, while the U.S. decentralization mode seems to also have led to a recognition of a need for a more centralized portfolio strategy component, management based on a portfolio strategy seems to have been much less common elsewhere. Such inputs, in fact, seem less readily acceptable in many national business settings. The notion of lower levels' participation in a firm's strategic decision making has been winning ground widely. We see no necessary conflict between this and following a planning approach as outlined in this book. In fact, the strong emphasis on developing interactive communication channels that is a key element of the planning approach outlined here should provide a strong impetus to more participative management. This kind of resistance may therefore be due largely to traditional preconceptions that planning means centralization. It should be pointed out, however, that when it comes to the adaptive aspects of planning the challenge typically will be to be able to come up with opportunistic, innovative, and timely changes of strategic directions. Within an existing organization there will of course always be a tendency toward preserving the status quo, particularly given that only a small fraction of a firm's management will be exposed to product/market-based business strategizing, the major focal point for adaptation, while most managers will be exposed only to aspects of such general strategies. Thus, it seems necessary to call for a sense of realism when determining the levels and forms of participation during the early stages of the planning process, so that a necessary capability to execute adaptation can be maintained, which in the long run of course will be fundamental for the job security of everyone involved. In some countries government regulation and/or union pressure makes it difficult to find such a reasonable mode of front-end participation, thereby causing potentially serious long-term adaptive problems.

We have now concluded our discussion of barriers to implementing planning in multinational corporations. Given that we restricted ourselves to issues related to the planning process and did not deal with key substantive strategic choices that might face the multinational, our discussion has been intentionally brief. It should, however, be noted that the design and implementation of strategic planning within the multinational corporate setting in many respects represent the ultimate in challenges when it comes to skillful situational design of the planning systems. In these settings, more than anywhere else, careful tailor-making within the corporation seems essential, taking advantage of the flexibility options we have discussed for making planning a more relevant tool in the various national settings. Overly standardized planning approaches, implemented more or less uniformly across the company, definitely do not seem to meet the multinational corporation's planning needs. Surprisingly, many multinationals still seem to fall short in meeting these tailor-making challenges.

There is one difficult problem that remains to be discussed, namely, how to develop an operational measure of risk in complex corporate settings. This will be the topic of our next section.

Risk Aversion in Planning

We have discussed the significance of risk in several instances throughout this book. Our emphasis has been on the importance of formulating a relatively explicit assessment of one's risk exposure. This might facilitate the pursuance of strategic resource allocation in such a way that a risk/ return trade-off might be achieved. Our task in this section is to suggest ways for developing a more explicit concept of risk exposure in strategy formulation and implementation. It is our experience that risk taking often might be seen as something bad when it comes to planning and that minimizing risk often becomes an implicit objective of the planning effort. A more appropriate approach would be to seek selected risky investments so that the firm's overall risk/return posture may come in line with its overall capabilities for risk/taking. By not doing this a company might neglect a potential competitive advantage over less resourceful companies.[6]

We shall discuss two aspects of risk taking in this section. First, we shall discuss how a formal strategic planning approach actually might encourage excessive risk averseness in large, diversified, hierarchical organizations unless risk assessment is approached more explicitly. Second, we shall briefly address the need for having management's own risk-taking preferences reflected in planning choices; what might be the right resource allocation choice for one decision-maker may be too risky for another.

We recall from Chapter Three that we have established a pragmatic measurement of risk assessment. Let us now discuss how this might be used to counteract the tendency toward the excessive risk aversion often found in large, hierarchical organizations. Let us first illustrate why risk aversion might become a problem. When an organization is considering taking a risk it will evaluate whether it is strong enough or not to pursue this exposure. This will largely depend on the extent of discretionary reserves the organization has at its disposal. What might seem to be an overly high risk for a manager at the strategy center level, given his limited resources as well as an incomplete perception of the resources of the company as a whole, may seem a reasonable and appropriate risk to take when seen from an overall corporate perspective. Thus, there may be a natural tendency toward more and more risk aversion the further one descends down the general management levels in the organization.

There are two aspects of the design of a strategic planning system in particular that might facilitate the counteraction of such bottom-up risk aversion. As discussed in earlier paragraphs of this section, an explicit statement of risk exposure might facilitate the review of plans at higher organizational levels from a risk-taking perspective. It might permit upper-level management to get a more complete view of the range of risk/return strategic alternatives that exist, not only the more conservative ones, as well as to endorse risk taking on a selective basis. Second, a portfolio strategy point of view is essential when it comes to the corporate level's risk/return assessments. Each major resource allocation decision will have to be evaluated in the context of the nature of the risk exposure that the firm already has been committed to. Only by taking such a corporate-wide view can the firm's resource capacity to be exposed to risks be matched with its actual risk/return commitments.

Let us now turn to the role of the individual decision-maker's preference toward risk taking in planning. We recall that an individual's attitude toward risk is in fact part of the person's personality. While there are ways to determine executives' risk preference functions, we do not feel that it will be necessary in most cases to go through such procedures. Instead, it suffices to develop some broad classification of each key manager's risk-taking attitudes in terms of general risk-taking philosophy and degree of consistency in risk taking over time. Over time, then, as management is becoming more experienced in making use of strategic planning as a management tool, a gradual establishment of a risk preference image will take place for each executive. When a particular executive submits his plan, corporate management will be in a position to review and evaluate this within the context of the manager's general risk taking attitude. Corporate management may then also be in a position to pay particular attention to the plans of those managers who have been shown to be oscillating in their risk-taking attitudes.

This concludes our brief discussion of the handling of risk as a potential barrier to the evolution of effective planning. Needless to say, the roles of the various executives as participants in the planning process will have a major impact on the risk-taking patterns that actually emerge in an organization. We shall have an opportunity to pursue this further in Chapter Seven when we discuss in more detail the roles of various executives in the planning process.

When Should Strategic Audits of Planning Needs Be Carried Out and by Whom?

The analysis of a corporation's needs for planning provides a static view of how the company and its businesses stand in terms of strategic strengths and weaknesses at one particular point in time.[7] It is useful for

management at certain intervals to be presented with a reasonably complete and consistently developed picture of the particular situational
setting at hand—what strategic and financial constraints there are and
what particular needs the company has for planning. It is easy to develop
the argument that such a strategic assessment analysis should be carried
out before a formal corporate strategic planning system is installed. This
will provide the necessary direction for designing capabilities into the
planning system.

As a planning system starts to function after it has been properly
tailor-made and installed, the system itself will provide an update of what
the emerging new planning needs will be. It will consequently typically
not be necessary to carry out a complete new independent strategic
planning need assessment analysis on a continuous basis.

It might be useful, however, to carry out ad hoc strategic position
audits of particular divisions, particularly if a given business is facing
exceptional changes in its business climate as well as when major strategic
shifts are being contemplated, such as a major expansion or withdrawal.
In such instances, in-depth data on an ad hoc basis might be useful
independently of the planning schedule. Not only will this allow for
enough detail in the data. It will prevent holding up the corporation's
entire planning effort to provide the data for the strategic analysis of the
exceptional business setting.

When candidates are being identified for potential acquisition there
is also a need for a strategic audit analysis of the new business. There may
of course be problems gathering parts of the data in such instances, but it
will normally still be possible to come up with a useful analysis. Given
that the efforts involved in carrying out such a thorough acquisition
analysis will be considerable, it might be useful to develop a stepwise
analytical scheme. This might help weed out at an early stage acquisition
candidates that look relatively unpromising, so that only the more attractive candidates will pass the preliminary screenings and receive a full
strategic audit treatment. We have already discussed aspects of this
earlier in this chapter in connection with how to avoid overloading the
planning system.

At some intervals, however, there might be a need to repeat a
full-blown strategic audit for the entire company. This may be needed as a
basis for a major overhaul of the planning system which now and then
may be necessary. There seems, in fact, to be a life cycle for many a
corporate planning system; after some years in place the present system
might be abandoned and a new system installed. This might happen in
connection with a major reorganization and/or management reshuffle.
The strategic position audit is of course a useful tool at such times. One of
the arguments that has been made in this book, however, is that it would

be ideal to have the corporate planning system subjected to a relatively continuous process of improvement and incremental updating, thereby making it unnecessary to perform frequent major overhauls of the planning system. Given the high costs of such major overhauls, not only in money terms but also in terms of the disruption they might cause in the managerial strategic process, it seems clear that too-frequent major changes in the planning process should not become the norm. Therefore, we have argued for a "managing the evolution of the system" approach earlier in this chapter.

Who should carry out the strategic position audits? Given that an audit might trigger a set of one-shot decisions of potentially far-reaching consequences for the individual managers regarding such issues as the redefinition of boundaries between product/market elements and the relative importance of each business, a central involvement in an ad hoc activity of this kind might diminish a corporate planning executive's effectiveness and credibility as a party in the ongoing continuous corporate planning process. The line executives, too, will typically have so much personally at stake that they might not be effective participants in this process. In order not to lose credibility for the ongoing planning work that is supposed to follow from the strategic audit, it might be useful to draw on temporary expertise from outside the main line of the organization to carry out the strategic audit analysis—either an in-house consultant group or outside consulting help. This might better assure an objective audit and protect against the danger of bias that could enter the analysis if it is carried out by managers who are directly involved in the businesses. We shall pursue this issue further in Chapter Seven when we discuss the roles of various stakeholders in the corporate planning process.

Summary

In this chapter we have discussed a number of important issues with respect to managing the evolution of a strategic planning system so that the system can remain current and effective over time. At the outset we established the need for managing the evolution of a corporate planning system on a more or less continuous basis. This necessity was due to the fact that a firm's situational setting, and thereby its needs for planning, typically would be changing frequently due to environmental changes as well as due to the fact that strategic decisions taken internally might also affect the firm's own setting. Thus, the design of a planning system would be in need of frequent updating in order to facilitate the development of new planning capabilities to meet the emerging needs.

We also stressed the need to manage the evolution of a planning system not only in a narrow sense but to recognize that an important aspect of this management task will be to ensure consistency among the elements of the broader strategic management system. Given that the changing situational setting and the firm's evolving needs thus will be the basis for the tailor-making of all the subsystems, it is pertinent to run a consistency check of how the design of the various subsystems fit together. Given that the responsibility to maintain the various subsystems often rests with different people in the organization—the planning system with the corporate planner, the budgeting system with the corporate controller, and so on—it becomes a difficult issue to maintain an adequate, cross-sectional systems consistency.

In the remaining sections of the chapter we then discussed a number of issues that might become barriers to the implementation of effective planning systems. A common problem can be found when the planning system becomes so detailed, elaborate, and inflexible that it simply represents too high a burden on line management's time and energy. We discussed several ways of cutting down such overloading of the planning system and also pointed out that the development of a more focused strategic direction might allow senior management to free some of the time that would otherwise probably have to be spent on near-term direction setting.

We also considered various strategic filters, notably a group structure's tendency to lead to suboptimal portfolio strategies, as well as the problems that might arise in developing sound business plans when the definition of product/market element patterns was illogical. In both these cases we could see that the organization's structure could hamper the development and implementation of sound strategies.

The so-called matrix organizational structure which is often found in complex organizations creates special problems for planning, above all because of the excessive time involvement normally required by management for carrying out planning in such a setting. We discussed how a division of labor between an adaptive and an integrative dimension might facilitate keeping this planning task within a more reasonable context.

We discussed how the concept of risk needed to be explicitly dealt with in the planning process to attain a proper degree of risk averseness within an organization. We also stressed the pertinence of having the risk preferences of key individual executives taken into account when reviewing planning proposals.

Finally, we addressed the question of when and how strategic audits of planning needs should be carried out, with particular emphasis on by whom.

NOTES

1. The following articles and books address important aspects of the task of managing the evolution of the strategic planning system: William H. Newman, "Strategy and Management Structure," *Journal of Business Policy* (Winter 1971–72); Larry E. Greiner, "Evolution and Revolution as Organizations Grow," *Harvard Business Review*, 50 (July–Aug. 1972), 37-46; H. Igor Ansoff, Robert P. Declerck, and Robert L. Hayes, "From Strategic Planning to Strategic Management," in *From Strategic Planning to Strategic Management*, eds. H. Igor Ansoff, and others (New York: Wiley-Interscience, 1976); Erich Jantsch and Conrad H. Waddington, *Evolution and Consciousness: Human Systems in Transition* (Reading, Mass.: Addison-Wesley, 1976); Bo L. T. Hedberg, Paul C. Nystrom, and William H. Starbuck, "Designing Organizations To Match Tomorrow," in *Prescriptive Models of Organizations*, eds. Paul C. Nystrom and William H. Starbuck (Amsterdam: North-Holland, 1977), 171-183; Allan T. Malm, "Approaches to Social Systems Design," in *Management Studies*, ed. Lawrence H. Benningson (Lund, Sweden: Student Litteratur, 1977), 143-164; Edgar H. Schein, "Increasing Organizational Effectiveness Through Better Human Resource Planning and Development," *Sloan Management Review*, 19, no. 1 (Fall 1977), 1-20; and Gerald Zaltman and Robert T. Duncan, *Strategies for Planned Change* (New York: Wiley-Interscience, 1977).

2. Several authors have addressed the issue of consistency between a firm's internal structure and external environment and/or among subsystems within the internal structure; see, for instance, Alfred D. Chandler, Jr., *Strategy and Structure* (Cambridge, Mass.: M.I.T. Press, 1962); Rensis Likert, *The Human Organization* (New York: McGraw-Hill, 1967); Gene W. Dalton, *Motivation and Control in Organizations* (Homewood, Ill.: Irwin, 1971); William H. Newman, "Strategy and Management Structure," *Academy of Management Proceedings* (Aug. 1971); R. P. Rumelt, *Strategy, Structure and Economic Performance* (Boston: Division of Research, Harvard Business School, 1974); and John P. Kotter, "An Integrative Theory of the Behavior of Formal Organizations," *Harvard Business School Working Paper* (Boston: Harvard Business School, 1976).

3. See J. C. Athanassiades, "The Distortion of Upward Communication in Hierarchical Organizations," *Academy of Management Journal*, 16 (June 1973), 207-226.

4. For the roles of a matrix organization structure as part of the strategic system, see Jay R. Galbraith, "Matrix Organization Design: How To Combine Functional and Project Forms," *Business Horizons* (Summer 1974); J. R. Galbraith, *Designing Complex Organizations* (Reading, Mass.: Addison-Wesley, 1973); David I. Clelland, and William R. King, "Organizing for Long-Range Planning," *Business Horizons* (August 1974); Stanley M. Davis, "Two Models of Organization: Unity of Command Versus Balance of Power," *Sloan Management Review*, 16, no. 1 (Fall 1974); 29-40; William Goggin, "How the Multidimensional Structure Works at Dow-Corning," *Harvard Business Review*, 52 (Jan.–Feb. 1974), 54-65; Stanley M. Davis and Paul R. Lawrence, *Matrix* (Reading, Mass.: Addison-Wesley, 1977); and Stanley M. Davis and Paul R. Lawrence, "Problems of Matrix Organizations," *Harvard Business Review*, 56 (May–June 1978), 131-142.

5. See John S. Schwendiman, "International Strategic Planning: Still in its Infancy," *Worldwide P & I Planning* (Sept.–Oct. 1971); K. A. Ringbakk, "The

Corporate Planning Life Cycle—An International Point of View," *Long Range Planning*, 5, no. 3 (Sept. 1972), 10-20; Louis T. Wells, ed., *The Product Life Cycle and International Trade*, (Boston: Division of Research, Harvard Business School, 1972); Peter Lorange, "La Procedure de Planification dans les Entreprises Multinationales," *Revue Economique et Sociale*, 31 (March 1973); 111-120; Peter Lorange, "Formal Planning in Multinational Corporations," *Columbia Journal of World Business*, 8, no. 2 (Summer 1973), 83-88; R. Mazzolini, "European Corporate Strategies," *Columbia Journal of World Business* (Spring 1975); George A. Steiner and Hans Schollhammer, "Pitfalls in Multinational Long Range Planning," *Long Range Planning*, 8, no. 2 (April 1975), 2-12; Peter Lorange, "A Framework for Strategic Planning in Multinational Corporations," *Long Range Planning* (June 1976); and Heinz Thanheiser and Peter Patel, *Eine Eimpirische Studie der Strategischen Planung in Diversifizierten Deutschen Unternhemen* (Fountainebleau, France: INSEAD, 1977).

6. Peter F. Drucker, "Long-Range Planning Means Risk-Taking," in *Long Range Planning for Management*, ed. David W. Ewing (New York: Mc-Graw-Hill, 1972), and Ben C. Ball and Peter Lorange, "Managing Your Strategic Responsiveness to the Environment," *Sloan School Working Paper* (Cambridge, Mass.: Sloan School of Management, M.I.T., 1978).

7. Analogous ideas to the one of carrying out a strategic systems audit have been suggested by Ferguson *(strategic concept audit)* and by Smith *(strategic information profiles)*; see Charles R. Ferguson, *Measuring Corporate Strategy* (Homewood, Ill.: Dow Jones-Irwin, 1974), and Theodore A. Smith, *Dynamic Business Strategy: The Art of Planning for Success* (New York: McGraw-Hill, 1977).

chapter seven

Executives' Roles in Planning

Introduction

As stressed throughout this book, the planning process is a strategic decision-making process. Thus, it will be only through proper involvement by executives that the strategic process will work. It is therefore necessary to discuss appropriate roles for various groups of executives in the planning process. There will of course never be one role model that will be equally applicable to all corporate settings. Here again we shall face a contingency-approach issue. Although it obviously would be inappropriate to consider executives' styles as factors that can be controlled as part of the planning systems design process, we are still facing a set of issues analogous to the ones discussed in the previous three chapters, namely, that the appropriateness of different managerial styles for involvement in planning will depend on the given situational setting. The purpose of this chapter, then, is to point out major role choices for various executive positions in different situational settings, so that the various executive team members can develop appropriate styles of involvement.

As a prelude to our analysis, we shall start with a further delineation of some of the behavioral aspects of planning. First, we shall discuss the specific role alternatives facing the CEO and senior line executives, such as group or division heads as well as strategy center managers. Then we shall focus on the different roles that the corporate planner might have. He might be involved with the design or improvement of the planning process itself. Or on the other hand, he might be offering substantive advice to the line on what strategic decisions to take. To conclude the chapter, we shall discuss briefly the roles of the board of directors as well as outside consultants in the planning process.

A Behavioral Process

As we have seen throughout this book, the diverse set of business activities being pursued within a large corporation calls for specialized input from those who are closest to the business. At the same time there will be a need for coordination of this potentially diverse set of actions so that the company can move in the most favorable direction. A major purpose of a corporate planning system is to facilitate common direction setting within a diverse organization. Without some mechanism for developing a sense of direction for a company with its many power constituencies and factions, it will be difficult for an organization to move substantially in a desired strategic direction. [1] Without a common focus which is at least understood and shared to some degree among the management team, a sense of factionalism is likely to develop. Well-intended organizational talent and energy might be spent pulling in opposite directions. Even the most brilliant, insightful, and persuasive CEO cannot succeed unilaterally in setting the strategic direction that his company should be going in. The planning approach discussed in this book is intended to facilitate this organizational direction-setting task.

It should therefore be stressed again that one important condition for being able to reach an overall strategic sense of direction among the managers is that the planning process must be interactive and iterative. It is necessary that the specialized skills and viewpoints of various managers throughout the line be allowed to interact with the more general management viewpoints of the organizational levels above. For instance, the CEO will depend on the specialized business inputs of his various division managers, who will be closer than he to their particular business settings; he will consider these inputs in an overall corporate context. Similarly, the head of a particular division will have to rely on the specialized inputs of his various functional department managers. He will have to be the one who takes the overall point of view of the business, above all in attempting to channel the functional strengths into cross-functional strategic programs that enhance the strategic progress of the business as a whole. The planning process should therefore unlatch the firm's specialized as well as general management resources. It is essential to have a relatively free-flowing two-way interaction in order to achieve good planning. Blockage of such communication channels might have deteriorating effects on the quality of planning.

Before discussing guidelines for making the planning process an effective communication vehicle, let us raise another related behavioral concept, namely, that the process should be iterative. Given the typically complex nature of the strategy formulation and implementation task, it is, of course, unlikely that the various participants in the planning process will be able to come up with their finalized inputs as the result of their first attempt. Few, if any, are able to see the ultimate strategic solution. A more likely set of events will be that plans are developed through a series of iterations, back and forth among the managers of the planning process. This can be achieved only through a relatively open two-way communication channel.

A significant requirement for all effective systems of communication is that the various tasks be clearly identified and delineated: Which managers should be involved? What should be discussed? When during the process should this be? The conceptual planning scheme that has been developed provides exactly this type of focus. It specifies when objectives, strategic programs, or budget-related issues should be discussed and what questions each group of managers should be concerned with at each stage. This should facilitate a clearer sense of role identification among the managers in the planning process.

Similarly, by providing a set of rules for communication, the planning system will provide a safeguard mechanism so that the various managers can be heard when appropriate. This is particularly important in a large corporation, where it often might be difficult for managers down the line to raise a concern as part of the routine operation. It is much easier for a subordinate manager to present his points of view in the yearly planning cycle than if he has to take the initiative to raise an ad hoc strategic issue on his own on an exception basis. Thus, the planning system provides an important mechanism for formalized bottom-up communication. A similar top-down communication mechanism is of course also critical, but this may often constitute less of a bottleneck in that senior management might feel more free to communicate with subordinate managers.

A relatively open two-way process of developing a course for the strategic direction of the firm will most likely add to the effect of instilling a sense of commitment to this set of plans. Not only will it be more difficult for a manager to depart from a widely communicated previously agreed-upon direction, but there will be considerable group pressure on each executive to deliver. A strategy center manager, for instance, will know that fulfillment of his part of the corporate plan will be essential to the overall corporate success and that a slip might have broad repercussions throughout the organization. A disciplined team spirit for strategy fulfillment accountability might emerge.

In our experience the disciplinary pressure of having to stick to a committed direction frequently provides a sobering experience for the CEO and his senior management. This means that the CEO will not be as free to impose unilateral ad hoc shifts in the strategic direction. In many cases this might represent a definite potential for strengthening the quality of decision making in that spur-of-the-moment decisions that break with a systematically established prior strategy might less easily be taken. Even though some loss of flexibility might be the result, it often pays to take time to assess why the old strategy would be invalid. Ad hoc superimposed strategic changes by senior management will frequently be seen as a breach of the planning contract by the rest of the company's management. Such decisions will typically be resisted by the organization and might be difficult to implement despite their merit. Needless to say, such unilateral top-down spur-of-the-moment strategic decision making taken outside the context of the planning system tends to undermine the effectiveness of the planning system as a strategic decision-making vehicle. Ironically, the CEO will probably be the one to lose the most from this.

Being fundamentally a behavioral process, planning is likely to be affected by management's style in several ways. First, the effective manager within the operating context of a strategic planning framework will probably be the one who possesses such personal qualities as flexibility, open-mindedness, the ability to listen, and tolerance. With less flexible management types planning is less likely to succeed. Second, patience and discipline are necessary style ingredients for managing within a planning context. Often it turns out to be particularly difficult for action-oriented line executives to reconcile themselves to the fact that orderly strategic decision making takes time. Finally, it should be stressed that good planning means hard work. It is normally an intensive, time-consuming process. Participating in review meetings and undertaking revisions might seem a never-ending effort before finally reaching an agreement on a strategic direction to follow. Only when the managers are realistic about the amount of time that planning will take, being willing to commit sufficient time and intellectual involvement, will there be a realistic possibility that effective planning might materialize.

What has been briefly touched upon in this section is the need to recognize several general implications for management's style stemming from the fundamental fact that we are dealing with a behavioral process. Let us now move to a discussion of the specific roles of the various manager groups in planning, starting with the CEO.

The Chief Executive Officer's Role in Planning

The CEO is the person ultimately responsible for strategic decision making within the firm. Although he might have delegated larger or smaller parts of this task, he is still responsible. Given that a strategic planning system is intended to facilitate better strategic decision making, it is clear that the system must be designed to suit the needs of and the decision-making style of the CEO.[2] Unless the CEO is able to understand and feel comfortable with the rationale for the particular design, he will probably not make much use of the strategic planning system as an integrated part of his decision making. In line with this, he must be assured that the system reflects his own basic business aspirations and beliefs. Let us, then, structure our discussion around the following three issues: What management style characteristics should be taken into account when designing the planning system? How can the planning system be integrated as a tool in his decision-making process? What will be the CEO's role in the actual design of the planning process?

It does not require extensive observations to conclude that there is a wide diversity of management styles among the CEOs of large corporations. This will of course depend on many underlying factors, such as the career pattern of the CEO, his ambition on behalf of his company, pressures from outside interest and power groups, and so on. Let us consider the following two hypothetical CEOs and see how their management styles are likely to be different. On the one hand, we have a CEO who has risen to the top spot of a large, capital-intensive corporation through a series of internal promotions. He may be around 60 when he takes over as CEO, and the mandatory retirement age may be 65. The financial situation of the company is comfortable. The board of directors is relatively passive, and there is no single large stockholder. A CEO in this position might well adopt an outlook of not rocking the boat. His major concern is probably to preside over a firm which is continuing in its steady success and basic mode of operation of the past and to be in a position to hand over the helm of a sound ship to the next CEO when mandatory retirement occurs. There will be little pressure for changes from the predominantly inbred organization (of which the CEO is a typical representative). Similarly, the CEO sees little reason to take major long-term risks that might pay off a long time after his retirement. On the contrary, about the only real pressure the CEO occasionally might feel is from financial analysts and the stock market: no short-term surprises, steady quarterly performance. The basic outlook of this CEO is therefore relatively short-run. He will feel more comfortable with a planning system which emphasizes integration rather than adaptation. He typically does not see much of a need for a planning system that would put explicit emphasis on identifying and ameliorating structural and/or financial portfolio pressures.

The contrast might be a CEO who takes over the top spot at a relatively young age, so that he has, say, about 20 years of tenure ahead in the job. Further, he might have been brought in from the outside some years ago with extensive experience running several different businesses as a strategy center and a division manager. The company may be fairly diverse, and because of a high degree of growth through acquisition, there may not be one distinct internal corporate style of management. The company has shown a strong financial performance in the past; however, during the recent few years its performance has slackened somewhat when compared with a selected number of relatively similar companies. This CEO has strong ambitions for his company, putting pressure on the corporation for higher performance and being willing to make long-term commitments that might take the firm into quite different strategic directions. The planning system that this CEO would find useful and be comfortable with would probably emphasize relatively more adaptation. It might facilitate putting pressure for longer-term strategic performance excellence on its divisions, accentuated by explicit competition among the divisions for the available corporate resources for their expansion. The system might further emphasize structural portfolio readjustment pressures by supporting the CEO's efforts through occasional channeling of funds to acquisitions.

The above examples should of course not be interpreted as having general value per se. They are merely intended as points in case to suggest that the CEO's style and aspirations for the company and himself will be critical when it comes to delineating a useful design of a planning system. Among the factors that might affect the design are the length of remaining time in the CEO's tenure and whether he is inbred or not. In each situation it is necessary to delineate critical elements of that CEO's style and preconceptions.

Let us now move to the second issue relating to the CEO's role in planning, concerning how he is to integrate planning into his decision-making style. We shall claim that as a prerequisite for that to take place the CEO must accept that he will get only as much out of the system as he puts into it. Thus, if he is not willing to interject himself actively into the process, but rather takes a more or less neutral or aloof role, critical top-down inputs will be missing from the planning process. Besides biasing the decision-making process itself, he might also cause adverse psychological effects on his organization through this form of planning behavior. Consider, for instance, a CEO who has announced to his organization his intention to strengthen strategic decision making through promoting a strategic planning system. When the actual work on the planning cycle takes place, however, the CEO takes a relatively low-key position with regard to providing inputs to and reviewing substantive matters of the objectives-setting and strategic programming cycles. In contrast, when the culminating step in the narrowing down process—the budget—is being presented, the CEO comes on strongly with sweeping suggestions for change. This causes modifications not only of the budget itself but also of several strategic programs, and it raises doubt about the fundamental relevance of some of the objectives. The strong, indirect signal to the organization in this case is probably clear. Despite his lip-service commitment to strategic planning, the CEO will in fact be more oriented toward relatively shorter-term, internally oriented, and integration-related issues. The line managers are likely to remember this in subsequent years and will prepare objectives and programs in such a way that they will fit into an anticipated budget, dominated by the CEO's integrative emphasis. Thus, we see that the entire core purpose of the planning process as a vehicle for identifying the relevant strategic options and of narrowing down these options is likely to be biased. Lack of front-end participation by the CEO coupled with a budget-dominated review style in this case becomes a major barrier to effective strategic planning.

It follows that the CEO must be willing to devote a sufficient amount of time and degree of intellectual involvement to the planning process in order for it to function. Some CEOs might state that although they want to devote the time required, they simply do not have enough time available due to other pressing activities. The real irony of this quite common line of argument is not only that it signals that planning is likely to fail but that it frequently is based on a false assumption. The key question when it comes to time spent is whether planning might facilitate the freeing of time now spent on ad hoc fire-fighting activities as well as on disentangling a strategically unfocused budget. In one large, successful, highly diversified company we studied, we found that exactly this had happened to the CEO's time-spending pattern. The added strategic focus being brought to the company through increased emphasis on objectives setting and on strategic programming gradually allowed the CEO to free time he previously had to spend on an exceedingly elaborate and cumbersome budgeting process. In another company the CEO was able to free considerable time previously devoted to capital budgeting approval as he was able to shift his emphasis from a detailed review and approval/ rejection of each particular investment project proposal to a review of the strategic programs. Given that an investment would be part of an already approved program and that the strategic relevance of the investment would thereby have been established, the CEO was able to treat the individual proposals in less detail.

An effective strategic planning system is above all, then, a tool intended to assist the CEO in doing a better job in his overall strategic decision-making task. It follows that the CEO will therefore have particularly strong incentives for making planning work. If not willing to let his strategic decisions unfold within the framework established by the planning system, the CEO is handicapping himself above all. Similarly, if not willing to commit the necessary amounts of time and intellectual involvement, the CEO handicaps himself again.

Let us now turn to the third issue raised in relation to the role of the CEO in the planning process, namely, what should be his involvement, if any, in the design of the strategic planning system. Further, to what extent should he have a knowledge of the detailed functioning of this system? Most CEOs will probably state that the design of the strategic planning system as well as its monitoring are tasks that belong to the corporate planner and his department. Given the lack of time that typically plagues a CEO, this is a very understandable position. However, the design of the strategic planning system and the way it is managed will have a vital impact on how strategic planning might function, as we have seen throughout this book. Consequently, it is necessary that the CEO be reasonably certain that the planning system is designed and managed in a way that facilitates a planning emphasis consistent with his intentions. There are two concerns that need to be raised in order to facilitate this.

First, it seems necessary that the CEO know enough about the general aspects of planning that he can feel reasonably comfortable about how the process in fact works within his company. Without this sense of what has been going on in order for the planning outputs to have been developed, it will be difficult for him to feel entirely comfortable about taking a position with respect to the substantive strategic issues he will have to decide on through the process. In particular, he should have a reasonably good perception about the amount of effort, the degree of professionalism, and the sincerity of commitment to the plans that have gone into the planning documents he receives. By being familiar with the functioning of the process the CEO can better calibrate what emphasis to put on the various planning outputs as a basis for his strategic decisions. Stated more succinctly, the CEO must be involved.

Second, it follows that the power to control the actual design and execution of the strategic planning system is an important one, since influencing the planning system might be an effective if indirect way of promoting strategic direction. Hence, the CEO should maintain the broad responsibility for this task in his own domain. This means that he should stress that the corporate planning department, which often has the task of designing and managing the planning system, operate strictly as an extension of his own office. Changes in the planning process should have the clout of being sponsored by the CEO, prepared through the staff support of the corporate planning department. Thus, the CEO should retain ownership of the strategic planning system.

Neither of the above two responsibilities should significantly tax the CEO's time. It is critical that he be sensitive to these issues when he delegates tasks to the strategic planning department consistently with this. Some CEOs, however, might not feel content with taking such a passive role of minimum involvement in the development and management of the planning system. These CEOs have found that the design of the planning system has the potential to offer such an effective indirect tool for changing the strategic direction of a company that they want to be directly involved in this function. If, for instance, a company is facing an increasingly complex environment because of acquisitions or because of increasingly turbulent business surroundings, the CEO might approach the issue of how to take advantage of this indirectly by modifying the planning system so that it more adequately copes with the new setting. One move in this direction would, for instance, be to institute more sharply targeted formalized environmental scanning procedures. Increasingly, we have examples of CEOs who actively and deliberately modify the structure of the strategic planning system in order to achieve a change in the strategy that they want their firm to follow.

As stated throughout this book, an important strategic planning system situational design issue is to tailor-make the structure of the strategic planning system to the particular strategy that is being followed. There is seemingly a contradiction between this and what was stated in the previous paragraph, where it was implied that a strategy emerges as an output from the planning system. Does structure follow strategy, or does strategy follow structure? We shall elaborate on several key issues behind this apparent contradiction, and we shall see not only that the two viewpoints can be easily reconciled but that this will have consequences for the CEO's role in planning.

Former Energy Department Secretary Schlesinger is quoted as saying that the major task of planning is to develop strategies that are sufficiently robust so as to allow for opportunism within the general confines of the robust strategic direction. The issues arising from this are twofold: How does a corporation develop a good and sufficiently robust strategy? And how does the company go after opportunities (and avoid threats) within the general confines of such a robust strategy? We have previously stressed that an initial strategy is seldom formulated from scratch through a formal strategic planning cycle. Instead, the strategic decision-making pattern of the firm's past will play a significant role in an explicit strategy statement. In addition, ad hoc special-purpose studies on specific strategic issues will typically play a major role in sharpening a formalized statement of the firm's strategic position. As examples of such ad hoc strategic positioning attempts we have discussed the ad hoc strategic audits. A more robust formal statement of the firm's general strategic posture will come out of this.

The strategic planning system, then, would facilitate operationalization and fine-tuning of the basic robust strategic thrust by providing the mechanism for reassessing the rationale for one's strategies through the annually recurring adaptation- and integration-related stages of the planning cycle. Given this, there should be no doubt that the design of the structure of the strategic planning system must be tailor-made to the basic robust strategy at hand, i.e., that planning structure should follow strategy.

However, at some point down the evolutionary path of implementation of the robust strategy, there might be a perception of a need to modify the basic strategic thrust, beyond the incremental fine-tuning that results from the completion of each year's planning cycle. It will be in such instances that the CEO may want to modify the structure of the planning system in order to change the robust strategy. Thus, when seen in such an evolutionary context we might say that planning structural changes might precede strategic changes in order to facilitate major but relatively rare strategic reorientations.

To summarize our position with respect to the CEO's role, then, we generally find it useful that the CEO actively influence the design and evolution of the strategic planning system in such a way that it reflects the situational reality and that he use his leverage to modify the strategic system at discrete intervals in order to induce major strategic changes.

The Line Management's Roles in the Planning Process

Let us now turn to a discussion of the roles of the other line management groups in planning, excluding of course the CEO, whom we discussed in the previous section. We shall find it useful to distinguish between the role of line general managers, such as those who head a division or a strategy center, and line managers who represent a particular function.

A line general manager, such as a division or strategy center head, should normally be in a position with little or no ambiguity in terms of the role that he is expected to play in the planning process. Given that the overall pattern of the planning process has been established from the corporate level, it will soon become apparent to the corporate level as part of the top-down/bottom-up interaction if a division manager is out of phase with his planning attempts. The line general manager will face a strict schedule for preparing aspects of his business plan. The effects of being out of phase in time and quality might be twofold and might have quite serious consequences. First, the corporate level will have to make portfolio strategizing and resource allocation decisions based on a pattern of business opportunity data which in fact will not be comparable across all the businesses, given that the quality and reliability of the inputs will vary from division to division. This might cause serious dysfunctions in the portfolio strategizing. Second, a division with insufficient quality in its planning thrust might end up shortchanged in the interdivisional competition for funds. It is therefore important that a division manager be able to develop relatively accurate and relevant plans and that he ap-proach the task of planning in a professional manner. His challenge is to perceive the key adaptive and integrative strategic issues facing his busi-ness from a general management point of view.

Given that the effectiveness of the company's planning process as a whole might suffer when one division manager does not carry out his planning task, it is indeed pertinent to try to prevent this from taking place. We shall look at two types of causes for potential lackluster divi-sional planning and also indicate what might be appropriate senior man-agement action for ameliorating this problem. One reason might be a resistance by the division manager to cooperate in the planning effort. Such a situation is not uncommon, particularly during the initial start-up periods of planning. This might be caused by such emotions as "I've been successful in this business for a long time—why should I do it differ-ently?" "I do not have time for this, because someone has to run the business." Or "This is just another of corporate management's fads; next year there will be something else." The resistance might be more calcu-lated, based on the perception that planning might diminish the power of the division manager. A strong division manager, for instance, might feel that a less explicit resource allocation process based on a one-to-one, not a portfolio-type, divisional-corporate interaction might provide him with more leeway. The corporate level can of course not tolerate such forms of resistance. The CEO might communicate this to the division manager directly, during the corporate review period. Resistant divisions will be requested to go back to the drawing board and come back adequately prepared. Partly, too, the point might be communicated indirectly by penalizing those divisions in the funds allocation process that have not satisfactorily documented how the funds are to be spent strategically. Such an approach might be expensive, however, and the CEO will not want to carry such a policy too far by distorting the resource allocation process. Given the seriousness of divisional noncooperation, the CEO will sooner or later have to face up to the issue of when to remove those division managers who do not want to cooperate. Lack of action by the CEO on this point might seriously strain the usefulness of planning as a meaningful strategic decision-making tool.

We are of course dealing here with an aspect of the more fundamental issue of strategic planning's effect on potential redistribution of power within the organizational hierarchy of a corporation. Given that a more explicitly focused corporate portfolio strategy opens up the potential for a more systematic redistribution of resources among the elements of a portfolio, one might deduce that comprehensive formal planning in many instances might imply a redistribution of power away from more autonomous divisional business-centered nuclei and toward the corporate office. As such, it is not surprising that division managers might resist planning. For the same reason it should be equally clear, however, that such resistance must be kept within limits by the CEO.

Another major reason why division managers might not perform satisfactorily in planning has to do with lack of familiarity with the task of thinking in a strategic mode. For many managers there will have to be a period of learning before becoming comfortable as business strategists. For others, however, the likelihood might be slight, at best, that their development will catch up through learning. Such a lack of aptitude to function as a good business strategist would indeed be a serious deficiency on the part of the division manager. Eventually, this is likely to lead to his removal.

In summary, then, a division manager does not have to be concerned about the issues of how to design and manage the planning system, per se; this task has been taken care of at the corporate level. However, the division manager must be able to understand the rationale for the design of the planning system well enough to be able to provide those substantive planning inputs that the system requires. When it comes to participation within the system he will have no choice other than full cooperation in order to excel. For the successful business manager, planning thus must become analogous to a language that he is expected to master and to be thoroughly comfortable with.

Let us now turn to the functional line executives and discuss their roles in planning. As pointed out earlier, the functional departments will play a rather informal role during the objectives-setting stage. During the strategic programming stage, however, they will play a key role in conceiving ways to implement the strategic directions of the businesses. Thus, they face a set of derived strategic tasks. The functions possess critical strategic resources for making this happen, primarily critical management talent and technological skills. They will be bringing to the process specialized functional skills, preferably of an outstanding quality. The yearly programming cycle will serve primarily as a vehicle for summing up the status of a more or less continuous and primarily interfunctional set of unstructured or semistructured activities. This is intended to conceive new programs as well as improve and implement existing ones. The focus or general direction for the company to take is more or less given; the issue for the functional executives is how to come up with program suggestions to make this happen. This process typically calls for highly creative inputs. This is generally not easy because it will be difficult to prescribe a common structure in terms of steps to follow in this part of the process. Thus, the functional executives' roles in planning tend to be less formal and quite ambiguous as well.

The interface between the functions and the annual formal plan can at times be a traumatic and frustrating experience for the functional managers. This planning stress might be brought on them partly because of the requirement for communication and coordination along intuitive and diffuse patterns across clearly defined functional boundaries, partly because the temporary nature of strategic programs prevents the development of more long-term and permanent interpersonal ties, and partly because of the difficulty in seeing the overall strategic rationale from a narrow, functional basis.

The Roles of the Planners

In our discussion of the roles of the planners, we shall find it useful to distinguish between the corporate-level planning executive and planners at the division and functional levels.[3] This is in line with what was proposed during our discussion of the roles of the CEO and the line executives in the planning process. We distinguished there between the task of developing a strategic planning system that would fall primarily under the CEO's jurisdiction versus the tasks of operating within the system by providing the substantive inputs to the planning process to be performed by the line. We shall discuss the roles of the corporate-level planner first.

There are two major groups of tasks that might be conceived of for the corporate-level planner. There will of course be a need to contribute to the various substantive strategic decisions that will have to be taken at this level. Examples might be to assist in acquisition studies or to give advice to the CEO on the relative merits of the planning documents submitted by each division. We shall, however, delay our discussion of the corporate planner's role in substantive strategic decision making and instead initially focus on the other major group of tasks, namely, to play the instrumental role in the design and implementation of the strategic planning system as well as to administer or manage the planning process.

This task is in essence at the center of what this book is all about. Central issues thus would be to facilitate the design of a strategic planning system through choice of an appropriate conceptual scheme for strategic planning and through tailor-making this scheme to the particular situational setting at hand. Other central issues would be to facilitate the implementation of the planning system by discussing it with the line executives and assisting the line in making use of the system. This leads to a third set of issues, namely, to be responsible for the improvement of the system, such as modifications, extensions of scope, or changes in emphasis. Finally, we have the task of physically coordinating the often vast number of diverse activities associated with a company going through a planning cycle, such as preparing an updated planning manual; disseminating a planning calendar; distributing common background assumptions to the line such as common economic assumptions; collecting divisional output drafts at each planning stage; arranging for time, place, and agenda for planning review meetings; and so on. The job of running the planning function is exhaustive and challenging.

Maybe the biggest challenge with respect to the planner's job of managing the system stems from our emerging recognition that rather than dealing with a planning function in the narrow sense, planning should be seen as one of several critical elements of an overall strategic decision-making system. This, as we have seen, attempts to encompass in a coordinated and consistent fashion the tasks of identification of strategic options, of narrowing down these options, of monitoring progress toward the fulfillment of the targets set, and of reconciling the motivating of individual managerial behavior with the strategic direction desired. It will probably become exceedingly critical that the emerging managerial function of managing the evolution of this broader strategic system be well performed. It is particularly important to take a unified point of view when it comes to this management function, given that lack of consistency among the elements of the broader strategic system might jeopardize its overall effectiveness as well as the effectiveness of its parts, despite the fact that a given subsystem when seen in isolation might appear to be performing satisfactorily.

Traditionally, different corporate-level staff functions have been responsible for managing aspects of this overall strategic system. For instance, the corporate planner might be responsible for the parts of the system relating to objectives setting and strategic programming, the corporate controller might be responsible for the budgeting and monitoring stages, and the executive development function might be responsible for the management incentives aspects. There is a need to unify and coordinate these responsibilities. Whether the corporate planner or one of the other staff members is designated to head up this task is not relevant; the key is that one executive is actually given the overall responsibility.

The task of managing the planning system, i.e., of being an effective custodian of planning as a strategic decision-making process, is thus not only increasingly important but increasingly complex as well. It is increasingly important because of the central role the planning system is expected to play in facilitating strategic change within the company. It is increasingly complex because of the fact that we are dealing with one overall strategic system that needs to stay consistent and current, not a set of separable, more or less independent subsystems. It might be reasonable to speculate, then, that the position of being responsible for the overall strategic corporate planning process should be held by a senior staff executive. The candidates for the job should thus have a broad enough systems background so as to be able to comprehend the various parts of the overall strategic system. This person should be working in close cooperation with the CEO in order to be able to manage the thrust of the system in a direction that corresponds with the CEO's strategic outlook. Thus, the planner must have a style which allows him to work relatively easily with the CEO—the boss must develop confidence and trust in his planner. Given that the increasing importance of such an overall strategic decision-making system is likely to become recognized by a wider stratum of managers who will be expected to be participants in the planning process, it is finally an advantage that the corporate planner knows his way around the company. To be able to draw on a wide body of personal contacts, developed through a working career in the company, will be a definite advantage. By appointing a company person to the planner's post, and not bringing in an executive from outside for the job, one might expect that some of the apprehension that line typically might have for the corporate planner might be lessened.

corporate says: Hire planner FM which company

Let us now turn to the other major potential task of the corporate planner, namely, to be involved in analyzing and even in deciding on parts of the substantive issues that are brought up through the planning process. There are several aspects of this task that might be raised. One is the corporate planner's role in providing common background assumptions on certain factors such as the overall economic outlook as well as what common figures might be relevant to use for wage rates, interest rates, currency rates, and so on. A second is the planner's role in consolidating substantive planning inputs from the divisions, checking for mechanical errors such as in the arithmetic, as well as performing a general analysis of the effects of the proposed planning inputs, with particular emphasis on funds-flow feasibility from a corporate point of view. A third role would be the planner's responsibility to pass judgment on the appropriateness of various substantive strategic decision alternatives. The nature of the first of these roles is such that it should be seen in isolation from the other two in that making background information available to the planning process does not represent a direct involvement in strategic decision making. This is in contrast to the last two roles, which intervene more directly in the functioning of the strategic decision-making processes. While the second role refers to the functioning of the management process and the third role refers to the substantive strategic choices that will have to be made, there is room for confusion with respect to these two interrelated roles, as we shall see below.

The dynamic and industrious corporate planner will of course attempt to play a dual role, emphasizing an involvement in the management of the planning process as well as attempting to have an impact on the substantive strategic issues that will have to be decided on as part of the planning task. Unfortunately, however, this dual task involvement pattern might cause friction within the organization and ultimately might diminish the corporate planner's ability to carry out both his process-related and substance-related tasks. We shall see that there are several reasons why it might be difficult for the corporate planner to fulfill the two types of tasks. First, the process of identifying relevant strategic options and deciding which to pursue and in what ways is a task which might significantly change the strategic direction of the firm. The line will have to carry out these changes. It would therefore also be appropriate to place a significant part of the responsibility for fulfillment of strategic performance squarely on the line. The line executives, who will have to live with the plans, should also feel that they are dealing with their own plans. Consequently, accountability for one's stated strategic positions is a corollary element for the interactive narrowing down aspect of the planning process. Rightly, line executives will be likely to resist the notion that staff executives have a major influence on critical strategic choices. The prevailing feeling would be that these executives will not be as close as the line to the businesses and also that the staff might more easily walk away from their decisions. The likelihood of such line resistance to inputs from the corporate planner is probably particularly high when the corporate planner is new to the company as well as when he does not have a line background from within one or more of the company's businesses.

A second and related reason why the corporate planner might run into resistance if attempting to have an impact on the substantive strategic direction setting stems from the interrelationship with his other task, managing the planning process. We have already discussed how modification of the structure of the planning system might affect the firm's strategic direction. Thus, the corporate planner might have an indirect impact on the substantive strategic course that the firm takes. To carry out rational and pragmatic modifications of the planning system is of course within the domain of the corporate planner's task and should not be challenged by the line. If, however, the corporate planner also tends to get heavily involved in substantive issues, then a feeling might easily develop among line managers that the corporate planner is attempting to set the rules of the game and be a player in the game as well. The line will naturally resist letting one of the players have such a substantial advantage by controlling the rules.

What emerges is a trade-off situation when it comes to these potentially dual process- versus substance-oriented types of roles of the corporate planner. On the one hand, the corporate planner should undertake the task of managing the planning process well. However, his task effectiveness with respect to this is likely to diminish if he allows himself to get overly involved in substantive strategic decision-making matters. On the other hand, he might be a staff confidant of the CEO, relied on and respected by the CEO for his sound judgment on substantive matters. If a staff executive in such a position is chartered with undertaking the corporate planner's task of managing the planning process, he too will probably fall into the trap of wearing two hats. The result is that he most likely will have to compromise either on the effectiveness of his substantive strategic decision-making involvement or on his effectiveness as a custodian of the strategic planning process.

Given the difficulty of combining the two potentially conflicting roles of the corporate planner, a sensible solution might be to assign the two tasks to two different executives or offices. The executive in charge of corporate planning would then concentrate on the task of managing the strategic planning process. As already pointed out, this is a critical management task in itself and will probably take on even higher importance given the notion of having to reckon with an overall strategic system, as we have advocated in this book. It definitely does not seem prudent to risk the possibility of this planning function being carried out less effectively by adding a substantive strategizing task element and potential role conflict to the corporate planner's responsibilities. His key priority should be to improve the planning system's effectiveness.

The task of counseling the CEO on substantive strategizing matters should rest with one or several corporate staff assistants to the president. These should be executives whom the CEO feels comfortable with, both in terms of respecting their judgment and trusting their loyalty. Ideally, such executives should have strong backgrounds in the operations of the company, and they will normally hold quite senior titles. Together with the CEO they form the senior management team.

Let us illustrate how the dilemma of the duality of the corporate planner's role was tackled within a large oil and energy-related company. In this firm the two types of tasks were delineated in considerable detail, providing for a clear split between the two purposes. This was done by letting the corporate planning group consist of not two but in fact four distinctive subunits. A unit called *planning process administration* oversaw the functioning of the planning process and was the only process-oriented unit. The other three units emphasized aspects of substantive planning. Notably, there was one group for strategic analysis of the submitted business plans. Another group, called *corporate strategy analysis and development*, focused on strategic aspects of the corporate portfolio's properties, including identification and analysis of acquisitions and/or divestitures, as well as assisting in the implementation of such tasks. Finally, a group was charged with macroeconomic analysis and compilation of special-purpose background statistics, primarily to serve as common inputs to the line's planning process. This company seems to have been quite successful in delineating between the process-related and the substance-related tasks so that they do not interfere with each other. Also, there seem to have been benefits from instilling a mode of specialization in terms of who should be carrying out different aspects of the substance-related tasks. Given the formidable work load at hand when it comes to analysis and resolution of substantive planning issues in companies of this size, this degree of delineation might be a sheer necessity.

In practice, there unfortunately tends to be at least two common types of forces that jeopardize the clear division of labor that we have recommended for achieving effective role definitions of the planner's tasks. First, a corporate planner entrusted with the management of the planning process might find it exceedingly difficult to discipline himself to stick to his low-profile, process-oriented, hands-off role by not becoming excessively involved in substantive strategic issues. There might be a natural tendency for him to attempt to build up his influence on substantive matters as he perceives that he is in reasonably firm control of the planning process. It might indeed be hard for the successful corporate planner to stay away from a gradually increasing involvement in substantive issues as he matures in the process job. He might even see this as the only direction he can go in order to continue a satisfactory professional development. Unfortunately, such a misconception might easily be the first step toward the downfall of the planner. Instead, he should pursue his professional development within the planning process area by taking on greater responsibility for developing a better overall integrated strategic system.

Another potential problem stems from the common tendency among corporate planners to allow themselves to get temporarily involved in a fire-fighting capacity during the period of start-up of strategic planning, particularly by doing a large part of the initial planning themselves. It may be particularly frustrating to the corporate planning group that the line executives are still so far away from thinking and acting strategically. In their frustration about what they perceive as slow progress toward the development of more involved strategies, the corporate planners may not be able to resist the temptation to step in and help the line in the development of their plans. This may happen even though the corporate planner might be perfectly clear about the fact that planning should be a function of the line. However, the planner will justify his temporary substantive involvement as intended only to get things started so that progress can be faster. Unfortunately, the effects from this type of well-meant but less well-conceived intervention by the corporate planning groups are almost universally negative. The line will typically fail to accept the plans that are being developed for them. They will feel a lessened pressure for developing strategic thinking on their own. The corporate planning staff will be perceived as meddling in substantive matters and may be seen by the line as a threat. There is also the danger that the planner's own perception of the importance of a strict process involvement posture might be compromised as time goes on. In short, the entire basis for making satisfactory progress with planning through evolution might easily be undermined at the outset through such actions. At best, the misconceived eagerness of the corporate planning staff might lead to a delay of planning progress; at worst it might diminish altogether the chances of making planning work.

Let us now shift the focus of our discussion to the roles of the planners at lower organizational levels within the corporation. Let us first consider the tasks of the planner within a business division. Let us recall that the role of a division manager in planning, above all, will be to contribute bottom-up inputs relating to the business that he is associated with for the resolution of where the company and its parts should go and for choosing alternative strategic programs for the business for getting there. The systems framework for developing and delivering these substantive planning contributions has been provided by the corporate planning department. Thus, the role of the division planner, maybe more fittingly labeled the business planner, will be to assist the general manager of the division in the development of his substantive business plans. The division planner's role in many ways will be analogous to that of the CEO's corporate-level senior staff assistants. The focus is on substantive strategic choices. The rationale for the need for a planner's position is, above all, to relieve the division manager of some of the substantive strategic analytical work that he otherwise would have to carry out. Further, the division planner might be of use to the division manager in giving advice on evaluating and choosing among the substantive alternatives.

It follows that the actual role definition of a division planner will depend on his particular division manager. Therefore, it is difficult to give general suggestions with regard to the division planner's role beyond the general statement that it will be substance-oriented in nature. The success of his task will depend on whether he is able to develop a highly personalized relationship with his division general business manager. This will largely be dictated by whether the division manager finds his analysis and advice on the various substantive strategic alternatives useful.

Let us turn finally to a brief discussion of the roles of planners at the functional level. As stressed before, the strategic roles of the various functional departments are derived from the business strategies and occur primarily through their participation in the strategic programming activities, where the emphasis is heavily on interfunctional cooperation. Thus, at the functional level it might be useful to assign a planning executive the responsibility for the planning of a particularly important strategic program. A major focus for such planning would be to facilitate better cross-functional integration. A unique feature of these strategic program planners' tasks would be the temporary nature of their planning missions. As soon as a particular strategic program is completed, the planning task will be finished. It seems essential that the planners in question recognize the temporary nature of their roles. Too often a planning organization might add some sense of permanence to the management of a strategic program, deviating from more realistic management actions to keep the program moving toward its completion.

In many organizations we find even large staff executive groups carrying out marketing planning, production planning, R&D planning, and so on. Given the point of view taken in this book regarding the derived strategic roles of the various functions, we do not see a need for functional planners as such. Rather, the planners should be assigned to strategic programs, as discussed above. Often, however, labels such as production planning or marketing planning are quite misleading; these tasks often refer to quite well-defined, near-term tasks that will have to be carried out within strategic program contexts. A major part of these activities may be related to the development of inputs for the operating budget and to the execution of these action programs as well. Let us, however, stress that long-term functional planning in isolation from the other functions seems to have little merit.

As a way of summarizing the span of role alternatives for planning executives it is useful to consider Exhibit 7-1. As can be seen, we have indicated three role alternatives for the planner: *catalyst,* *analyst,* or *strategist.* Also we have indicated two major types of tasks for the planner. He may contribute more or less effectively toward better functioning of the planning process. Also, he may be more or less effective in enhancing sound, substantive strategic decisions. As we have argued, the corporate

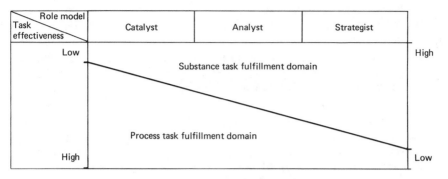

Task effectiveness	Role model		
	Catalyst	Analyst	Strategist

EXHIBIT 7-1   Trade-off Between Process Effectiveness and Content Effectiveness for Different Role Alternatives of Planning Executives

planner might find himself in a trade-off position if he tries to do an effective job along both dimensions. It is not easy to wear two hats in a *pure planner* ↓ *Catalyst* satisfactory manner. We also argued that the primary task domain for the corporate planner should be process effectiveness. Hence, the most appropriate as well as normally the safest role profile for him would be to act as a catalyst. Only rarely will he succeed in maintaining his process involvement effectiveness while attempting to increase his role in substantive strategic decision making. The CEO's corporate-level planning assistants, on the other hand, should be expected to emphasize the role of strategist, providing advice and recommendations on strategic decisions that are to be taken. Thus, we see that when it comes to the role of corporate planners at the corporate level there seems to be a dichotomy between process and substance, and it may in fact be unrealistic to attempt to combine the two roles. The continuous trade-off picture in Exhibit 7-1 may, therefore, not even be realistic. To make our summary complete, let us stress again that planners at lower levels in the organization will be concerned primarily with substantive issues and will consequently not face a similar role trade-off dilemma as is the case at the corporate level.

The Role of the Board of Directors in Planning

Let us now turn to a brief discussion of the role of the board of directors in the planning process, assuming that the board is composed primarily of outside directors. (The inside directors will presumably play the roles laid out for the CEO and the senior line officers, already discussed.) We see two distinct roles for the board. One might be to influence certain types of strategic decisions by facilitating the recognition of corporate-level needs for changing portfolio direction due to financial pressures as well as structural pressures. In fulfilling this role the board members would benefit from some understanding of the rudiments of the strategic planning process. A second role would be as a watchdog to check whether the strategic decision-making process seems to satisfy a minimum aspiration level of excellence and professionalism. We shall discuss each issue in turn.

Traditionally the board of directors is involved in approving next year's budget as well as in the formal approval of large capital expenditure decisions. We have previously discussed how such decisions should be evaluated in terms of their fit as elements of broader strategic programs. As such, judging the merit of various strategic program alternatives represents the crucial strategic decision, not the capital expenditure appropriation per se. However, the traditional role of the board is often not focused on the strategic issues but will instead be closer to what we might call rubber stamping of project appropriations. A potentially more useful role for the board would be involvement in the evaluation of the decisions of the major strategic thrusts of the firm. As such, the board should play a role in the approval of the emerging corporate-level outcomes from each of the objectives-setting, strategic programming, and budgeting cycles. Primarily, the board should be kept informed in order to be able to achieve a better understanding of the strategic direction of the firm; it should normally not play an active role in strategy formulation as such.

The benefits from a more focused strategic involvement by the board might be useful in two areas in particular. As has been discussed widely, the board is expected to take a strong lead in overseeing the company's stance on social responsibility issues. Such issues can probably be meaningfully analyzed only when related to the social acceptability of strategies. To focus on evaluating the acceptability of events that are taken out of their strategic context might more easily lead to biased judgments. Thus, the board needs to understand the rudiments of the overall strategic direction in order to carry out its role of social accountability.

A second useful area of contribution for the board members might be in providing the company access to information about a wider set of opportunities. This might be particularly valuable when assessing the corporate-level portfolio planning procedures. Here, opportunities for acquisitions and/or divestitures in particular might be brought up by members of the board.

There is another important function for the board when it comes to planning, namely, ensuring that the professionalism of strategic decision making is maintained in the corporation. Board members might ask themselves whether management in fact manages strategically and strives for excellence. Such probing by the board should help keep alive the issue of whether senior management's aspirations for the company are satisfactory. It is above all within the context of probing into the firm's planning activities and reviewing the plans that the board will have its primary chance of adding a more long-term view to senior management's aspirations.

It follows from the above that board members normally should have a minimum degree of understanding of how the planning system functions in order to be able to perform the tasks discussed. One approach to this that was taken by one company, with sales of three billion dollars and active within a high-technology business, was to hold a workshop with the board and senior management in attendance to discuss the structure and the functioning of the planning system. The board members felt that without such a background understanding of how the strategic processes work it was becoming next to impossible for them to make a positive contribution to the strategic direction setting.

The Role of Outside Consultants in Planning

Not unexpectedly, the area of strategic planning and analysis has become a thriving field of management consulting. In our opinion there is quite a span of potential roles for consultants to play in this area, but confusion about these roles might be dysfunctional. Let us therefore delineate at least three distinct areas of consulting tasks that should call for different modes of involvement by the outside consultant.[4] First, we have the task of carrying out an assessment of one's strategic setting in order to update one's needs for planning either at the business level, the corporate level, or both. We recall that such assessments typically will not be carried out every year and that they often require familiarity with specialized analytical techniques (as seen in Chapter Three). Analogous to a medical checkup, such an analysis might frequently touch upon issues that are highly sensitive to the management involved. All these considerations should suggest that it might be beneficial to make use of outside consultants to bring an objective approach to the strategic assessment analysis. It will of course be necessary for the consultants to establish close cooperation with the firm's own management in such instances in order to ensure a realistic input of company-specific background information.

A second area where outside consultants might play a useful role would be in carrying out specific, one-shot analyses of substantive strategic choices. Here the consultant would work in a capacity similar to the CEO's staff assistants for analysis and recommendations of substantive strategic issues. He will in fact be in a working capacity quite similar to the strategic substance-oriented corporate- or division-level planner.

When it comes to bringing in outside consulting assistance to facilitate improvements in the functioning of the strategic planning system, however, our position is that the consultant's role might be more limited. To be useful in such instances a careful role and task delineation should be undertaken. The only way to implement a planning process within a company is if this strategic way of thinking is adopted by the line management. Thus, we are dealing primarily with the task of changing a style, or a process, not with the task of searching for some specific solution to a problem, as we were in the two previous situations. For such a change to develop there seems to be no way around impressing on the line that it must help itself through learning by trial and error. Thus, there will be no shortcut or substitute to having the line, including senior management, intimately involved in establishing planning themselves. A consultant might play a useful role as a facilitator of this self-help approach. Specifically, he can be of assistance in suggesting the design of aspects of the process, keeping in mind, however, the caveat that the design of the system should be done under the auspices of the CEO and the line. Issues that fall into this category might be the preparation of planning instructions (often labeled the planning manual), the establishment of a planning calendar, as well as the delineation of how to modify the budgeting, monitoring, and incentive systems to make them consistent with the planning system. Further, an outside consultant might play a useful role as an educator during the start-up period by explaining aspects of the system to various line units and communicating the overall rationale of the approach. He might also play a role as a catalyst during the planning reviews, particularly when it comes to facilitating a more open-ended and free-flowing mode of communication among the executives involved. Thus, we see that an outside consultant can be a useful although peripheral resource in advising and guiding the line during their attempt to implement the planning process.

Unfortunately, there still seems to be a widespread misconception among some companies that a planning system can be installed through a shortcut by means of an intensive outside consulting effort and that outside consulting resources can beneficially be drawn on in preparing the actual plans. In our opinion this will not provide the line with a sufficient opportunity to internalize the strategic management process mode. Nor are plans developed by outsiders likely to create a necessary sense of internalization, commitment, and ownership among the line. In summary, then, although outside consultants play useful roles in carrying out strategic audit tasks and in analyzing and offering recommendations on specific substantive strategic issues, when it comes to influencing changes on the strategic planning process itself they should be more advisors and catalysts.

Summary

We have discussed the roles of various executive groups in the planning process. A few general conclusions emerge which seem to be particularly important. The first is that the CEO's role in planning is a central one; in fact he is the owner of the planning system. It is hard to justify the costs of developing a planning system unless the CEO intends to make use of the system for substantive decision making directly as well as for influencing strategic direction through evolving the system. Second, the line plays a key role in the development of plans. The planning documents should represent the line's views of their strategic positions and tasks and as such should be developed by the line. While a corporate planner should be responsible for the management of the strategic planning process, he should leave it to the line to get involved in the substantive strategic decision making. If not, his effectiveness as custodian of the strategic planning system is likely to diminish rapidly. However, while the substantive planning issues at the corporate level should be dealt with by the CEO and his team of top management advisors, planners at the divisional level should be seen as assistants to the division manager on substantive matters.

The role of the board of directors in planning is one of attempting to understand the planning process enough to approve the firm's overall, broad strategic direction, in contrast to the more or less common rubber stamping of capital expenditure projects and the annual budget. Also, the board might play a role in facilitating the necessary degree of professionalism in strategic management. Outside consultants are potentially useful in carrying out strategic position audits as well as in doing specific strategic issue substance analyses. However, the outside consultant's role should be seen as more limited in terms of carrying out the planning process itself.

We stressed that the role of the corporate planner might be expected to increase in importance with the growing recognition of the position's evolutionary role for two reasons: partly because the planning system needs to be seen as part of a broader set of systems, presenting a more challenging managing task, and partly because of the importance of managing and manipulating the strategic system as an indirect way for achieving strategic change.

NOTES

1. See A. Morrow, D. Bowers, and S. Seashore, ed., *Management and Participation* (New York: Harper & Row, 1967); R. D. Beckard, *Organization Development: Strategies and Models* (Reading, Mass.: Addison-Wesley, 1969); and W. G. Bennis, *Organizational Development: Its Nature, Origins, and Prospects* (Reading, Mass.: Addison-Wesley, 1969).

2. See, in particular, Walter B. Schaffir, "Strategic Business Planning: Some Questions for the Chief Executive," *Special Study No. 63* (New York: Presidents Association, 1976). See also R. Tannenbaum and F. Massarik, *Leadership and Organization* (New York: McGraw-Hill, 1961); Fred E. Fiedler, *A Theory of Leadership Effectiveness* (New York: McGraw-Hill, 1966); and Robert F. Neuschel, "Corporate Strategy: The C.E.O. as Kingpin," *McKinsey Quarterly* (Summer 1977).

3. See E. H. Schein, *Process Consultation: Its Role in Organization Development* (Reading, Mass.: Addison-Wesley, 1969); George A. Steiner, "Rise of the Corporate Planner," *Harvard Business Review*, 48 (Sept.–Oct. 1970), 133-139; Peter Lorange, "The Planner's Dual Role—A Survey of U.S. Companies," *Journal of Long Range Planning*, 6, no. 1 (March 1973), 13-16; James K. Brown, "Planning and the Corporate Planning Director," *Report No. 627* (New York: The Conference Board, 1974); and Robert W. Ackerman, "Role of the Corporate Planning Executive," in *Strategic Planning Systems*, ed. Peter Lorange and Richard F. Vancil (Englewood Cliffs, N.J.: Prentice-Hall, 1977).

4. See E. H. Schein, *Process Consultation: Its Role in Organization Design* (Reading, Mass.: Addison-Wesley, 1969), and David A. Kolb and Alan L. Frohman, "An Organization Development Approach to Consulting," *Sloan Management Review* (Fall 1968).

chapter eight

Corporate Planning— A Synthesis

Introduction

In this concluding chapter we shall summarize the book's major thrust and discuss where planning stands today. Our pupose has been to set forth an operational concept of effective corporate planning which is based on matching the capabilities of a company's planning system to the particular needs for planning stemming from the company's strategic setting. We have described how such a planning needs/capability match might be reached and what it might take to maintain such a level of planning effectiveness.

Having restated the book's purpose, we shall briefly review the major components of our planning approach. Then we shall discuss how this approach can be useful in providing a capability for meeting some of the major planning problems that companies face today, notably a need to adapt to environmental opportunities and/or threats and to integrate more efficiently around their internal strength and weakness pattern. Finally, we shall attempt to see planning in a prospective view; without pretending that we know what the future may bring, we shall point out certain trends that we think may occur. We hope that this will bring about a more sharply articulated notion of the benefits and costs of corporate planning as a strategic decision-making tool for management. Only through a planning approach will companies be able to succeed in the years to come, we believe, not only because the planning approach offers an operational set of tools to cope with emerging challenges but also because of the competitive advantage to those firms which will make effective use of it.

A Rationale for Corporate Planning

There should be a number of important benefits to a corporation which institutes a strategic planning approach. The real test as to whether planning is worth its efforts, of course, will be whether it will contribute to the improvement and stabilization of the firm's bottom-line results over an extended period of time. It is, however, for all practical purposes, impossible to measure the benefits of planning in such a direct way, and we have not even attempted to come up with a direct benefits/cost measure in this book.

One might instead attempt to develop an indirect measure of the benefits from planning, partly by specifying a set of useful outputs from the process on substantive strategic decision making and partly by indicating the nature of positive changes in the firm's managerial decision-making process from adopting planning as a tool. Although we have not attempted to develop such an indirect benefits analysis either, we shall briefly list what we feel might be the more important benefit factors for improved substantive strategic decisions as well as for an improved strategic decision-making process.

The planning approach should provide a better sense of the strategic direction of an organization not only in terms of more strategically focused decisions at the business level stemming from a better understanding of the businesses but also by providing a corporate portfolio context that allows for a more directed allocation of strategic resources in order to influence the long-term overall direction and structure of the firm. In addition to developing a better sense of direction within the company, planning will also provide an early sensitivity to problem areas. Thus, the strategic decisions that are being made should not only be more strategically focused in general but also should translate into resources needed, tasks implied and by whom, measures of progress, as well as time-specific schedules of progress.

We shall indicate five positive impacts on a firm's decision-making process, although there certainly will be several others. First, the process might significantly assist in arriving at a proper strategy. This is of course exceedingly important in that there are very few executives who are able to develop superb strategies as a natural, informal, and highly personalized process. A second benefit should be that a more explicitly understood strategic direction for the company is likely to emerge. Third, a planning approach might provide the discipline for periodic strategic review; actions to ameliorate potential strategic problems are not easily initiated, in contrast to fire-fighting actions for tackling day-to-day problems. Fourth, a planning process should provide a basis for a more explicit division of labor among management at various organizational levels, thereby also providing a basis for a greater decentralization of strategic responsibility and of operating decisions. Finally, the planning process will provide the basis for systematic learning, i.e., as a vehicle for improving the organization's strategies based on experience from monitoring progress and analyzing deviations from the original strategic targets.

The benefits from planning listed in the two preceding paragraphs should be relatively plausible at this stage. We have seen, throughout the book, how these and other benefits are likely to emerge from planning. We have not, however, attempted to come up with explicit benefit measures in this instance either. Given the vast diversity of corporate settings and styles, we feel that it would be difficult at best, and probably quite useless, to attempt to measure the effectiveness of planning in a more exact way. Instead of attempting to prove why planning is a useful activity, we have assumed in this book that it is. Based on the premise that planning makes sense in general, we have advocated an approach which states that the maximum benefit a given firm might get from planning depends on how well the planning system's capabilities match the company's particular needs for planning. Thus, our position is that measuring the effectiveness of planning in an absolute sense has little meaning, given that some companies will be in better positions than others when it comes to achieving such benefits. Rather, we have argued, a more meaningful measure of planning effectiveness would be to assess how well a given firm is doing in meeting its particular potentials, i.e., how well it is able to match its planning capabilities with its planning needs.

Both the concepts of needs for planning as well as planning capabilities were operationalized by means of measuring adaptation and integration. Adaptation, as we recall, refers to the identification and pursuance of opportunities and/or threats in the firm's environment. Integration, on the other hand, refers to the pursuance of the long-term internal operating activity patterns of the firm in such a way that internal strengths are taken advantage of and developed while internal weaknesses are ameliorated. The needs for planning, both adaptive and integrative, stem from the particular strategic setting of the firm, as we have seen. The adaptive and integrative capabilities to meet these needs depend on the particular design and structure built into the planning system. A major purpose of this book, then, has been to come up with an operational approach for determining an organization's needs for planning and for designing a planning system in such a way that its capabilities become as relevant as possible. A second major purpose of this book has been to develop the argument for maintaining a planning system, i.e., for managing its evolution over time. Given that most firms' needs for planning will tend to change, often quite rapidly, as a function of environmental changes as well as due to strategic resource reallocations within the firm itself, it will be necessary to continue to modify a planning system so that it may maintain its effectiveness.

The decision-making focus on the planning process will be on how to better allocate the firm's scarce strategic resources. Financial resources, i.e., discretionary funds, will not be the only resource category in this context. At least equally important will be the allocation of the company's critical management talent to tasks where they can have the most strategic impact. The firm's technological know-how is a third type of strategic resource and should be treated in an analogous way. Planning means to make decisions, i.e., to come up with the best pattern of choice for how to make use of the firm's strategic resources, so that ultimately the firm may be able to more than replenish its strategic resource base. Only then, of course, can a company prosper.

Having now restated the rationale for our approach to planning, let us briefly revisit the major elements of our approach.

The Elements of the Approach

The first element in our approach is the emphasis on an overall strategic decision-making system consisting of five interrelated elements: objectives setting, strategic programming, budgeting, performance monitoring, and motivating. The task of this system, then, seen as a decision-making tool for the allocation of strategic resources, is to facilitate the identification of relevant strategic options; to narrow down these options by making a gradual commitment of resources to particular strategic directions, culminating in a set of action programs coordinated for the company as a whole; to monitor progress toward the fulfillment of objectives, both long-term and near-term programs; and to provide management with rewards for contributing to the fulfillment of strategic direction as well as near-term performance. The system, then, attempts to facilitate adaptation to environmental opportunities and/or threats as well as integration of the company's pattern of operating activities so as to capitalize on internal strengths and ameliorate internal weaknesses.

The second element of our planning approach provides a basis for a division of labor within the management hierarchy with respect to strategy formulation and implementation; specifically, three levels of strategy are being operationalized. At the corporate level we have a portfolio strategizing task which balances the company's various business activities. Thus, the key strategic issue here is to allocate the firm's resources to the businesses in such a way that the desired overall portfolio strategy can be reached.

At the division level the strategic emphasis will be on succeeding competitively within a particular business. The key strategic issue here, too, is resource allocation, but the focus of strategic choices will be fundamentally different: In what aspects of the business shall we commit ourselves in the creation of competitive strength, say building market share? A successful company cannot be involved in everything; strategic management implies making strategic choices and a sharpened strategic focus.

The third level of strategy involves the functional departments. The task here is to develop strategic programs for implementing a particular business strategy. These strategic programs will typically be interfunctional. This level of strategizing, then, differs, from the other two levels in at least three important respects. First, strategizing at the corporate and division levels implies a general management point of view, but specialized, functional viewpoints are the bases for strategic programming, brought together under the auspices of a business strategy umbrella. Second, although the tasks of portfolio and business strategizing are permanent, a functional strategic program will be much more temporary in nature. Third, this strategic programming will have a key role in determining how to implement a strategic direction set at higher levels but will not be fundamentally concerned with where to go.

The fourth element of the conceptual scheme is the notion of a behavioral process, with emphasis on learning and information handling. Thus, the scheme acknowledges the necessity to bring a relatively large number of managers into the planning process to share responsibility for and commitment to a particular direction for the firm. To achieve this the system must provide an opportunity for each relevant manager to set forth his arguments and for an orderly pattern of interaction. Given the often heavy need for considerable iterations, it is critical that the planning system provide an effective communication pattern among managers. It is also critical that the system allow for the accumulation of useful managerial experience among its participants. It is not a trivial task to develop and maintain a good strategic posture; only through learning and improvements over time can this be done.

The five-by-three communication framework for strategic planning should provide the basis for pursuing planning. Given an overall logical consistent focus, it permits the various aspects of planning to be addressed separately at different points in time while still enabling all of it to fit into an overall strategic trust. By having thus developed a "skeleton" for a strategic planning system, the next task is to discuss how this scheme might be implemented so that the system will respond to the needs of the firm today.

Responding to Today's Needs

Although there might be an unfortunate tendency among management to claim that the problems one is facing today are more complex than ever and that the future is more uncertain than ever, there is still truth in the fact that a few basic environmental shifts seem to have taken place. The "growth-forever" syndrome of the decades up until the early 1970s certainly seems to be gone. The culmination of this point might have been labeled growth without profits. Similarly, energy and other raw materials resource shortages may inflict more structural changes on the business environment than we have yet seen. Impacts from government regulations as well as from interest groups on business seem to have reached new levels and are branching out into new areas. Basic technological innovations are having as many shattering effects on several businesses as ever. Certainly, the need to keep up with and respond to the environment seems to have increased. Similarly, competitive pressures seem to be as strong as ever in calling for efficient modes of operation; today more than ever there seems to be a survival of the fittest. As a consequence, today's planning challenge should be seen in a dual perspective: It should enable the company to adapt better and quicker to environmental opportunities and/or threats. Also, however, it should facilitate the handling of the integrative challenges facing the firm. In each given situation a proper balance between the adaptation and the integration emphases of planning thus becomes more critical than ever.

Given the increased volatility and complexity of a firm's environment, some managers might assert that while planning might have been workable in the more stable settings of the past, it is certainly no longer a viable tool given today's rapid changes. Such a view of planning, however, is in fundamental contrast to the approach developed in this book. What we have aimed at is to develop a concept of planning which is explicitly fit to deal with today's turbulent environments—by seeing a set of plans as an initial bench-mark which then will be modified as needed in a way consistent with what surfaces through the subsequent monitoring. Thus, our planning approach is attempting to turn the firm into a self-corrective system, entirely analogous to a rocket homing in on a target.

There are several issues which emerge which are important in influencing the adaptive/integrative planning balance viewpoint; we shall point out five examples of such issues that we see as particularly pertinent to today's setting.

First, there is a need to emphasize an appropriate top-down participation by senior management in starting off the planning process so that a realistic picture can emerge of the CEO's expectations for the firm and his preconceptions as to how far and in what direction the firm might go. More than ever the CEO must be firmly part of planning. Second, there is a need for responses by the divisions to the CEO's initiative by assessing the nature of opportunities and/or threats within one particular business. This would involve an analysis of how to predict and respond to a particular environmental factor to which a business strategy might be exposed. An opportunistic business outlook is more essential than ever, emphasizing one's competitors, creative moves, and quick responses. Third, a corporate review of the business opportunity assessments should be carried out within the context of a portfolio strategizing task, i.e., a review of all divisions' inputs to an overall portfolio pattern as well as response to and interaction with each division contingent on the other inputs. Thus, a sequential corporate review of the divisions would not be satisfactory. More than ever the corporation will be in need of an innovative portfolio strategy on top of its business strategies, i.e., an active strategic component to be the value added at the corporate level. Fourth, the attempt to formulate a set of objectives should be kept in decision-oriented focus in that it will be necessary to choose which businesses to emphasize relative to others. The expected effects from such shifts in emphasis within the portfolio will be to close the planning gap between the CEO's initial expectations and the expected performance output of the tentative portfolio. A fifth aspect of the design tools which seems to become increasingly critical is the development of *strategic control* to monitor progress not only toward the fulfillment of budgets but also toward the fulfillment of specific strategic programs as well as more general objectives. This also allows for an explicit incorporation of management incentives so as to reinforce managers' contributions toward strategic direction—increasingly critical, given the emergence of a highly individualistic new breed of professional managers.

In addition to the above viewpoints on planning which seem to have become increasingly important for directly influencing the adaptive/integrative balance thrust of a company's planning, we have operational ways of improving adaptation or integration through the design of the planning system itself. Chief among them is the linking of the various elements. Other design tools relate to the formats of the plans, the types of review processes employed, and the layout of the planning calendar.

A proper perspective of corporate planning as a management tool today, then, recognizes that the state of the art is sufficiently developed to provide critical support for strategic decision making. This results from our increasing understanding of how to focus the planning system in a particular direction, toward a more appropriate adaptation/integration balance, as well as from our ability to specify in operational terms the nature of the particular needs for planning and to design the systems to meet these needs.

Emerging Trends and Challenges

About the pressures facing the firm during the years to come, we can of course only speculate. However, it seems reasonable to expect that the need to strategize will become even stronger in the future. Thus, a corporate planning system will increasingly become a tool that senior management can use to influence the strategic direction of the firm. In this respect three considerations should be noted. The first reinforces the need to manage the evolution of a strategic planning system so that it will remain sufficiently up-to-date to be effective, as would be required given the planning system's role as a critical strategic tool. The second consideration deals with the need to manage the planning system so as to anticipate strategic shifts that management will want to carry out, i.e., as a vehicle to facilitate and reinforce strategic change. The third deals with the new and important role of the corporate planner as a custodian managing the planning system.

The need to manage the evolution of the planning system will probably become increasingly important due to a combination of two forces. First, a strategic planning system which is reasonably effective in the first place will have an impact on the actual strategic choices and decisions that are being made. These strategic decisions will in turn change the situational setting of the firm. This, however, will probably imply changes in the needs for planning, i.e., a need to revise the planning system too. Thus, the system must be updated in order not to self-destruct. Equally important in this respect will be the realization that the planning system no longer can be seen as a relatively broad-gauged, crude tool but as an increasingly precise, multifaceted vehicle. Hence, the need for a more continuous updating effort emerges, where previously less frequent revisions of the planning system might have sufficed.

The issue of making use of the planning system as a vehicle for reinforcing strategic changes is an important one. Increasingly there seems to be a realization that strategic change seldom occurs as a consequence of dictates by senior management when it comes to the substantive aspects of a decision but rather as a function of senior management's manipulation of the administrative systems of the firm. Particularly, organizational changes have been used by senior management as a vehicle for inducing new strategic direction. Instead of using such a sweeping tool exclusively, the planning system might emerge as another useful vehicle for the CEO to use in setting strategic direction. Particularly important is the opportunity that this offers to change the planning system in advance to ensure more immediate and focused strategic shifts.

This brings us to the role of the corporate planner. The corporate planner should continue to focus on maintaining the system and not become more involved in the substance of strategic decision making. However, his task of managing the planning system is likely to become increasingly important. To do an adequate job he will need to have a good sense of the strategic direction which senior management is pursuing. Thus, the corporate planner might be seen as a member of the senior management team, close to the CEO.

In summary, it seems reasonable to predict that a strategic planning system might become a distinct competitive advantage to those companies able to develop effective systems. This, however, will require an increasing emphasis on keeping the system's evolution under close scrutiny and control as well as ensuring that the system's focus is consistent with the strategic direction actually contemplated by senior management.

Summary

We have put forward in this book a discussion of strategic planning as a decision-making tool which can be summarized from three angles. From a retrospective point of view the elements of planning that have been introduced might be summarized into a unified conceptual scheme which integrates three distinctive strategic levels, five distinctive stages of tasks, and one interactive as well as iterative communication process. From a perspective point of view the system can be seen as a vehicle for responding to particular planning needs that have been identified, notably the increased need to pay attention to a proper adaptation/integration balance. From a prospective point of view we can expect a planning system to become more and more the central tool for facilitating strategic change, the operationalizing element of the emerging notion of a dual strategic/ operational mode of managing.

Name Index

Subject Index